Mystery and Detection
Thinking and Problem Solving with the Sleuths

Jerry D. Flack
University of Colorado at Colorado Springs

Illustrated by Gay Graeber Miller

1990
TEACHER IDEAS PRESS
A Division of
Libraries Unlimited, Inc.
Englewood, Colorado

TEACHER IDEAS PRESS
A Division of Libraries Unlimited, Inc.
P.O. Box 3988
Englewood, CO 80155-3988

Library of Congress Cataloging-in-Publication Data

Flack, Jerry D.
    Mystery and detection : thinking and problem solving with the sleuths / Jerry D. Flack ; illustrated by Gay Graeber Miller.
        xx, 246 p. 22x28 cm. -- (Gifted treasury series)
        Includes bibliographical references and index.
        ISBN 0-87287-815-5
        1. Critical thinking--Study and teaching.   2. Problem solving.
    3. Gifted children--Education.   4. Detective and mystery stories.
    I. Title.   II. Series.
    LB1590.3.F57   1990
    371.95'6--dc20   90-40103
                                                                CIP

Gifted Treasury Series
Jerry D. Flack, Series Editor

Inventing, Inventions, and Inventors: A Teaching Resource Book. By Jerry D. Flack.

Mystery and Detection: Thinking and Problem Solving with the Sleuths. By Jerry D. Flack.

This book is dedicated to my lifetime friend, honored colleague, and fellow mystery enthusiast, M. Elizabeth Nielsen, Ph.D.

Table of Contents

Preface xiii

Introduction xv

1 Problem Solving with Mysteries and Detectives 1

Models for Problem Solving and Sleuthing 1

Mr. Sherlock Holmes: A Role Model for Students and Teachers Alike 4

Using *Mystery and Detection* 9

    The Role of the Library Media Specialist 9

    Classroom Environment 10

    Essential Book Resources 10

    Creating a Web of Intrigue 12

    A Mystery Writer's Notebook 16

    Mystery Quotes 16

Notes 17

Teacher Resources 17

2 The Language Arts 19

Meet a Mystery Author 19

A Letter from a Professional 20

Case Study 21

Tools of the Trade 22

Mystery Desk 24

Traces 26

2   The Language Arts—*Continued*
Language Arts Activities...28
   Sampling Mystery Fare...28
   Critical Reading..30
   Critical Reading Questions...30
   The Mystery Story Elements...31
   Types of Sleuths..32
   Sleuth Search...34
   Reporting Mysteries..37
   Biographical Studies...39
   A Mystery Profile...42
   A Literary Mystery...44
   Fictional Biographies...45
   Write a Letter to Sherlock Holmes..47
   Vocabulary..47
   Gruesome Grammar...48
   Murderous Verse...50
   Mystery Newspapers...54
   Fairy Tales: They're Positively Criminal!..55
   Literary Trivia..55
   Class Detectives Club..56
   It Was a Dark and Stormy Night...57
   Solving Mysteries Creatively/*The Mystery of Edwin Drood*.....................58
   Writing a Mystery Story...59
   Mystery Story Starters...61
   Create an Authors' League...62
Notes..63
Teacher Resources...63
Classic Mysteries..66
Mystery Reading List for the Language Arts...67

3   The Arts...69
Meet the Author and Meet the Illustrator of *Mystery and Detection*..................69
A Letter from a Professional..70
Case Study...72
Tools of the Trade...74
Mystery Desk..76
Mystery Windows..77
Traces..79
The Arts Activities...80
Creative Dramatics..80
   Awareness Activities...80
   Movement, Pantomime, and Improvisation.......................................81
Radio Dramas...85
   Listening..85
   Creating Radio Mystery Dramas..85
Readers Theatre...87
Music..87
   Creating a Mystery Theme...87

Visual Arts...89
   Cartooning...89
   Photography..92
Arts Projects..93
Dance..101
Notes..101
Teacher Resources...102
Mystery Reading List for the Arts...105

4 The Social Studies..106
Meet an Anthropologist...106
A Letter from a Professional..106
Case Study..107
Tools of the Trade..108
Mystery Desk..110
Traces...111
Social Studies Activities..112
Research—Probes and Inquiries...112
Teaching Research and Independent Inquiry Skills.................................112
   Selecting a Topic...113
   Asking Questions..114
   Observing the Environment..117
   Finding and Evaluating Resources..118
   Taking Notes..121
   Organizing and Outlining Data..121
   Planning the Inquiry..121
   Sharing Information...123
   Evaluating the Inquiry Process...124
Historical Research..124
Psychology..125
   Psychological Sleuthing...125
   The Psychology of Mysteries...126
Economics...127
   Welcome to Mysteryland..127
   The Case of Aunt Sadie's Will...127
   Wall Street Crimes..128
Geography...128
   In Holmes's Footsteps...128
   Geographical Explorations...131
Archaeology...131
   Sleuthing through the Past...131
   Archaeological Investigations...132
Political Science and Debate...135
Notes..136
Teacher Resources...137
Mystery Reading List for the Social Studies...139

5 Future Studies 141
Meet a Science Fiction Author 141
A Letter from a Professional 141
Case Study 143
Tools of the Trade 145
Mystery Desk 146
Traces 147
Futures Activities 148
    The 3 P's — The Tools of Futurist Detectives 148
    Trending 150
    Cross-Impact Matrix 151
    Futures Wheel 152
Computer Crime 155
Are We Alone? 159
Robots as Criminals 160
Mystery Catalogs Circa 2090 160
Literature Studies 161
Scenarios of the Future 162
Notes 163
Teacher Resources 164
Mystery Reading List for Future Studies 166

6 Crime and Punishment 167
Meet an Attorney 167
A Letter from a Professional 167
Case Study 169
Tools of the Trade 171
Mystery Desk 173
Traces 174
Crime and Punishment 176
    Human Resources 176
The Vocabulary of Crime and Punishment 176
    Catching Crooks 178
    The Statistics of Crime 178
    Famous Criminals and Famous Crimes 179
    Crimebusters and Other Heroes 182
    Scotland Yard 183
So You Want to Be a Detective 184
Solving Mysteries 185
The Search for Clues: A Forensics Simulation 190
Computer Crime and Punishment Simulations 190
The Funny (and Far) Side of Crime and Punishment 191
The Crime Beat: Reporting Crime 192
An Advocacy Trial 194
Notes 207
Teacher Resources 207
Computer Simulations 209
Mystery Reading List for Crime and Punishment 210

Bibliography of Mysteries for Students and Teachers 211
    Primary Grades 212
    Middle Grades 213
    Secondary Grades 216
    Teachers and Library Media Specialists 219

Answer Key 221

Index 235

Preface

Mystery and Detection is the second volume of the Libraries Unlimited Gifted Treasury Series. Like its predecessor, *Inventing, Inventions, and Inventors: A Teaching Resource Book*, this volume attempts to provide qualitatively differentiated resources and teaching strategies for teachers, library media specialists, administrators, and parents charged with the education of our gifted and talented youth.

Currently, there is a great national discussion about the perceived lack of quality of education in the United States. Critiques of American education such as Allan Bloom's *The Closing of the American Mind* and E. D. Hirsch, Jr.'s *Cultural Literacy: What Every American Needs to Know* have spent months atop the nation's best-selling books lists. Reports by the Carnegie Foundation for the Advancement of Teaching (*High School*), the National Commission on Excellence in Education (*A Nation at Risk*), and a host of other similar reports commissioned by business, governmental, and educational agencies have examined the quality of education provided our youth and have found it wanting—American youth of today seem to lack the fundamental storehouse of information thought necessary to be literate citizens. Moreover, most of the critics of contemporary education call not just for the rigorous teaching of basic information but for the urgent need to teach thinking skills. The cry of alarm cited in *A Nation at Risk* is typical:

> Many 17 year-olds do not possess the "higher order" intellectual skills we should expect of them.
> Nearly 40 percent cannot draw inferences from written material; only one-fifth can write a persuasive essay.[1]

Seemingly overnight, thinking skills are in vogue.

The teaching of thinking skills alone, in a vacuum divorced from meaningful content, is suspect. The *sine qua non* of all the volumes in the Gifted Treasury Series is that rigorous content and challenging thinking processes must be fused if significantly differentiated learning is to truly occur. *Mystery and Detection* is no exception to this rule. Challenging contemporary and classical literature is referenced as the foundation for teaching gifted students critical thinking, research, and independent study skills.

Media are indispensable tools in the education of gifted learners. Thus, the critical roles of the library media center and the library media specialist are emphasized in this and other volumes of the Gifted Treasury Series.

Another hallmark of the Gifted Treasury Series is its practical ideas and strategies. Creativity and freshness are, of course, premium concerns, but are never promoted at the expense of practicality. Teachers, library media specialists, administrators, and parents can trust that the ideas and strategies recommended in *Mystery and Detection* not only work—they work well.

Notes

[1]The National Commission on Excellence in Education, *A Nation at Risk: The Imperative for Educational Reform* (Washington, D.C.: U.S. Government Printing Office, 1983), 9.

References

Bloom, Allan. *The Closing of the American Mind.* New York: Simon and Schuster, 1987.

Boyer, Ernest L. *High School: A Report on Secondary Education in America.* New York: Harper & Row, 1983.

Hirsch, E. D., Jr. *Cultural Literacy: What Every American Needs to Know.* Boston: Houghton Mifflin, 1987.

National Commission on Excellence in Education. *A Nation at Risk: The Imperative for Educational Reform.* Washington, D.C.: U.S. Government Printing Office, 1983.

Introduction

Using the Mystery Genre

"Why mystery stories?"

"Is mystery literature appropriate fare for gifted and talented students?"

"Should not *all* students be challenged to develop their thinking and problem solving skills? Why a mystery unit just for the gifted and talented students?"

These are but a few of the pertinent questions that students, parents, teachers, media specialists, administrators, and other school patrons may ask about the focus and content of *Mystery and Detection*. I'll focus here on the answers to these important questions.

Why Mysteries?

I make no apologies for introducing students to mystery literature. I want bright students to be introduced to the joys of reading a good mystery. I believe the mystery genre has been kept in the educational closet too long. Personally, I have found a lifetime of enjoyment in reading mysteries. Sometimes when the world seems to crowd in on me, or become a bit too confusing, I find reassurance, solace, and just plain enjoyment from the well-ordered world found in mystery literature. Indeed, I trace my great love of reading, in part, back to a specific, early encounter with a Sherlock Holmes story. I was a reluctant reader until required to read a story by Sir Arthur Conan Doyle in a junior high school English class. Suddenly, I was hooked. I wanted to read more of these wonderful stories about Holmes's and Watson's grand adventures. I am sure there are thousands of other would-be readers in schools just waiting to be turned on to the magic of words via a Holmesian tale.

No one should hesitate to share the joy he or she finds in reading well-written detective stories. Freud and Jung are two intellectual giants reputed to have been devotees of this genre. At least two presidents of the United States, Abraham Lincoln and Franklin D. Roosevelt, wrote mysteries for intellectual enjoyment and satisfaction. The cerebral challenge involved in most detective stories and novels is just one of the reasons for introducing students to mystery literature.

While there are poorly written mystery tales, there are also some extraordinarily fine examples of classical and contemporary mystery stories and novels. The duty of the adult, whether teacher, library media specialist or parent, is to direct students to the finer examples of the genre, and to help children and adolescents develop a literary taste that helps them distinguish the sublime from the ridiculous. Happily, even at the primary grade levels, many excellent mysteries are being authored today which are highly suitable for student use. Throughout this book, sterling examples of detective fiction for both children and adolescents will be listed.

Moving Beyond Sherlock Holmes

While I believe the mystery genre provides cerebral challenges and reading enjoyment for bright students, I also believe it is only a beginning point for inquiry.

A word about the terms "mystery" and "detection" may be in order here. Throughout *Mystery and Detection*, these words are viewed in at least two ways. As an entry point, both terms will be treated literally. That is, specific examples of the mystery literary genre will be discussed and recommended, and the detection skills and procedures of fictional sleuths will be examined. But, such references and discussions should not be viewed as an end in themselves. Rather, both in the text and, hopefully in classrooms and media centers where the text is used, literal discussions will serve as catalysts to spark student interest in the much larger and *real* mysteries of life and the universe, as well as the sleuthing skills required to unravel and understand them.

The Multilevel Benefits of Mysteries

From the early works of Wilkie Collins and Conan Doyle, through the writings of Dorothy Sayers and Agatha Christie, to today's mystery tales by authors like P. D. James and Charlotte MacLeod, mysteries provide a social and historical perspective of the times in which they are set or have been written. Mystery writers like Ellis Peters, whose mysteries are set in the monastaries of the Middle Ages, provide windows through which readers may glimpse the past. The knowledge of social class systems and manners of various historical eras in the English-speaking world, even the delivery of the mystery story itself to readers (serialization of the Holmes stories in the *Strand Magazine* and radio broadcasts in the 1930s) constitute educational bonuses on top of the reading pleasure students derive.

Mystery stories also reinforce fundamental values which may be sorely missing from other media young people encounter in today's entertainment world. Almost universally, three basic values are exemplified in mystery literature. The first of these values is inviolate: goodness triumphs and evil is vanquished. British mystery writer P. D. James describes mysteries as modern morality tales: "The crime novel is a moral form. Murder is uniquely wrong, and the resources of society are exerted to bring the perpetrator to justice. It's probably the most moral kind of fiction we have, in that respect."[1]

Second, brains rather than brawn prevail. Yes, a detective may occasionally have to use his or her fists, an umbrella, or even a gun to defend and protect the innocent, but the detective's use of reason (or the "little grey cells" as Hercule Poirot would say) is what ultimately leads to the triumph of good over evil. Finally, the sanctity of human life is upheld religiously in good detective fiction. The blow-your-enemy-up, huge-body-count, Rambo-style mentality is not found in the pages of MacLeod, James, Christie, Sayers, or Doyle. Agatha Christie's sleuth, Miss Jane Marple, brings culprits to justice and rights the grievous wrong of the taking of human life without killing off half the British countryside in the process. And she is not alone. In good mystery fare, the brain—not the automatic rifle—is the ultimate weapon, and it is used for the good of humanity and the preservation of a society of laws and order.

Why Mysteries for Gifted Students?

Anyone who doubts the appropriateness of the mystery genre for gifted and talented students should examine the challenging vocabulary (e.g., torpor, puerile, chimerical) found in the classic mystery stories of Conan Doyle and Edgar Allan Poe, or read one of P. D. James's modern morality tales.

If *Mystery and Detection* consisted of nothing more than an annotated bibliography of mystery fare with assorted directed reading questions about mystery stories and novels, then critics would be correct in charging that it should be directed to *all* students. I would quickly add that I have no objection to the reading of mysteries by students of all abilities and aptitudes. Indeed, as an English and reading teacher of students with a wide variety of needs, I have used mysteries to motivate and teach students who are reluctant readers and those with specific learning disabilities. Many of the ideas and suggestions in this text can be used fruitfully with all students.

However, the *chief* focal point of *Mystery and Detection* is the gifted student population. The readings, resources, strategies and investigations proposed and recommended are intended to challenge the most able pupils. Holistic and interdisciplinary learning are among the hallmarks of curriculum for gifted students. The chapters in *Mystery and Detection* accent several of the major academic disciplines: reading and the language arts, the fine arts, and the social studies; additional chapters are devoted to future studies and crime and punishment. Both of these latter chapters examine math and science connections.

I am confident that teachers and library media specialists will find enough breadth and depth in the recommended materials and strategies in this book to meet the widely varying academic needs of all gifted and talented students they serve. The learning experiences set forth in this book stem from student encounters with good examples of the mystery genre. The lessons and activities have significant potential for developing the writing, research, communication, planning skills, and innate creativity of talented students. Mystery and detection are exceptionally broad and rich topics of study through which the needs, interests, and learning styles of gifted and talented students may be accommodated. Myriad possibilities for interdisciplinary study exist for classes and individuals. Similarly, there are fertile opportunities for independent inquiry. Utilizing a single mystery story, for example, disciplines as varied as literature, philosophy, science, law, medicine, sociology, and psychology may be addressed. Beyond the basic lessons in literature and critical thinking orchestrated by the classroom teacher, students may identify areas of special interest for further research and study. The class logician can have a field day analyzing and critiquing examples of reasoning found in fiction and in real life legal cases. The would-be pathologist can investigate and learn about the more than thirty ways blood samples may be analyzed in a police laboratory. A young author can practice his or her writing skills utilizing the mystery genre and perhaps even establish a mentorship with a local mystery writer. The future Perry Mason can become the classroom legal expert.

Of course, all such investigations and inquiries are predicated on the willingness of the gifted student to *want* to learn. More and more, my experience leads me to accept the accuracy of the definition of giftedness proposed by Joseph Renzulli. Dr. Renzulli's definition is based upon the proposition that no single criterion should be utilized to identify giftedness. Rather, the University of Connecticut scholar suggests that giftedness is the interaction among three particular traits: above average ability, creativity, and task commitment.[2] I place particular emphasis on the task commitment component. I contend that gifted students deserve an education appropriate to their native abilities and talents. But, it is also my conviction that gifted students must respond to the challenges provided. Schools should not be in the business of labeling students just to ordain an elite class. Labeling is, at best, a necessary condition. The label "gifted" should exist to tell educators that particular students require special services and considerations. It is then incumbent upon these designated students to rise to the occasion when appropriate challenges are provided. Whenever a particularly difficult case was set before Sherlock Holmes, he accepted the challenge with relish. He threw all his energies into the pursuit of justice. He brought all his abilities to bear on the case. True, Holmes is a fictional character, but that does not lessen the importance of his actions and deeds. The presumption of this book and its activities is that "giftedness" is not a badge to be worn on a letter sweater. Rather, it is a whole way of being. It is characterized by an intense desire to learn, sustained by personal ambition and pride, and ultimately manifested in creative works.

The Morality Issue

Since mystery literature is so inextricably tied to criminality and ethics, it is worth commenting on these issues as they relate to gifted students. Much has been written and spoken about the gifted, their interest in ethical matters, and their morality. Some of the more hysterical advocates for gifted students have publicly claimed that unless gifted students are challenged in the schools, they may be prone to crime. Though the case of Leopold and Loeb is more than a half century past, the public is still dismayed and mystified as to why two young men from privileged backgrounds, one of whom was highly gifted, would wantonly and senselessly murder another youth. When a bright youth is arrested for a computer crime, the story receives national focus and attention. As I write these words, elsewhere in the nation, funeral services are being conducted for four high school honor students whose unsupervised experiment with constructing a homemade pipe bomb ended in a devastating tragedy.

The acknowledged father of gifted education research, Lewis Terman, probably began the public discussion of the moral behavior of the gifted with his now classic report in the first volume of *Genetic Studies of Genius* published in 1925. Among his many generalizations about gifted students, Terman wrote: "The gifted child of nine or ten has reached a stage of moral development which is not attained by the average child until age thirteen or fourteen."[3]

After thirty-five years of investigation of the same subjects, Melita Oden, writing in the fifth volume of the classic *Genetic Studies of Genius*, summarized what was then known about gifted subjects. The summary includes this statement:

> Indications are that the group does not differ greatly from the generality in the extent of personality and adjustment problems as shown by mental breakdown, suicide, and marital failures. The delinquency rate is but a small fraction of that found in the generality.[4]

Terman himself cautioned against unwarranted generalizations based upon his research. Contemporary researchers cast doubts about the generalizations he did make because of limiting factors associated with the selection of the subjects. Regardless, Terman's generalizations have been seized upon by educators and used as a rationale for the inclusion of teaching strategies based on Harvard Professor Lawrence Kohlberg's six-stage moral development hierarchy.[5]

Two Canadian researchers, Susanne P. Lajoie and Bruce M. Shore, reviewed the literature on delinquency among the gifted. They found the entire issue of gifted delinquency is very much confounded by other variables such as socio-economic status and learning disabilities.[6] Another Canadian, Margaret Parker argues forcefully for the need to rechannel the energies of gifted youths prone to delinquency in more positive and socially acceptable directions.[7]

My own experiences with gifted youth lead me to believe that the vast majority are not overly inclined toward delinquency. More critically, I believe that delinquency or its absence are chiefly the result of factors well beyond my control as a classroom teacher. Nevertheless, a little additional insurance can do no harm. Mysteries are splendid morality tales. Crime does not pay, nor is it glamorized in mystery fiction. Gifted students whom I have taught have attended to and profited from discussions of real-life and literary dilemmas oriented to Kohlberg's postulated hierarchy of moral development. Finally, more than a few students I have known have been dazzled by the sophistication of modern police detection technology and skills shared by experts visiting the classroom. Any student even remotely prone to delinquency may give more than a little pause to any thoughts of breaking the law after learning about the detection devices at the disposal of law enforcement agencies today!

The mystery genre is a rich, vital, and fertile domain of study for gifted and talented students. Properly approached, the topic is of sufficient breadth and depth to provide the challenge needed to meet the academic needs of virtually all gifted students.

Notes

[1]P. D. James, "Woman of Mystery," *Vis à Vis* 3 no. 5 (May 1989): 74.

[2]Joseph S. Renzulli, "What Makes Giftedness: Re-examining a Definition," *Phi Delta Kappan* 60 (November 1978): 180-84, 261.

[3]Lewis M. Terman, *Genetic Studies of Genius* (Volume 1) *Mental and Physical Traits of a Thousand Gifted Children* (Stanford, Calif.: Stanford University Press, 1925), 638.

[4]Lewis M. Terman, and Melita H. Oden, *Genetic Studies of Genius* (Volume 5) *The Gifted Group at Mid-life* (Stanford, Calif.: Stanford University Press, 1959), 143.

[5]For a detailed discussion of the use of Dr. Lawrence Kohlberg's moral dilemmas with gifted and talented students, see C. Maker June, *Teaching Models in Education of the Gifted* (Rockville, Md.: Aspen Systems Corporation, 1982), 137-76.

[6]Susanne P. Lajoie and Bruce Shore, "Three Myths? The Over-Representation of the Gifted among Dropouts, Delinquents, and Suicides," *Gifted Child Quarterly* 25 no. 3 (Summer 1981): 138-43.

[7]Margaret Parker, "Bright Kids in Trouble with the Law," *G/C/T* 9 (September/October 1979): 62-63.

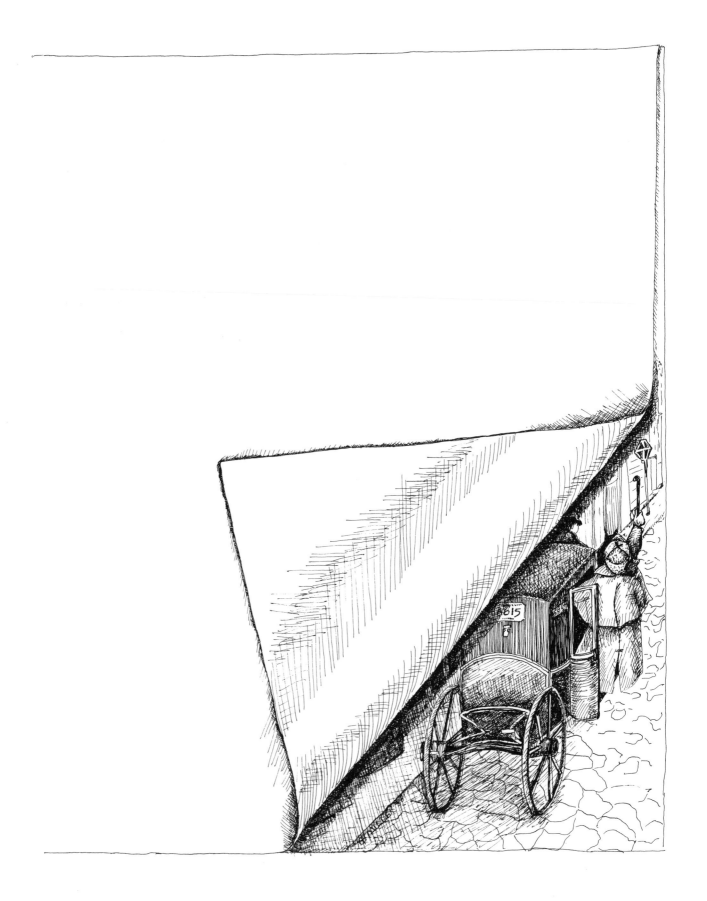

1

Problem Solving with Mysteries and Detectives

Models for Problem Solving and Sleuthing

I have worked in the field of education for nearly a quarter of a century. I have observed all manner and ages of students approach, tackle, and solve problems. As I have watched kindergarten students, graduate students, and professional colleagues engage in problem solving, the similarity between their behaviors and those of master detectives has not escaped my attention. Perhaps, at heart, we are all sleuths. Maybe this is why we like Nancy Drew and the Hardy Boys as youth and why, as adults, we cuddle up with tales of Hercule Poirot or Lord Peter Wimsey just before day's end. Is it just an accident that Sherlock Holmes is the most famous literary creation in the English language? I do not think so. Hence, I approach an educational definition of critical thinking and problem solving with a definite awareness of its close similarity to good, old-fashioned sleuthing.

Sherlock Holmes, the sixth grade science fair entrant, and the archaeologist share certain common, generic stages in solving problems. First, there is a motivational set. The motive may be an extra credit grade for a school child, the fulfillment of a job assignment for a worker, or the sheer joy of pursuing truth and righting wrongs for Sherlock Holmes. Once the task of detection or problem solving has been accepted, the hunt is on.

Good problem solvers and detectives are bloodhounds for facts and clues. They leave no avenue of possible relevance unexplored. They are systematic. Once their data have been assembled, they bring past experience and learning to bear in sorting, saving, and organizing data pertinent to the investigation. A hypothesis or prediction follows which is confirmed or disproved. A denouement or resolution is the final stage. Things are tidied up. The acclaim and awards are enjoyed or disappointing results are acknowledged. The problem solver or detective proceeds to new avenues of research, brand new ventures, or new cases.

Of course, detection, whether in the field of science, the arts, or on the pages of an Agatha Christie novel, is not always neat and tidy. Problem solving can be messy as well as precise. Hence, each "problem solving/ sleuthing" definition (see figures 1.1 and 1.2) should be seen as a generalization rather than absolute prescription from which there is never any variance. Some problem solvers depend upon a period of incubation, waiting and hoping for flashes of insight. Great detectives and great scientists sometimes follow hunches and intuition rather than logic; individual problem solvers may add or delete steps in the problem solving/sleuthing process as they idiosyncratically and heuristically approach and solve problems.

Any analysis of the problem solving/sleuthing model needs to consider the problem solver as well as the process. The affective characteristics and traits of problem solvers and detectives need to be considered. Risk taking, tolerance for ambiguity, and a burning rage to know are all personal qualities which cannot be prescribed, but which surely affect the outcome of any scientific exploration, artistic searching, or murder mystery investigation.

All of the activities and strategies recommended in *Mystery and Detection* emphasize at least one of the problem solving/sleuthing steps. Many of the projects utilize all the steps in combination. The following graphic symbols will be used throughout the text to call attention to particular activities which are especially geared to or emphasize a particular stage in the process.

MOTIVATION

SEARCH

ANALYSIS

HYPOTHESIS

VERIFICATION

RESOLUTION

ALL LEVELS

Figs. 1.1 and 1.2.

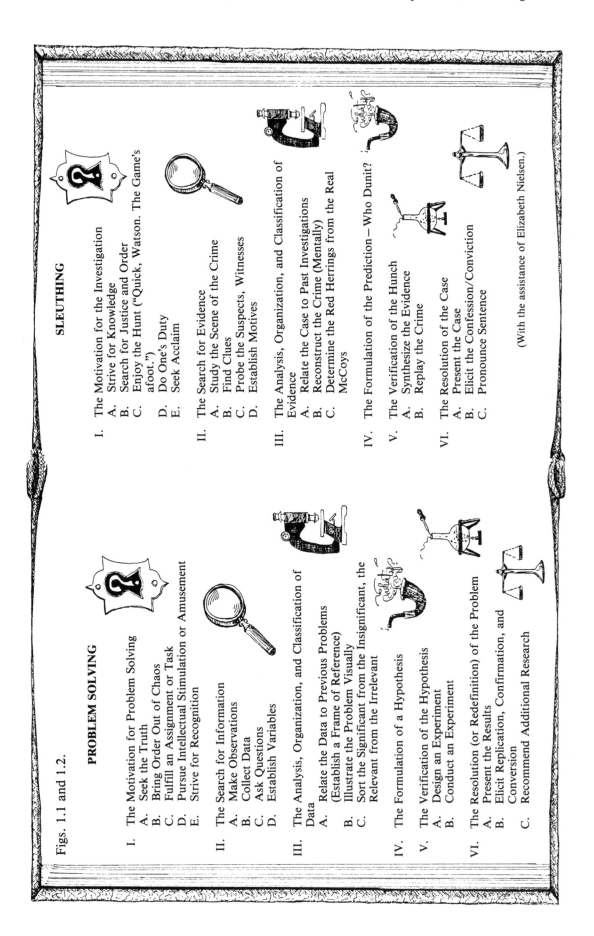

PROBLEM SOLVING

I. The Motivation for Problem Solving
    A. Seek the Truth
    B. Bring Order Out of Chaos
    C. Fulfill an Assignment or Task
    D. Pursue Intellectual Stimulation or Amusement
    E. Strive for Recognition

II. The Search for Information
    A. Make Observations
    B. Collect Data
    C. Ask Questions
    D. Establish Variables

III. The Analysis, Organization, and Classification of Data
    A. Relate the Data to Previous Problems (Establish a Frame of Reference)
    B. Illustrate the Problem Visually
    C. Sort the Significant from the Insignificant, the Relevant from the Irrelevant

IV. The Formulation of a Hypothesis

V. The Verification of the Hypothesis
    A. Design an Experiment
    B. Conduct an Experiment

VI. The Resolution (or Redefinition) of the Problem
    A. Present the Results
    B. Elicit Replication, Confirmation, and Conversion
    C. Recommend Additional Research

SLEUTHING

I. The Motivation for the Investigation
    A. Strive for Knowledge
    B. Search for Justice and Order
    C. Enjoy the Hunt ("Quick, Watson. The Game's afoot.")
    D. Do One's Duty
    E. Seek Acclaim

II. The Search for Evidence
    A. Study the Scene of the Crime
    B. Find Clues
    C. Probe the Suspects, Witnesses
    D. Establish Motives

III. The Analysis, Organization, and Classification of Evidence
    A. Relate the Case to Past Investigations
    B. Reconstruct the Crime (Mentally)
    C. Determine the Red Herrings from the Real McCoys

IV. The Formulation of the Prediction—Who Dunit?

V. The Verification of the Hunch
    A. Synthesize the Evidence
    B. Replay the Crime

VI. The Resolution of the Case
    A. Present the Case
    B. Elicit the Confession/Conviction
    C. Pronounce Sentence

(With the assistance of Elizabeth Nielsen.)

Mr. Sherlock Holmes:
A Role Model for Students and Teachers Alike

Mr. Sherlock Holmes appears to be an exemplary role model for both gifted students and their teachers. Holmes was a true student of all disciplines. He recognized the need to study science and mathematics as well as history, art, and languages. He never knew in advance which of the many disciplines he would need to call upon to solve a mystery. He believed education to be a lifelong pursuit. Mr. Sherlock Holmes is probably most famous for his unswerving faith in the power of the intellect. Gifted students *and* their teachers could do far worse than to emulate the intellectual and pedagogical behaviors of the well-known resident of 221 B Baker Street.

Figure 1.3 is an essay written by Dr. Ron Abrell. Dr. Abrell sums up the sterling qualities found in the character of Mr. Holmes which contemporary educators would do well to emulate. It is reproduced here with the permission of Dr. Abrell and *The Clearing House: A Journal for Middle Schools, Junior and Senior High Schools.*[1]

(Text continues on page 9.)

Fig. 1.3. Dr. Ron Abrell's article on character qualities.

MR. SHERLOCK HOLMES:
TEACHING EXEMPLAR EXTRAORDINARY

A keen observer of educational theory and practice must necessarily note the education profession's lack of interest in the use of literature as a tool for teaching. Yet, literature offers an unusually rich store of fictional characters from whom all educators can learn much. One such fictional character is none other than Mr. Sherlock Holmes of 221 B Baker Street. In the view of this writer, Sherlock Holmes constitutes a model whose personal characteristics, love of truth, concern for his fellow man, and teaching ability exemplify the best in pedagogy.

Before taking a look at the world's most celebrated sleuth as a teaching exemplar, perhaps it should be pointed out that Holmes had a vital interest in education and spoke to its importance on several occasions. That the famous detective believed in education is made quite clear by a remark made to Dr. Watson as the two passed through Clapham Junction on one of their returning journeys to London. Watson writes that:

> Holmes was sunk in profound thought, and hardly opened his eyes until we had passed Clapham Junction. "It's a very cheering thing to come into London by way of these lines which run high and allow you to look down upon the houses like this."
>
> I thought that he was joking, for the view was sordid enough, but he soon explained himself.
>
> "Look at those big, isolated clumps of buildings rising up above the slates, like brick islands in a lead-coloured sea."
>
> "The Board Schools."
>
> "Lighthouses, my boy! Beacons of the future! Capsules, with hundreds of bright little seeds in each, out of which will spring the wiser, better England of the future...."[1]

Not only did Holmes believe in formal schooling but he repeatedly insisted that education in the classroom be applied to the human experiment and tested in the laboratory of life beyond the classroom. Throughout all of the adventures and memoirs of the world's most renowned detective, Dr. Watson underscores the fact that Holmes is a well-educated man who is highly trained in his profession. However, Holmes is a person who applies his education to the most difficult problems and is first, last, and always a man of action who

achieves measurable results. In "The Musgrave Ritual," the following exchange takes place between Reginald Musgrave and Sherlock Holmes: "But I understand, Holmes, that you are turning to practical ends those powers with which you used to amaze us?" " 'Yes,' said I, 'I have taken to living by my wits,' "[2]

Like all great teachers, Sherlock Holmes loved his profession and lived for his art. Just as great teachers are preoccupied with their work and continually dream about what they might accomplish in the future, Holmes was totally obsessed with his work. In "The Adventure of the Copper Beeches," Holmes tells Watson that "it is one of the curses of a mind with a turn like mine that I must look at everything with reference to my own special subject."[3] As a person who worked "for the love of his art rather than for the acquirement of wealth,"[4] Holmes' magnificant obsession with his work is indeed exemplary and inspirational for all those who truly love the profession of teaching. The point is well made by Watson in the following passage from "The Man with the Twisted Lip":

> Sherlock Holmes was a man ... who, when he had an unsolved problem upon his mind, would go for days, and even for a week without rest, turning it over, rearranging his facts, looking at it from every point of view until he had either fathomed it or convinced himself that his data were insufficient.[5]

Holmes' level of commitment to and love for his profession exemplifies the attitude of excellent teachers everywhere when he says to a client concerned about rewarding him for his services, "As to reward, my profession is its own reward."[6]

Sherlock Holmes also possessed many personal characteristics which teachers might do well to emulate. He realized the importance of appearance and dress, knowing that they announce the practicing professional's attitudes, moods and values. Holmes also dressed for the particular situation in which he was to become involved so that he might better communicate with his clients. Like teachers who dress in a way that establishes a tone for interacting with students of varying backgrounds, Holmes observed the sartorial customs and fashions that his clients in their particular situations felt comfortable with. Not only did the

(Fig. 1.3 continues on page 6.)

celebrated detective assume many different disguises in order to trick or mislead the culprits of his cases, but he also disguised himself in order to establish contact and rapport with clients and criminals alike.

Sherlock Holmes also possessed that special blend of self-confidence and humility which characterizes distinguished teachers. His alert manner, upright carriage, impeccable dress, keen powers of observation, quick wit, clever repartee, and ability to comment at length on a broad spectrum of subjects denote and communicate a measure of self-confidence that all teachers could utilize. In "The Musgrave Ritual," Holmes tells Watson that he is "recognized both by the public and by the official force as being a final court of appeal in doubtful cases."[7] Holmes' self-confidence may be seen in nearly every case on which he works as he consistently informs his clients that justice will soon be done, the culprit will soon be behind bars, and that the criminal will receive sufficient punishment. In sum, Holmes knows that he is among the best in his profession and he knows that he is going to succeed because he, like all of the great teachers, makes use of knowledge, observation, and reason. Holmes indeed thought that knowledge, observation, and deduction were the three qualities which make the ideal detective. These qualities helped him assert that, "In my inmost heart I believed that I could succeed where others failed....[8] Certainly, the same qualities and the attitude to succeed where others fail give rise to that level of self-confidence which undoubtedly assists teachers in becoming highly successful.

The self-confidence displayed by Sherlock Holmes was balanced nicely by the humility that nearly always accompanies great detectives and teachers alike. Holmes knew that in the larger affair of human progress, many of his achievements were trifling and trivial. While Holmes' replies to Watson's recurring amazement frequently took the form of "elementary," "superficial," and "commonplace," these expressions do not represent egotism but show humility in that they communicate insignificant bits of information. Although supremely confident, Holmes repeatedly manifests humility during all of his cases. Perhaps a passage from "The Adventure of The Copper Beeches" reveals Holmes' humility as it really was. In answer to Watson, who was thinking how repelled he was by his friend's egotism, Holmes retorts:

> "No, it is not selfishness or conceit,"
> said he, answering as was his wont, my
> thoughts rather than my words. "If I claim
> full justice for my art, it is because it is ... a
> thing beyond myself."[9]

Throughout some fifty-six short stories and four novels which constitute *The Complete Sherlock Holmes*, the eminent private-eye admonishes Watson to remind him of his shortcomings and any over-confidence he may have. That such is the case is amply illustrated in "The Yellow Face," an episode in Norbury in which Holmes felt that he had overlooked the obvious. In his own words, "Watson," said he, "if it should ever strike you that I am getting a little over-confident in my powers, or giving less pains to a case than it deserves, kindly whisper 'Norbury' in my ear, and I shall be infinitely obliged to you."[10]

Although time does not permit citing examples here, even a casual reading of the Holmes' adventures and memoirs reveals that the fabled sleuth had many of the qualities which any teacher worth his salt possesses. Holmes is dependable, creative, enthusiastic, empathetic, intelligent, knowledgeable, insightful, imaginative, polite, punctual, and reliable. Conan Doyle characterizes him as a tireless worker who sees a task through until it is accomplished. Holmes is a realist who works toward the ideal, always striving to make the world a little more reasonable and humane. Although much of what he observes causes him to feel pessimistic at times, Holmes comes off as an optimist who believes he can make a difference. Like all great teachers, he wants to do something of lasting significance in his life. When Holmes tells Watson that his "life is spent in one long effort to escape from the commonplaces of existence,"[11] he is indicating that he is dissatisfied with the way things are. In actuality, Holmes lived the major part of his life moving from this "escape from the commonplaces of existence" to moving toward transcending the existential anxiety that grips all sensitive persons. His was largely a life of action devoted to the triumph of good over evil, intelligence over insanity, and logic over crime.[12]

The group of characteristics which most distinguish Sherlock Holmes as a human being and a professional is precisely those qualities which all great teachers possess and strive to develop. Specifically, Holmes is unique among detectives and other ordinary professionals because of his natural curiosity, inquiring mind, and thirst for truth. He is a seeker of answers, is in perennial quest of wisdom, and makes the "faculties of deduction and of logical synthesis"[13] his "special province."[14]

Holmes' curiosity and inquiring mind are evident in all of the cases on which he worked and can be illustrated by quoting the following from "The Blue Carbuncle": "He [Peterson, the commissionaire] brought round both the hat and goose to me on Christmas morning, knowing that even the smallest problems are of interest to me."[15] Again, in the same adventure in which he is pursuing a clue centering around a hat, Holmes tells Watson, "Its owner is unknown. I beg that you will look upon it not as a battered billycock but as an intellectual problem."[16]

Holmes always sought the truth and searched for answers wherever such took him and for however long was necessary. As the master himself puts it, "I shall take nothing for granted until I have the opportunity of looking personally into it."[17] Elsewhere, he states his tenacity when in pursuit of truth in the following way: "I make a point of never having any prejudices and of following docilely wherever fact may lead me...."[18] The constant, consistent, and careful way in which Holmes searched for the truth can also be viewed from an exchange taking place in "The Adventure of the Priory School," with Watson writing: "Holmes," I cried, "this is impossible." "Admirable!" he said. "A most illuminating remark. It *is* impossible as I state it, and therefore, I must in some respect have stated it wrong."[19]

Solutions to Holmes' cases had to come from data, as aptly recorded by Dr. Watson in "The Adventure of the Copper Beeches": "Data! data! data," he [Holmes] cried impatiently. "I can't make bricks without clay."[20] The importance of data is repeatedly underscored by Holmes throughout his cases and is made clear by Watson in "The Adventure of the Speckled Band": "I had," said he [Holmes] "come to an entirely erroneous conclusion which shows, my dear Watson, how dangerous it always is to reason from insufficient data."[21]

As for the particular act of teaching itself, Holmes shares much with the most competent of teachers. Dr. Watson, among other things, may be viewed as a student who not only sits at the feet of the master but also works at his side. Holmes makes Watson a helper, colleague, factotum, and sounding-board in solving problems. Holmes was excellent at establishing relationships and making one feel at ease. That this is so is obvious in "The Blue Carbuncle," in which Watson calls upon Holmes who is deep in the midst of work. Watson greets Holmes with the following: "You are engaged," said I; "perhaps I interrupt you." Holmes' reply is, "Not at all. I am glad to have a friend with whom I can discuss my results."[22] Throughout the Sherlock Holmes' stories, Watson always seems to be bungling, stumbling, and interrupting but Holmes constantly brings out the best in his student by praising, questioning, reinforcing, and encouraging the novice. It is not just what he brings out in Watson that counts, but also the qualities he puts into the doctor. The confidence, pride, and desire to know and succeed that Holmes gives Watson is evident in the three following passages:

Holmes tells Watson, "Now, I'll state the case clearly and concisely to you, Watson, and maybe you can see a spark where all is dark to me."[23]

Holmes informs one of his clients: "This is my friend, Dr. Watson. He has been of most vital use to me in several of my cases, and a lucky chance has made it possible for me to bring him out and associate him with this investigation."[24]

Watson writes: "I can see nothing," said I, handing it [an ordinary black hat] to my friend,"
"On the contrary, Watson, you can see everything. You fail, however, to reason from what you see. You are too timid in drawing your inferences."[25]

Holmes was a master at boosting the confidence and morale of both the good doctor and his clients. In all of his cases, he enthusiastically compliments Watson and his clientele with such adjectives as "excellent," "capital," "brilliant," and "superb." Not only did the noted detective anticipate what has come to be known as "Reward or Reinforcement Psychology," but he also was an educational psychologist of sorts. Although Holmes was not given to the jargon and special argot of the psychologists of today, he ranks among the first to see persons as individuals but as individuals caught up in groups. He was convinced that there are patterns of human behavior and given a fact, one can deduce a cause, and given a particular situation, one can hypothesize a probable result. This concept is beautifully illustrated when Holmes says, "You can ... never foretell what any one man will do, but you can say with precision what an average member will be up to. Individuals vary, but percentages remain constant."[26] Similar to all great teachers, Sherlock Holmes was a life-long student of all human behavior.

As is the case with outstanding teachers everywhere, Holmes excelled in communication. He was superb at putting his clients at ease and was a careful and sincere listener, interrupting only for some important detail. He was unusually competent at what George Herbert Meade called "taking the role of the other" or putting himself in the other person's place, thus improving his chances for picking up the subtle nuances of what was being said. Holmes was good at asking questions and drawing out his clients. The climate he set for interaction was typically characterized by warmth,

(Fig. 1.3 continues on page 8.)

concern, confidentiality, and openness without any possibility of condemnation. Of special note was his interest in and ability to interpret the nonverbal, both of which are faithfully recorded by Dr. Watson time and again in *The Complete Sherlock Holmes*. Three Sherlockian epigrams which give evidence of this include such quips as: "You see, Watson, but you do not observe" "I have trained myself to notice what I see"; and "My dear Watson, you look but you do not really see." In all of his cases, Holmes startled his clients and Watson himself with his remarkable understanding of non-verbal behavior. Characteristic of the importance Holmes placed on the meaning of nonverbal clues is a social transaction with Watson in "The Resident Patient." Watson expresses incredulity at a Holmesian inference by saying, "But I have been seated quietly in my chair, and what clues can I have given you?" Holmes replies, "You do yourself an injustice. The features are given to man as the means by which he shall express his emotions, and yours are faithful servants." Watson then queries, "Do you mean to say that you read my train of thoughts from my features?" Holmes' answer to the question is in the affirmative, "Your features, and especially your eyes."[27]

Finally, the trait that clinches Sherlock Holmes as a teaching exemplar extraordinary is his humanism. In all of his work, the famed detective combines good will with good taste, honorable intentions with high-minded spirit, and compassion with common sense. The humanism extended by Holmes to the thief in "The Blue Carbuncle" is the humanism which all great teachers extend to their erring students:

> After all, Watson, I am not retained by the police to supply their deficiencies ... I suppose that I am commuting a felony, but it is just possible that I am saving a soul. This fellow will not go wrong again; he is too terribly frightened. Send him to jail now, and you make him a jail-bird for life.[28]

Conclusion

It has been the purpose of this piece to show potential which literature may hold for shedding light upon the profession of teaching. Sir Arthur Conan Doyle's Sherlock Holmes was chosen as an example of how the paths of literature intersect with those of the teaching profession. Holmes was portrayed as a teaching exemplar par excellence and as one who shares many of the qualities possessed by the great teachers. His

portrait, as conceived in this paper, intended to show that he also stands as one from whom all teachers can learn much.

In summary, Sherlock Holmes loved his profession, lived for his clientele, and worked steadily in behalf of humankind in its entirety. He taught by example and championed humaneness, reason, and the development of the mind. Although the virtues which he and all great teachers exemplify are in short supply, one has the feeling that their importance is both elemental and as the master himself might say: "Elementary, my dear Watson, elementary!"

Notes

1. Sir Arthur Conan Doyle, *The Naval Treaty* in *The Complete Sherlock Holmes* (Garden City, New York: Doubleday & Company, Inc.), pp. 456-57.

2. _____. "The Musgrave Ritual," p. 388.

3. _____. "The Adventure of the Copper Beeches," p. 323.

4. _____. "The Adventure of the Speckled Band," p. 257.

5. _____. "The Man with the Twisted Lip," p. 240.

6. _____. "The Adventure of the Speckled Band," p. 259.

7. _____. "The Musgrave Ritual," p. 387.

8. Ibid., p. 388.

9. _____. "The Adventure of the Copper Beeches," p. 317.

10. _____. "The Yellow Face," p. 362.

11. _____. "The Red-Headed League," p. 190.

12. _____. "The Adventure of the Copper Beeches," p. 317.

13. Ibid.

14. Ibid.

15. _____. "The Blue Carbuncle," p. 246.

16. Ibid., p. 245.

17. _____. "The Boscombe Valley Mystery," p. 202.

18. _____. "The Reigate Puzzle," p. 407.

19. _____. "The Adventure of the Priory School," pp. 549-50.

20. _____. "The Adventure of the Copper Beeches," p. 322.

21. _____. "The Adventure of the Speckled Band," p. 272.

22. _____. "The Adventure of the Blue Carbuncle," p. 244.

23. _____. "The Man with the Twisted Lip," p. 233.

24. Ibid., p. 237.

25. _____. "The Adventure of the Blue Carbuncle," p. 246.

26. _____. *The Sign of Four*, p. 137.

27. _____. "The Resident Patient," p. 423.

28. _____. "The Adventure of the Blue Carbuncle," p. 257.

Using *Mystery and Detection*

There are several common features in each chapter of *Mystery and Detection*. These features or segments are intended for duplication and student use. They appear under these headings:

A Letter from a Professional

Case Study

Tools of the Trade

Mystery Desks

Traces

A "Letter from a Professional" is a letter directed to students from a dedicated and successful professional in a field or discipline related to the subject matter at hand. These professionals share with students how they work to solve problems. Each chapter also contains a case study relevant to the content and discipline of the chapter. The case studies illustrate the problem solving and sleuthing models at work. In "Tools of the Trade," students are asked to consider the professional tools needed by persons operating within the province of each of the various disciplines or topics addressed.

Two visual mysteries or puzzles have been created for students in each chapter. The childhood or adult desks ("Mystery Desks") or work tables of famous people representative of the disciplines are shown. The pictures contain well-placed clues readers need in order to determine the identity of the owners of the mystery desks. The utilization of problem solving and sleuthing skills will help the patient and persistent detectives in the classroom figure out the mysteries of the desks.

Likewise, good detectives in the classroom will delight in solving the puzzles which appear in "Traces" in each chapter. Traces, like footprints in the sand, are clues, that if carefully examined and studied, reveal a famous incident or episode from fiction, art, or real life. The drawings have special relevance to the chapters in which they appear. For example, the traces drawing found in the chapter on language arts is a scene from *The Wizard of Oz*.

The focal point of each chapter is the description of educational activities for classroom, library, or home use. At the conclusion of each chapter, reading lists and other pertinent resources for both students and teachers (or parents) are listed. A bibliography of mysteries appropriate for elementary and secondary school students may be found at the end of the book.

The Role of the Library Media Specialist

A major feature of each volume in the Gifted Treasury Series is an emphasis on the importance of the role library media specialists play in the education of gifted students. In every school, the library media specialist should be an integral and indispensable member of the curriculum planning team in gifted child education. It is nearly impossible to imagine completing a successful mystery unit without the full cooperation and participation of the library media specialist. He or she can be of invaluable help in creating a collection of appropriate mysteries for students of various ages and abilities. He or she can assist students in the many and varied investigations suggested throughout this text. He or she can assist in the location of difficult-to-find print and audiovisual resources, and direct students to human resource persons such as pathologists, criminologists, and local mystery authors. A creative library media specialist may also seize the opportunity to engage in some chilling story telling based on the mystery theme. The library media center can truly be the Scotland Yard upon which young scholar/sleuths converge. The library media specialist, sleuth par excellence, who guides their myriad investigations may well be the Commander Adam Dalgliesh of the school. Whether in teaching gifted students how to search for information, analyze evidence, check the veracity of sources, or use media tools to prepare an unbeatable case, the library media specialist can and should be a significant mentor for gifted and talented students.

Classroom Environment

A classroom where mystery and intrigue are to be the center focal point should definitely have allure and mystique. Movie posters of Sherlock Holmes and Agatha Christie characters may decorate walls. Video stores and poster shops are excellent sources of such material. Teachers and library media specialists should always be alert to free and inexpensive bulletin board material. Because of the popularity of mystery figures, mystery-oriented material is not difficult to locate. Figure 1.4 is an example of advertising which alludes to the great Sherlock Holmes. Such advertising not only calls attention to the topic at hand, it reinforces in students' minds the universal appeal of mysteries.[2]

A learning center is a definite must. The learning center may include mystery games like Parker Brothers classic board game, Clue® or any of the many games based upon the exploits of Sherlock Holmes which may be found in mystery book stores or games stores. Magazines like *The Armchair Detective* should be available for student reading.[3] Catalogs from mystery bookstores provoke student interest and reveal the breadth of choice within the mystery genre.[4] Classic works of detective fiction should be in the learning center or on an adjoining reading chart. Note that the school library media specialist can be especially helpful in selecting mysteries which are appropriate for the age and grade level needs of students. Advance teacher planning should utilize the assistance and talent of the library media specialist in selecting nonfiction books which are relevant to the mystery unit. Many titles are cited throughout this book. Essential books to keep available throughout the study of mysteries are listed in the section "Essential Book Resources." Additional nonfiction books might include biographies of famous mystery writers, real-life detectives (e.g., Pinkerton), famous crimes and criminals, or books about police procedures such as fingerprinting.

Essential Book Resources

There are several prime resources which teachers should consult before starting the mystery unit with students. Generally, these same resources should be available throughout the unit for use by both teachers and students. Here, as elsewhere throughout the entire book, only the names of authors and titles will appear in the chapter text; complete bibliographic information about resources will be found at the end of the chapter in which each title is named. Here are the prime resources (see bibliography for complete publication information):

Franklin W. Dixon, *The Hardy Boys Detective Handbook*.

Michael Hardwick, *Sherlock Holmes: My Life and Crimes*.

Jane Horning, *The Mystery Lovers' Book of Quotations*.

Phil McArdle, and Karen McArdle, *Fatal Fascination: Where Fact Meets Fiction in Police Work*.

Barbara Norville, *Writing the Modern Mystery*.

Dilys Winn, *Murder Ink: The Mystery Reader's Companion*.

Dilys Winn, *Murderess Ink: The Better Half of the Mystery*.

Fig. 1.4. (Reprinted with permission from AT&T.)

Before you choose a long distance service, take a close look.

You may be thinking about choosing one of the newer carriers over AT&T in order to save money.

Think again.

Since January 1987, AT&T's rates have dropped more than 15% for direct-dialed out-of-state calls. So they're lower than you probably realize. For information on specific rates, you can call us at 1 800 222-0300.

And AT&T offers clear long distance connections, operator assistance, 24-hour customer service, and immediate credit for wrong numbers. Plus, you can use AT&T to call from anywhere to anywhere, all over the United States and to over 250 countries.

You might be surprised at how good a value AT&T really is. So before you choose a long distance company, pick up the phone.

AT&T
The right choice.

Creating a Web of Intrigue

Ascertaining what students already know about mysteries and mystery literature is a beginning point for a mystery unit. The use of the webbing technique is a highly effective tool for this purpose. Ask students to brainstorm all they know about mysteries, mystery writers, and detectives. Who are their favorite mystery writers? How many famous fictional sleuths can they name? What new things would they like to know about mystery literature and the art and science of detection? The completed web, displayed on the bulletin board, may serve as a guide in assigning student projects and activities for individual and small group investigations and an outline for projects and inquiries for the entire class. Figure 1.5 is an example of a web a class might create. The web illustrates the versatility the mystery unit has in accommodating a variety of learning interests and styles students exhibit, and the multidisciplinary nature of mystery inquiries. Figure 1.6 is an unfinished web teachers and library media specialists may use with students.

Two alternative approaches may be utilized to discern prior knowledge students bring to the mystery unit. In one variation of the web students first recall all they know about mysteries and detection via brainstorming as suggested above. However, do not web or connect the student responses. Instead, simply record all the responses on the chalkboard in the order they are given. When all discussion and volunteering of names, objects, and ideas ceases, move to the second step. Ask the students to suggest an effective means of categorizing the random information on the board. One student may suggest the following as a good way to categorize all the information:

CRIMES   SLEUTHS   WRITERS   FAMOUS CASES

The class then tries to place all the data they have volunteered into the four suggested categories. Another student might suggest that a temporal classification system (e.g., PAST, PRESENT, FUTURE) would work better. Still another student might suggest that geographical classes (e.g., UNITED STATES, GREAT BRITAIN, and OTHER NATIONS) would work well.

In this exercise, students not only reveal what they know about mystery and detection, but also use the thinking skills of classification and categorization.

Figure 1.7 is an example of a seat activity students can do. Provide each student with a copy of figure 1.7, which is an acrostic puzzle. Each student fills in the blank spaces with all the associations he or she can make about mystery and detection. The tough part is that all the names, objects, and ideas listed must begin with the letters listed on the left margins. The information they write down must fit the acrostic pattern: M-Y-S-T-E-R-Y. After students have had time to complete the acrostic sheet, a class discussion may proceed with the students sharing and comparing what they have written.

(Text continues on page 16.)

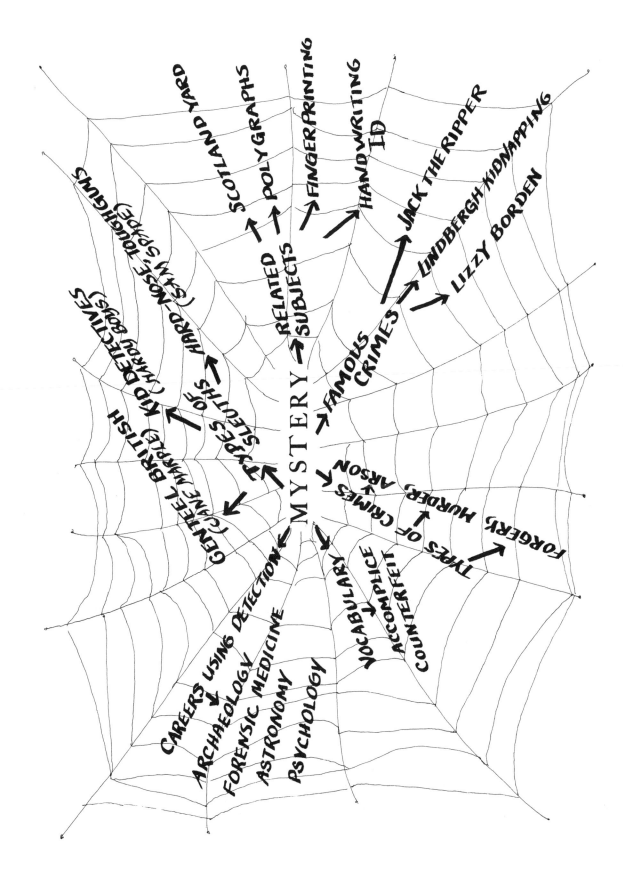

Fig. 1.5.

Fig. 1.6.

Fig. 1.7.

M _____

_____

_____

Y _____

_____

_____

S _____

_____

_____

T _____

_____

_____

E _____

_____

_____

_____

_____

_____

R _____

_____

_____

Y _____

A Mystery Writer's Notebook

From the first day of the mystery unit, every student should acquire the good habit of keeping a notebook or journal. The notebook can be the repository for reactions to class discussions, stories read, movies viewed, and ideas for plots and characters they wish to weave into an original detective story. New information they learn about fingerprinting or blood typing or a current crime in the news may be recorded in the notebook. Questions they want to ask and possible avenues of inquiry to follow to find answers may be logged in their detective's notebook. The young sleuth can create minute mysteries in his or her notebook for other students to solve. Apprentice detectives may wish to give their mystery notebook a special name such as "The Baker Street Tattler." The possibilities for journal entries are unlimited. The real point to be made is that students need to emulate one of the best behaviors of good detectives: always record evidence. Few students write as much as they should. The idea of keeping a detective's notebook may just be the "hook" some of the more reluctant students need to begin the practice of writing often. In this age of technology, students may wish to keep their detective notebooks on floppy disks.

Mystery Quotes

Quotes about and from mysteries can add spice to the mystery unit. Quotations written on the chalk-board, on cards in the interest center, or simply read orally at the beginning of a class session can provoke critical thinking and spark good discussions. For example, what does Holmes mean when he tells Dr. Watson, "You see, but you do not observe," in the story "A Scandal in Bohemia." A truly excellent source of mystery quotes is *The Mystery Lover's Book of Quotations* created by Jane Horning. Horning offers mystery lovers a comprehensive collection of quotes including sage words and advice found in classic mysteries as well as the thoughts of writers such as Chaucer and Shakespeare on mystery topics.

The following are examples of quotes which can be used to get students thinking about mystery, detection, and using plain good logic.

With method and logic one can accomplish anything.
> Hercule Poirot in "The Kidnapped Prime Minister," from Agatha
> Christie, *Poirot Investigates*

There is nothing more deceptive than an obvious fact.
> Sherlock Holmes in "The Boscombe Valley Mystery from Sir
> Arthur Conan Doyle, *The Adventures of Sherlock Holmes*

Crime does not pay.
> Chester Gould, speaking as Dick Tracy

There ain't many whys without becauses.
> Asey Mayo in Phoebe Atwood Taylor, *The Cape Cod Mystery*

Some circumstantial evidence is very strong, as when you find a trout in the milk.
> Henry David Thoreau, *Journal*

It is at the movies that the only absolutely modern mystery is celebrated.
> Andre Breton

I have never known anything to be of no significance.
> Detective Cuff in Wilkie Collins, *The Moonstone*

Many of Sherlock Holmes's best utterances are to be found in Dr. Ron Abrell's essay (previously in this chapter). Encourage students to be quote sleuths and to note and enter into their mystery notebooks intriguing quotes they find in their reading of mysteries.

Notes

[1]Ron Abrell, "Mr. Sherlock Holmes: Teaching Exemplar Extraordinary," *The Clearing House* 9 (May 1979): 403-7. Dr. Abrell's essay is published here with the permission of the author and the Helen Dwight Reid Educational Foundation. The publisher is Heldref Publications, 4000 Albemarle St., N.W., Washington, D.C. 20016. Copyright © 1979.

[2]The author wishes to thank AT&T for permission to reproduce their advertisement in this text.

[3]*The Armchair Detective* may be purchased from newstands and mystery book stores. Subscription information may be obtained by writing *The Armchair Detective*, 129 West 56th Street, New York, NY 10019.

[4]The Mysterious Bookshop, 129 West 56th Street, New York, NY 10019, (212) 765-0900; Foul Play Press, P.O. Box 175, Woodstock, VT 05091. *Sleuth Times*, 51 Main Street, Box 419000, Isleton, CA 95641.

Teacher Resources

Dixon, Franklin W. *The Hardy Boys Detective Handbook*. New York: Grosset & Dunlap, 1988.

This work is an excellent resource for younger students interested in police and detective procedures.

Hardwick, Michael. *Sherlock Holmes: My Life and Crimes*. Garden City, N.Y.: Doubleday, 1984.

Michael Hardwick has probably written more about Sherlock Holmes than any other person, including Conan Doyle. In this volume, he allows the great Holmes to tell his own story. See also Hardwick's *The Complete Guide to Sherlock Holmes*. New York: St. Martin's Press, 1986.

Horning, Jane. *The Mystery Lovers' Book of Quotations*. New York: Mysterious Press, 1988.

Horning has compiled more than 200 pages of sage advice and wit from the foremost writers in the genre.

McArdle, Phil, and Karen McArdle. *Fatal Fascination: Where Fact Meets Fiction in Police Work*. Boston: Houghton Mifflin, 1988.

The authors cover nearly every conceivable aspect of crime found in fiction and real life. In authoring the book, the authors worked closely with police personnel to make sure their facts about mystery and mayhem are correctly stated. The book is probably best used with secondary students.

Norville, Barbara. *Writing the Modern Mystery*. Cincinnati, Ohio: Writer's Digest Books, 1986.

A mystery editor who works with some of the finest writers of this literary genre tells readers how to write their own good mysteries.

Winn, Dilys. *Murder Ink: The Mystery Reader's Companion.* New York: Workman, 1977.

> This volume is sort of the Sears, Roebuck catalog of mysteries. Just about everything anyone would want to know about famous mystery writers, their sleuths, and their stories may be found within the covers of this book.

_____. *Murderess Ink: The Better Half of the Mystery.* New York: Workman, 1979.

> Winn more than makes up for any oversight of the feminine side of crime and detection in his first volume by creating this second volume exclusively devoted to notable women mystery writers, sleuths, and victims.

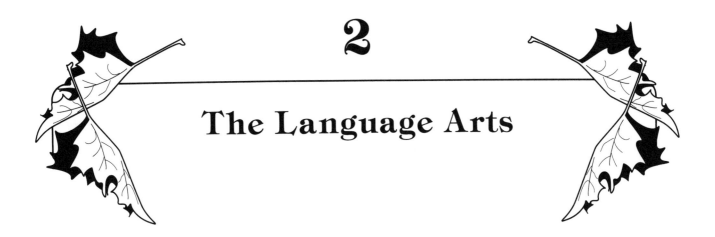

The Language Arts

Meet a Mystery Author

Charlotte MacLeod, like her fictional counterpart TV's Jessica Fletcher, is often described as "America's reigning whodunit queen." She authors superb mystery novels and lives in a small town in Maine. There the similarity between television's Jessica Fletcher and Charlotte MacLeod ends. Charlotte MacLeod is much too busy turning out well-plotted, delightfully clever works of fiction to have any time left over for solving real-life crimes. She has written more than thirty books for both juvenile and adult audiences, using her own name and the pseudonym Alisa Craig. Some recent juvenile titles include: *We Dare Not Go A-Hunting* (1980), and *Maid of Honor* (1984), both published by Atheneum.

Her most popular sleuths are Professor Peter Shandy, Sarah Kelling, and Max Bittersohn. Readers first encountered Peter Shandy, Balaclava Agriculture College's co-propagator of the Balaclava Buster rutabaga in *Rest You Merry* (Doubleday, 1978) and have delighted in following his adventures through such other MacLeod mysteries as *The Luck Runs Out* (Doubleday, 1979), *Wrack and Rune* (Doubleday, 1982), *Something the Cat Dragged In* (Doubleday, 1983), *The Corpse in Oozak's Pond* (Mysterious Press, 1987), and *Vane Pursuit* (Mysterious Press, 1989). Max Bittersohn, art investigator and detective, first meets Sarah Kelling while both are attempting to unravel a mystery about her prominent Boston family in *The Family Vault* (Doubleday, 1979). Their further exploits are recounted in *The Palace Guard* (Doubleday, 1981), *The Withdrawing Room* (Doubleday, 1980), *The Convivial Codfish* (Doubleday, 1984) and *The Recycled Citizen* (Mysterious Press, 1988) among others. This prolific writer's mysteries, under the pen name of Alisa Craig, include *Trouble in the Brasses* (Avon Books, 1989), and *The Grub-and-Stakers Quilt a Bee* (Doubleday, 1985). Author MacLeod has also penned articles for such diverse periodicals as *Cricket, Yankee,* and *Criminologist.* Figure 2.1 is a letter to students from Ms. MacLeod.

A Letter from a Professional

Fig. 2.1. A letter from Charlotte MacLeod, mystery writer.

Dear Reader,

To a mystery writer, the biggest mystery is why non-writers keep asking, "Where do you get your ideas?" Ideas are everywhere. You just see one you like, and grab it. The real question should be, "What do you do with an idea once you've claimed it for your own?"

First, you don't tell anybody. The surest way to murder a good plot is with a wagging tongue. What you do is jot your idea down as it first comes to you, then you start thinking about it.

What kind of mystery will this idea lend itself to? Would it be better as a short story or as a book? What age group would it appeal to? What other ideas does it suggest? How can these be connected to your basic plot? What characteristics will you need to act out your story? Who's going to do what?

That last question is the big one. For me, as for most mystery writers, the best way to develop a plot is to start with the finish. You decide what the real mystery is to have been, who'll be responsible for making it happen, and who solves it. Once you've done that, you start deciding how the action evolves and how the solution is arrived at. You jot down some more notes. And, repeat, you don't tell anybody.

Once the framework of the plot is established, some writers work out an elaborate outline. Before they start the first page, they know exactly what's going to happen in every chapter. Others, prefer to work from their preliminary notes, letting the story evolve bit by bit out of their imaginations, always keeping an eye on the established goal. That's what I do because I find it more fun.

Getting started can be terribly hard work, but you keep going. If you stop to revise what you've done, no matter how bad it is, you may spend the rest of your writing career doing the same paragraph over and over. You get it all down, then you revise.

If your idea is as good as you thought it was, you find that somewhere along the line, though usually not until you've done a great deal of desperately hard work, your characters seem to take over and start writing your story for you. Better still, you get help from everywhere. You open a book, turn on the radio, get into a conversation, and all of a sudden you find yourself being handed precisely the bit of information you need to take the next step toward your solution.

Even then it's not easy. You're a mystery writer, not a poet. You don't wait to get in the mood, you sit down and write. You keep on writing, then you write it all over again, and again until you've got it the way you want it. You read everything you can get your hands on, and analyze how other writers get their effects. You learn all you can about grammar and spelling. You add new words to your vocabulary as avidly as a miser adds money to his hoard, because words are your tools and knowing how to use them is your craft.

By now you may be thinking that the real mystery is why anybody's willing to do this much work with no guarantee of success. I've sometimes wondered, too, but the answer is simple enough. Have you figured out yet what it is?

Charlotte MacLeod

Case Study

Fig. 2.2. Language Arts Case Study.

There has never been another detective to equal the great Sherlock Holmes. In all of mystery literature he reigns supreme as the greatest master of detection through deduction. Holmes's acclaim was of such magnitude during the Victorian era that widespread mourning occurred in the English-speaking world when his demise at the Falls of Reichenbach became known in "The Final Problem" in 1893. Indeed, it is said the force of public opinion caused Holmes's creator, Sir Arthur Conan Doyle, to resurrect the master sleuth a decade later with the 1903 publication of "The Adventures of the Empty House." His fame and popularity have not waned. With the exception of the Bible and Shakespeare, more English words have been penned about Sherlock Holmes than any other subject. More movies (to date, 175 films with 61 different actors in the lead role) have been made about Sherlock Holmes than any other fictional character.

Dr. Watson's chronicle of "The Adventure of the Speckled Band" illustrates Holmes' classic approach to sleuthing or problem solving. He even includes a cautionary comment from Holmes about the pitfalls to which the problem solver can fall prey.

It is the spring of 1883, and Watson and Holmes share bachelor quarters at 221 B Baker Street. Almost immediately, Dr. Watson tells readers of the famed detective's motivation for accepting the case. Holmes accepts only those cases unusual enough to satisfy his great curiosity. He works not for wealth or financial gain but for "the love of his art."

Holmes begins his search for evidence the moment he first meets Helen Stoner of Stoke Moran in his sitting room. He listens to Miss Stoner's tragic tale, taking in every word. "Pray be precise as to details," he urges the witness. He takes in visual data as well, noting the bruises on Miss Stoner's wrist and correctly deduces that she has been cruelly treated by her stepfather, Dr. Roylott. After Miss Stoner's departure, he inquires at Doctors' Common to obtain still more data. Later, at Stoke Moran, Holmes thoroughly examines the grounds where gypsies, a cheetah, and a baboon roam freely. He also observes the sleeping chambers of Dr. Roylott and Miss Stoner in an attempt to reconstruct the circumstances surrounding the death of Miss Stoner's twin sister. The master detective hopes to prevent yet another tragedy.

Holmes analyzes the data and arrives at an initial prediction which turns out to be incorrect. Even the great Holmes can err: "I had come to an entirely erroneous conclusion which shows, my dear Watson, how dangerous it always is to reason from insufficient data." Reanalyzing his data, Holmes happily comes to the right conclusion in time to foil the evil Dr. Roylott. The case is resolved with the death of the murderer as his evil plan turns back upon him. The "Speckled Band," the deadly swamp adder, strikes him and not his intended victim, Miss Stoner.

"The Adventure of the Speckled Band" is typical of great detective fiction in that the reader is allowed to peer inside a great mind and witness an expert problem solver at work. Readers can follow the *deductive* line of reasoning followed by the great Holmes. In other detective fiction, readers follow the reasoning of the Belgian sleuth Hercule Poirot as he builds a case delicately, *inductively* adding clue upon clue to reach an indisputable conclusion. Readers may also peer into the mind of Miss Marple, another of Agatha Christie's sleuths, and observe an expert detective who uses *analogous* reasoning to find the guilty. The elderly spinster from the tiny British village of St. Mary Mead notes similarities between people and circumstances in a current case and people and past events in her small community as she searches for similarities that ultimately lead to the solution of the crime. It seems that a good mystery serves not only to entertain, but also as a primer on problem solving.

Tools of the Trade

Figure 2.3. is a sketch of a desk which might belong to a mystery writer. Duplicate the figure or use it as an overhead for class discussion. Ask students to brainstorm the "Tools of the Trade" that a mystery writer might need. How might the labels on the files in the filing cabinet read? Ask students to note that the bookshelf is empty. What books might a mystery writer need? There are no utensils or paraphernalia on the top of the desk other than a personal computer keyboard and monitor. Books on the table have no titles on their spines. What else may be missing? Is the area above the file cabinet a window (If so, what is the view?), a bulletin board, or some other object? Ask students to complete the picture of a mystery writer's studio by drawing in appropriate books and other items which would be the tools of the trade for a mystery writer.

This activity may be used as a pretest or diagnostic tool to determine how much students already know about the mystery genre; as a motivational tool to introduce a unit on mysteries; or, even as a posttest to ascertain how much students have learned about mysteries and mystery writing.

Fig. 2.3. Tools of the trade for language arts.

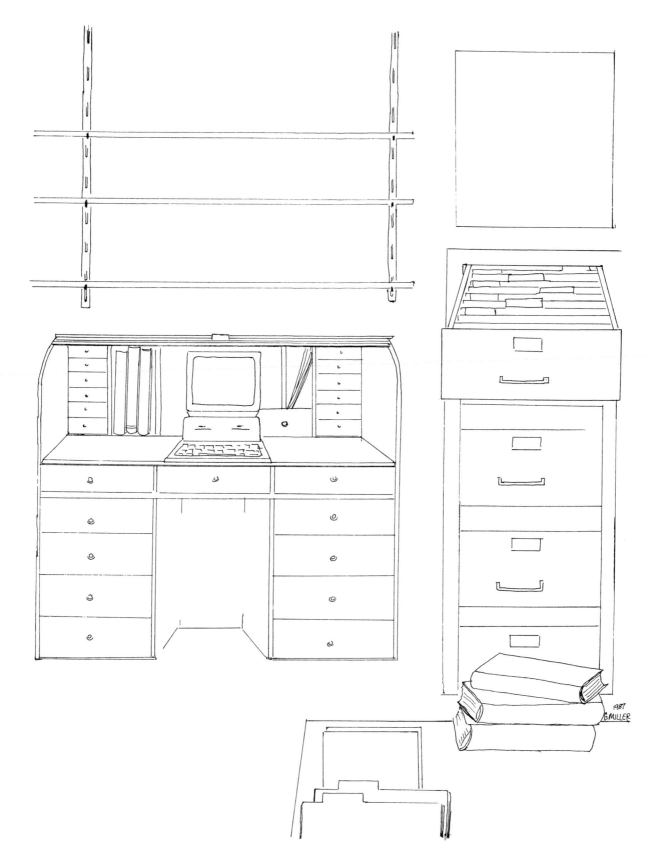

Mystery Desk

Figure 2.4 is an illustration of a desk which might have belonged to well-known siblings, three of whom became famous authors. Share the illustration with students and ask them to be good detectives in determining to whom the "Mystery Desk" might belong. Do not reveal the answer (found at the end of the book) to students too soon. If students have to ferret out the answer through careful examination of the clues provided, library research, and probing questions, they will be more likely to feel like true investigators and really enter into the spirit of a mystery/detection unit.

After students have deciphered the clues in figure 2.4, and have solved this mystery, encourage them to research the background of other famous (or infamous) people and create either childhood or adult desks to stump their classmates, siblings, parents, or other teachers. For example, how might desks belonging to the young Abraham Lincoln, Martin Luther King, Jr., and Eleanor Roosevelt have looked? This extension activity requires students not only to research the lives of the subjects, but periods of furniture as well. Considerable library research was utilized in creating all the desks which appear in this book so that each might be authentic not only in contents, but in period design as well. (See the letter to students found in "The Arts" chapter. The illustrator of this book describes her creation of the desks found in the book.)

Fig. 2.4. Famous author's desk.

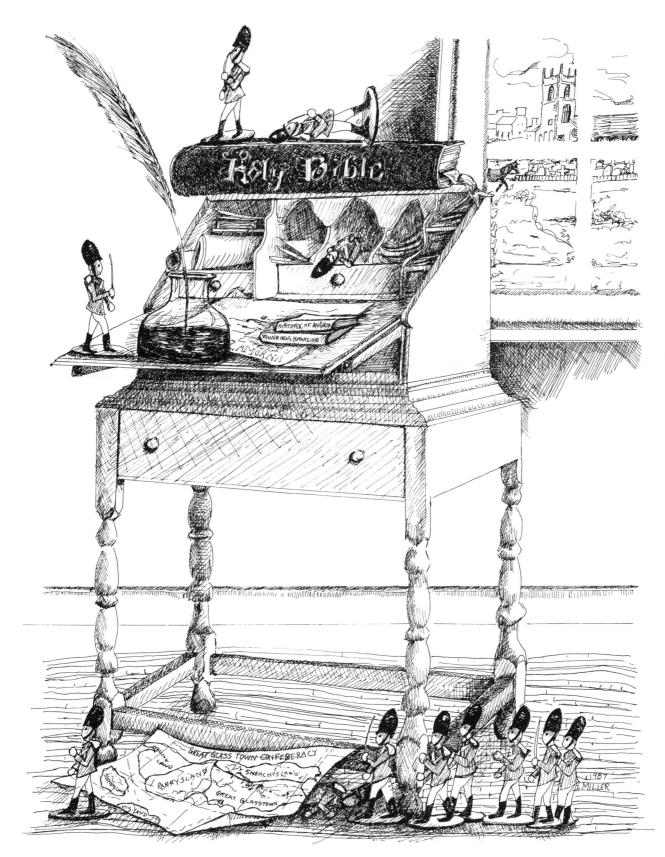

Traces

Figure 2.5 may be shared with the class as an overhead transparency or may be duplicated as a handout. It represents a bird's-eye view of the "traces", or tracks, of a famous literary event. Ask students to utilize the visual clues to determine the famous literary event depicted. They should note the traces and also use any other visual data in the drawing to discern the correct answer. As with the mystery desks, do not be too quick to help students determine the answer (found at the end of the book). As students behave like Sherlock Holmes in determining the correct response and verifying their answers, reasoned from the observable data, their motivation for the mystery unit will increase and they will develop greater confidence in their ability to think critically and problem solve.

Fig. 2.5.

Language Arts Activities

Sampling Mystery Fare

Happily, it is not difficult today to find good examples of the mystery genre for any age group. A representative reading list will be found at the end of this and all succeeding chapters and at the end of the book. No exploration of detective literature would be complete, however, without reference to the early masters. Capable students should begin sampling the rich heritage of detective fiction including:

Agatha Christie's *The Mysterious Affairs at Styles* (Bantam, 1983)

G. K. Chesterton's *Father Brown Omnibus* (Dodd, Mead, 1951)

Wilkie Collins's *The Moonstone* (Dodd, Mead, 1951)

Arthur Conan Doyle's *The Adventures of Sherlock Holmes* (Ballantine, 1975); *The Memoirs of Sherlock Holmes* (Penguin, 1987); *The Return of Sherlock Holmes* (Ballantine, 1975)

Dashiell Hammett's *The Maltese Falcon* (Vintage, 1984)

Edgar Allan Poe's stories such as "The Gold Bug" found in *The Unabridged Edgar Allan Poe* (Courage, 1985)

Dorothy Sayers's *The Five Red Herrings* (Harper & Row, 1986)

It is worth mentioning here that students do imitate the behaviors significant adults model, and teachers are significant adults who should be seen reading. Share with students both your current mystery reading tastes and talk about the detective heroes and heroines you may have had as a youth.

An excellent history of the genre may be found in *The Literature of Crime and Detection: An Illustrated History from Antiquity to the Present* by Waltraud Woeller and Bruce Cassiday. The authors begin their history with Greek playwrights Aeschylus and Sophocles and end with contemporary mystery authors such as Donald Westlake and Elmore Leonard.

The printed word is not the only source of excellent mysteries. Visual and auditory literacy can become an important and integral part of a mystery unit in the English/language arts classroom. The PBS television series "Mystery!" offers excellent dramatizations such as John Mortimer's "Rumpole of the Bailey" as well as first-class renderings of classics by Sayers, Christie, Doyle, and others. The series is offered weekly with excellent narrative explication by Vincent Price. Many of the programs are available in video format from either video stores or through mail order video catalogs. The Miss Marple Series includes "The Body in the Library," "A Pocketful of Rye," and "A Murder Is Announced." Agatha Christie's "Partners in Crime" stories which were also dramatized for "Mystery!" are widely available in VHS format from Pacific Arts Video. Several of Christie's Hercule Poirot mysteries have been filmed. HBO/Cannon videos presents the *Agatha Christie Collection* which includes three Poirot mysteries with Peter Ustinov as the Belgian sleuth. The titles are *Appointment with Death, Death on the Nile,* and *Evil under the Sun.* The same series features Angela Lansbury as Miss Marple in *The Mirror Crack'd.* Ingrid Bergman won her third Academy Award for her portrayal of a Swedish nurse in *Murder on the Orient Express.* Albert Finney received an Academy Award nomination for best actor for his portrayal of Hercule Poirot in the same film.

Some cautionary advice about the use of films and videos in a mystery unit. Many of the videos teachers might consider using in the classroom specifically state that they are packaged for home use only. Any other use, including classroom showings, constitutes a copyright infringement. Wise teachers will work with library media specialists to determine which films and videos may be ordered from media catalogs specifically for classroom use. Secondly, many people are quite rightfully concerned about the amount of time students are exposed to television and movies. An even better alternative to class showings of mystery films, is a viewing list of classic mystery films. Each student, in consultation with his or her parents, can select the video titles available from a local video store for shared family viewing.

A final caution: Feature films in the classroom and in the home, need to be screened in advance by parents, teachers and library media specialists as some films do contain profanity. Happily, when using a VCR, teachers and parents can fast-forward the tape past inappropriate dialogue or scenes.

Many fans of "Mystery!" believe the PBS series reached its pinnacle with the presentation of "The Adventures of Sherlock Holmes" starring Jeremy Brett. Filmed by Granada Television, Limited in Great Britain, the films are distributed by Simon & Schuster video in the United States. Titles such as "A Scandal in Bohemia," "The Blue Carbuncle," and "The Adventures of the Speckled Band" are available in VHS format in many video store outlets. They may also be ordered from *Signal*, a public television catalog, 333 Sibley Street, Suite 626, St. Paul, MN 55101. (A fun trivia footnote. In what other famous film have readers seen Jeremy Brett, whom many critics have dubbed the best movie Sherlock ever? Answer: More than two decades ago, the versatile British actor portrayed the character of Freddy Eynsford Hill in the Warner Bros. movie musical *My Fair Lady*.)

For information on other episodes of "Mystery!" contact "Mystery!" WGBH Education Foundation, 125 Western Avenue, Boston, MA 02134, (617) 492-2777.

The now classic Basil Rathbone series of Sherlock Holmes movie mysteries of the 1930s and 1940s are also available in video format. In 1988, Key Video reproduced—in glorious black and white—all fourteen of the Basil Rathbone/Nigel Bruce movies in the VHS format. The series is widely available for rental from video stores. (Order from Key Video, 39000 Seven Mile Road, Livonia, MI 48152.)

Rivalling the Basil Rathbone-Sherlock Holmes films in popularity in the 1930s and 1940s were the six *Thin Man* films starring William Powell and Myrna Loy as Dashiell Hammett's Nick and Nora Charles. Powell won an Academy Award nomination as best actor in 1934 for his portrayal of Nick in the original film. The six films are available from MGM/UA Home Video, Inc. While the films are entertaining, readers and potential viewers should be forewarned that a feature of Nick's character was his almost constant drinking of martinis. In these films from an era when the devastating effects of alcoholism were not, apparently, as well appreciated as they are today; the consumption of alcohol is all but glorified.

Father Brown, the sleuth of Chesterton's witty mysteries, is played by Alec Guinness in the delightful 1954 British film, *The Detective*, which is available in VHS format from Columbia Pictures Home Video.

Younger students may appreciate "The Mystery of King Tut's Tomb," originally an episode of the television series, "The Hardy Boys" starring Parker Stevenson and Shaun Cassidy. It is available from MCA Home Video.

Young Sherlock Holmes, a Steven Spielberg production, is yet another video to examine. It purports to portray the early character development and school experiences of Doyle's classic creation. A word of caution needs to be offered. The plot elements refer to both hallucinogenic drugs and an obscure religious cult which practices human sacrifice. The results are both graphic and visually frightening.

Of course, for older student audiences, the genius of Hitchcock films like *The 39 Steps* and *North by Northwest* should not be missed. *The 39 Steps* is based on John Buchan's book of the same title which is often cited as one of the best children's adventure books ever written. David O. Selznick's production of *The Third Man* is yet another classic mystery film as is John Huston's *The Maltese Falcon* featuring Humphrey Bogart as detective Sam Spade. Other film titles may be found with the apt assistance of the library media specialists and the use of a fine educational film catalog.

After a long, hard week at school, every good library media specialist or teacher is entitled to some joyous and relaxing laughter. So, after school lets out on Friday, complete your mysterious week with a stop at the local video store where you can pick up some popcorn and *The Pink Panther* (1964) and *A Shot in the Dark* (1964), both available from CBS Fox Video. While Sherlock Holmes would not approve of his style, Peter Sellers's Inspector Clouseau does give sleuthing a whole new twist.

Old-time radio broadcasts may also be used to introduce students to the mystery genre. Fortunately, representative samples of radio mystery broadcasts from the 1930s and 1940s are easily accessible in cassette format. "The Shadow," "Suspense," "Dragnet," "The Whistler," and "Yours Truly, Johnny Dollar" are just a few of the many mystery radio programs which will whisk students back to a time when there was no television and the listener's imagination played an integral part in the look, feel, and texture of the unfolding drama. Old-time radio dramas offer teachers a splendid opportunity to work on students' listening skills and provide them with some social history (many commercial cassettes contain the original commercials as well as the program text) of a bygone era while sampling the wide variety of mystery formats.

Critical Reading

In small group discussions, students should create their own lists of criteria to utilize in evaluating detective fiction. This is best attempted after students have read at least one short story and one novel. Students may compare their lists with those originated by professional authors, editors, and critics found in such books as *Murder Ink* and *Writing the Modern Mystery*. Students may want to add special criteria to use when evaluating movie, television, and radio versions of mystery literature. The criteria which evolve from this activity should be utilized in all future writings and oral discussions of mystery reading, listening, and viewing.

Critical Reading Questions

Teachers need to ask critical questions making students carefully examine what they have read. The teacher's questions should move students' thinking from the factual levels of knowledge and comprehension upwards to the analysis and evaluation levels of cognition. Questions should move beyond simply determining if the students know the plot, setting, major characters and resolution. Questioning strategies teachers could use in a book discussion of mystery literature might include the following:

What techniques did the author use to create a mood or feeling of suspense and intrigue?

What kind of reasoning (deductive, inductive, analogous) did the protagonist use to solve the crime?

Could you predict the solution? Trace your thinking. What steps led you to the solution? If you went astray, how did it happen? Did the author fairly or unfairly plant clues?

What kinds of questions did the detective ask which proved to be valuable in solving the case?

What observations did the detective make which proved to be of great value in solving the case?

What did you learn about reading mystery literature or the writing of detective fiction that you should remember for future reference?

How did the crafting of the story you read compare to classic mystery stories created by mystery masters like Edgar Allan Poe, Arthur Conan Doyle, Dorothy L. Sayers, or P. D. James?

What character traits, hobbies, or vocation does the author provide for the detective which make him or her interesting?

Is adequate data provided about the characters and suspects in order to make their motives and behaviors seem credible?

The Mystery Story Elements

There are notable exceptions, but most mystery fiction follows a fairly set pattern. After students have sampled some classic examples of the mystery genre, ask them to brainstorm all the elements common to mystery literature. Next, ask them to categorize the items, chronologically, according to when each occurs in a classic work of mystery. The list which emerges will serve students both in their evaluation of further mysteries read and in the writing of their own detective stories. In her excellent work *Writing the Modern Mystery*, Barbara Norville says the mystery story boils down to two things: cause and effect. The cause, she argues is desperation, and the effect is disaster.[1] In explicating this barebones formula students are likely to generate a list which may look something like the following:

1. A crime is planned and/or committed against a person (robbery, blackmail, murder), a place (vandalism), or an object (jewel theft). The crime must be of sufficient importance to warrant the efforts and time of the sleuth and the reader.

2. The crime is discovered.

3. The sleuth enters the drama.

4. The detective determines if there are any witnesses, fingerprints, etc. The sleuth determines what is known, has been seen, or heard.

5. The relevancy of each piece of evidence is considered. Frequently there are red herrings which may distract (temporarily) even a sleuth as great as Sherlock Holmes.

6. Suspects and motives are considered. A suspect must have a motive to receive serious consideration as the culprit. Motives, however, may not always be obvious. The sleuth may have to dig deep into a suspect's past to determine a motive well-hidden by time.

7. The sleuth forwards a hypothesis. Means, opportunity, and motive converge upon one suspect. The perfect crime has not occurred. The guilty party has slipped up somehow, and the sleuth has discerned the error.

8. A chase may occur as the detective zeroes in on the culprit.

9. Reason must prevail. At some point the sleuth shares the reasoning power utilized to determine the culprit. All the clues utilized by the sleuth have to be available to the reader as well.

10. Justice must prevail. It is not always meted out in a court of law. Justice may be served "poetically" as in "The Adventure of the Speckled Band," when the villain meets the violent death he had planned for his step-daughter.[2]

Types of Sleuths

There are many types of sleuths common to mystery fiction. Students can learn to identify types of detectives from their reading. Identification of styles of detection help students in the creation of their own detectives for original stories. The following types are basic. Students may wish to verbally or visually provide a profile of their images of sleuths. Figure 2.6 is an example of the all-purpose sleuth.

Kid Detectives. The Great Brain, Trixie Belden, the Hardy Boys, Nancy Drew, and their legion are popularly found in mystery fiction for young readers. These detectives are generally very bright and highly observant. They often outwit adults: both criminals and the police. They are shown to be helping law officials and the cause of justice. While adult sleuths frequently solve murder cases, the more youthful detectives typically handle less severe crimes.

Hard-Boiled Private Eyes. Largely an American contribution to the mystery genre, the no-nonsense, trenchcoat-clad, private man of few words investigator is a popular creation of 1930s mysteries. Dashiell Hammett's Sam Spade is the archetypal private eye. Humphrey Bogart popularized this type becoming the quintessential tough-guy private eye in Hollywood movies. Children will recognize this detective hero in the popular public service commercials about a Sam Spade-like hound who, dressed in trench coat, asks youth to help him take a bite out of crime.

Cerebral Sleuths. Sherlock Holmes and Hercule Poirot are the leaders of this class of crime solvers who simply cannot resist a puzzle. The formula is simple: a baffling crime is committed, the clues are revealed, and a race is on to see whether the reader or the sleuth will be the first to solve the riddle. Of course, the urbane detective always wins.

Ladies and Gentlemen. Lord Peter Wimsey and Jane Marple exemplify yet another character type. They are British and extremely well mannered. Good manners, gentility, and justice always prevail in their world. Tea time is not to be disturbed. Violence always occurs offstage. Their American cousin is Dorothy Gilman's grandmotherly Mrs. Emily Pollifax who occasionally has to miss a garden club meeting in order to work for the CIA.

Hardworking, Resourceful Police Officers. While a majority of mystery writers draw their sleuths from the ranks of private citizens, there are many excellent police detectives in mystery literature. Not all police officers are vain and as easily mislead as Doyle's Inspector Lestrade. Scotland Yard has produced P. D. James's poetry-writing inspector Adam Dalgliesh and Peter Lovesey's Victorian Sgt. Cribb. Tony Hillerman offers the painstaking, diligent sergeant Jim Chee of the Navajo Tribal Police.

Everyman/woman Sleuths. The "It's all in a day's work" sleuths are drawn from all types of professions and worldly circumstances. Chefs, bankers, jockeys, meter maids, and ballet impresarios are among countless everyman and everywoman characters who are somehow drawn into a crime which occurs in their profession or walk of life. Because they are puzzled or personally threatened, they become involved and manage to solve the crime. Dick Frances has popularized crime at the race track with detectives such as jockey Sid Halley. Mary Jane Latsis and Martha Henissart writing as Emma Lathen created bank executive John Putnam Thatcher who always becomes embroiled in a murder case while pursuing his banking duties.

Fig. 2.6. The all-purpose sleuth

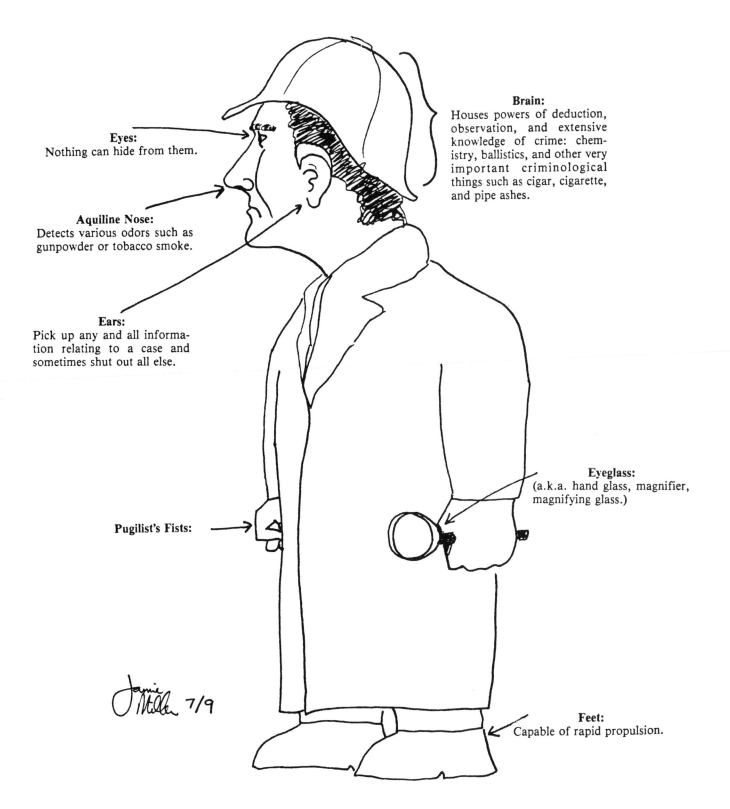

Eyes:
Nothing can hide from them.

Aquiline Nose:
Detects various odors such as
gunpowder or tobacco smoke.

Ears:
Pick up any and all information relating to a case and
sometimes shut out all else.

Brain:
Houses powers of deduction,
observation, and extensive
knowledge of crime: chem-
istry, ballistics, and other very
important criminological
things such as cigar, cigarette,
and pipe ashes.

Eyeglass:
(a.k.a. hand glass, magnifier,
magnifying glass.)

Pugilist's Fists:

Feet:
Capable of rapid propulsion.

It may be instructive to label categories of sleuths on a bulletin board and ask students to add names to each of the respective categories as new sleuths are discovered. Students may also want to discuss why they believe certain character types are more appealing than others.

Sleuth Search

Test the sleuth I.Q. of your students. Figure 2.7 is a game which asks students to match famous literary sleuths, in the left column, with their creators in the right column. If students need or want a second try, a second quiz is provided.

Fig. 2.7.

A. Can You Match These Sleuths with Their Creators?

Sleuths	Authors
1. Lord Peter Wimsey	A. G. K. Chesterton
2. Sam Spade	B. Dorothy L. Sayers
3. Hercule Poirot	C. Arthur Conan Doyle
4. Sherlock Holmes	D. Edgar Allan Poe
5. Peter Shandy	E. Phoebe Atwood Taylor
6. Father Brown	F. Dashiell Hammett
7. Philip Marlowe	G. Agatha Christie
8. Nero Wolfe	H. Charlotte MacLeod
9. Asey Mayo	I. Ellis Peters
10. Perry Mason	J. Raymond Chandler
11. Jim Chee	K. Emma Lathen
12. John Putnam Thatcher	L. Rex Stout
13. Brother Cadfael	M. Tony Hillerman
14. Rabbi David Small	N. P. D. James
15. Adam Dalgliesh	O. Harry Kemelman
16. C. Auguste Dupin	P. Erle Stanley Gardner

Fig. 2.7.

B. Match These Titles and Characters with Their Creators.

Titles, Characters	Authors
1. *The Case of the Vanishing Victim*	A. John Bellairs
2. "The Gold Bug"	B. Arthur Conan Doyle
3. Cam Jansen	C. Ellen Raskin
4. Nancy Drew	D. Donald J. Sobol
5. *The Curse of the Blue Figurine*	E. Zilpha Keatley Snyder
6. Frank and Joe Hardy	F. Charles Dickens
7. John H. Watson, M.D.	G. David Adler
8. *Encyclopedia Brown: Boy Detective*	H. Carolyn Keene
9. "Turtle" Wexler	I. Edgar Allan Poe
10. *The Egypt Game*	J. Agatha Christie
11. Tommy and Tuppence Beresford	K. Carol Farley
12. *The Mystery of Edwin Drood*	L. Franklin W. Dixon

Reporting Mysteries

Students can create their own casebooks of mysteries, keeping track of mysteries read, analyses of the quality of writing, reasoning evidenced, and general interest level. The "Mystery" form (figure 2.8) may be duplicated and utilized by students for both reading and television/movie viewing. Or, better still, ask students to create their own reporting form based upon class discussions, critical reading, and/or outside research. Additional questions might include the following:

Who are the witnesses?

Who are the suspects?

What are the motives?

What are the alibis?

How does the sleuth solve the mystery?

How are the guilty punished?

The students' mystery notebook is the ideal place for noting impressions of mysteries read, analyzing movies and television mysteries, original story ideas, newspaper clippings related to crimes and mysteries, new vocabulary encountered, research notes, and personal reactions to the mystery unit itself.

Fig. 2.8.

MYSTERY

Title _____

Author _____

    Pseudonym??
    (There is really no Emma Lathen; two women jointly write under the pen name Emma Lathen)

Setting _____

Crime Committed _____

Victim _____

Sleuth _____

    Distinguishing characteristics:

Whodunit? _____

What's your sleuthing IQ?   Dullard   Average Joe   Genius
                                      (circle one)

    Did you guess the solution before the author revealed it?

    What clues did you use? Were there red herring clues?

Is the book one in a series by the same author? _____ Did you like it well enough to want to read more books by the author? _____

Pretend the book is to be turned into a TV movie-of-the-week. Write a one-paragraph description for *TV Guide* summarizing the plot without giving away the ending. You may predict name actors to play the parts if you like.

Biographical Studies

Biography can be an integral part of any unit on mysteries. There are a number of excellent biographies written about such mystery authors as Poe, Christie, Sayers, Hammett, and Doyle. Indeed, real-life mysteries often surround the lives of the more famous whodunit authors. It has been argued that Sir Arthur Conan Doyle was the perpetrator of the Piltdown Man ruse, considered to be the greatest archaeological hoax of all time.[3] Doyle also became a real-life sleuth, using the methods he created for Holmes, when he came to the aid of an innocent man, George Edalji, wrongfully arrested, convicted, and sent to prison for the mutilation of animals in Great Wyrley, England in the early 1900s.[4]

The most authentic mystery Agatha Christie ever created was her own unexplained eleven-day, 1926 disappearance.[5] *Agatha Christie: How Did She Do It?* is a fifty-five minute film in which the official Agatha Christie biographer, Janet Morgan, explores the famous author's life and her craft. It is available from Home Visions Video.

Dashiell Hammett not only created Sam Spade, he also worked as a detective for the Pinkerton Detective Agency and hunted down a man who stole a Ferris wheel.[6]

The lives of masters of the mystery genre are enticing subjects for inquiries. Similarly, the lives of persons involved in real-life criminology are engrossing subjects for study. Allan Pinkerton, a native Scot, made his name an American household word through his detection skills. His sleuthing powers uncovered a plot to assassinate Abraham Lincoln in 1860, and he later set up the United States Secret Service at Lincoln's request. One excellent biography of Pinkerton's life for younger readers is *Allan Pinkerton: First Private Eye* by LaVere Anderson. Countless other names of mystery authors and real-life crime fighters will occur to students through reading and class discussions. Students can research the lives of mystery authors or famous subjects in criminology and share their information through a variety of means. After students have researched a subject's life, ask them to:

Plan a skit dramatizing a significant event in the life of the subject. Engage other students to help dramatize the event for the rest of the class.

Create a time line of events in the life of the subject. Display the time line in the classroom for other students to enjoy.

Create a scrapbook or bulletin board display of your own drawings depicting significant events in the subject's life.

Portray the subjects as they respond to significant questions about their life on a television talk show.

Write both the questions and responses and ask a classmate to serve as the interviewer. After adequate rehearsal, present the interview to classmates.

Pretend that you are the biographical subject and write a first person account of the most mysterious event in your life for a mystery magazine. Share the completed article with classmates.

Create a passport for the biographical subject. When and where did he/she travel? Prepare an accompanying short paper explaining the significance of the subject's travels.

Create a Gallery of Famous Mystery Authors in the classroom. Use words, pictures, drawings, and short biographical sketches to capture the personalities of famous authors whose works are being read by class members.

Create a journal or diary which might have been kept by the subject. The diary should contain at least ten revealing entries describing significant events in the person's life.

Create a board game based upon the facts and events in the life of a famous mystery writer. (Questions may also be related to characters, stories and novels created by the subject.) Games such as Trivial Pursuit® and Clue® may serve as models. Classmates can learn more about a famous author such as Agatha Christie by playing the game.

Join classmates who have researched the lives of other mystery writers in planning a special mystery banquet. How should the seating be arranged? What foods should be served? What should the evening's entertainment be? Imagine all the details needed for a successful gathering of the most accomplished mystery authors. For even more fun, proceed with the banquet as students portray their famous writers. Improvise conversations and events which might transpire.

Create a biographical mystery sketch. Design a visual portrait of a mystery writer or a fictional detective featuring words, symbols, and drawings that represent the subject's life and work. Classmates must decipher the clues in order to determine the subject's identity (figure 2.9 is an example). The subject of the mystery sketch is mystery writer Margaret Truman, the daughter of the late President Harry Truman. She was born in Missouri in 1924, was a singer, and now writes mysteries set in the nation's capital.

Library media centers will vary in the availability of biographical references. The following is a beginning list of selected biographies students and teachers may locate:

LaVere Anderson. *Allan Pinkerton: First Private Eye.* Garrard, 1972.

Charles H. Higham. *The Adventures of Conan Doyle: The Life of the Creator of Sherlock Holmes.* Pocket Books, 1976.

Janet Hitchman. *Such a Strange Lady: A Biography of Dorothy Sayers.* Harper & Row, 1975.

Dorothy B. Hughes. *Erle Stanley Gardner: The Case of the Real Perry Mason.* William Morrow, 1978.

Diane Johnson. *Dashiell Hammett: A Life.* Random House, 1983.

Bettina Knapp. *Edgar Allan Poe.* Frederick Ungar, 1984.

Charles Osborne. *The Life and Crimes of Agatha Christie.* Collins Ltd., 1982.

Fig. 2.9.

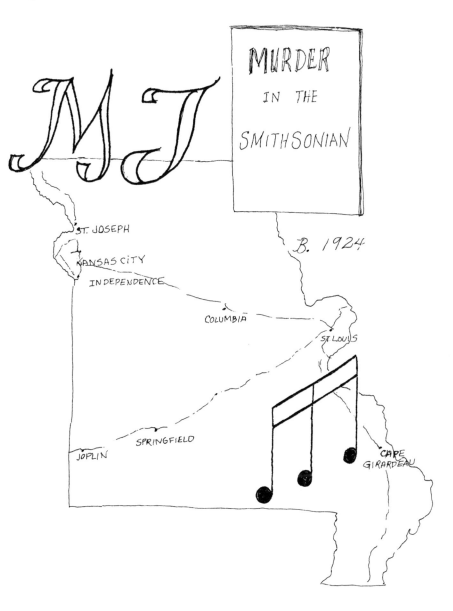

Three other biographical sources should be mentioned. Students can learn about a great mystery writer through her own words. Agatha Christie spent more than fifteen years writing her memoirs published as *Agatha Christie: An Autobiography*. In *Sleuths, Inc.*, Hugh Eames studies the problem solving skills of the great literary detectives like Sherlock Holmes and Sam Spade *and* their respective creators. Eames describes the real-life detecting skills Doyle, Hammett, Chandler and others employed in their lives. In *The Dangerous Edge*, Gavin Lambert also explores actual dramatic episodes in the lives of such mystery-creating giants as Wilkie Collins, Conan Doyle, and Alfred Hitchcock. Lambert suggests that the basis for the fiction practiced by these great writers may be found in the facts of their real lives. Figure 2.10 is a sample mystery profile.

A Mystery Profile

Fig. 2.10. Profile of Edgar Allan Poe

The Short, Unhappy Life of a Genius:
Edgar Allan Poe

EDGAR ALLAN POE

Edgar Allan Poe is the acknowledged father of the detective story. He is recognized as one of the greatest writers America has produced. He also lived a life filled with poverty, despair, and tragedy.

Poe was born in Boston in 1809, the same year as two other historical giants of the nineteenth century, Abraham Lincoln and Charles Darwin. His parents, Elizabeth Arnold and David Poe, Jr., were both stage actors. Edgar was their second son; a daughter would be born two years later. By the time this third child was born, the Poes had separated and Elizabeth Arnold Poe was destitute and terminally ill with tuberculosis. After the death of his mother, the young Edgar went to live with Mr. and Mrs. John Allan of Richmond, Virginia, who became his foster parents. John Allan, a merchant dealing in tobacco, coffee, and tea, took his business and his family to England in 1815. The family remained in England for five years where the young Edgar began his schooling. Allan's business did not prosper in England, however, and the family returned to Virginia in 1820.

As Poe grew into young manhood, his relations with his foster father soured. In 1826, Poe entered the University of Virginia which Thomas Jefferson had founded just two years earlier. There his brilliance was clearly demonstrated. He was a French and Latin scholar and read Greek, Spanish, and Italian. While his academic life was promising, his personal life was not. His first problems with alcohol surfaced in his university days, and he accrued gambling debts he was unable to pay and his foster father refused to pay. He was dismissed from the University of Virginia and returned home to Richmond in shame.

In the spring of 1827, Poe returned to his birthplace, Boston, where he published his first work, *Tamerlane and Other Poems*, and joined the army. He prospered in the army and eventually received an appointment to the military academy at West Point in 1830. During his army tenure, he was stationed at Fort Moultrie on Sullivan's Island in the harbor of Charleston, South Carolina. The region and its pirate lore was to become the subject of one of his most famous detective stories, "The Gold Bug." There is some question as to the specific reasons Poe left West Point in 1831. John Allan refused to send him the financial support money he needed; his drinking increased; and, he once again built up gambling debts. There is no doubt about his fate at West Point. In 1831, Poe was court-martialed and dishonorably discharged from the military academy.

The remainder of Poe's life is primarily a catalog of incidents of misery, poverty, and degradation. He lived mostly a hand-to-mouth existence, rarely having more than a few dollars at any one time. His stories and poetry were published in magazines and he achieved considerable fame during his lifetime, not only in the United States, but in England and France as well. He was paid little for his writings and his literary works were not protected by the kinds of copyright laws which exist today. His alcoholism and volatile personality made him a difficult and unreliable worker, and he floated from one writing and editing job to another. In 1845, his business fortunes seemed to take a turn for the better. He became the editor and proprietor of a magazine, *The Broadway Journal*, but within a year the journal ceased publication.

In 1836, Poe had married his cousin, Virginia Clemm. It was an improbable marriage, the bride being only thirteen years old at the time. Virginia Clemm Poe was in ill health much of her adult life. The poverty in which she and Poe often found themselves scarcely contributed to good health. She died in 1847, and Poe's final descent into an alcohol-induced madness rapidly accelerated. In October, 1849, Poe died a pauper.

There is little doubt of Poe's genius. In addition to being a language scholar and a great author and poet, he possessed exceptional skills as a mathematician. But Poe was also a tormented human being who was his own worst enemy. One of his biographers says this of Poe: "He was not a nice person. He was, moreover, a reactionary, a snob, and a racist whose works give offense to Blacks, to Jews, to ... almost anyone who is not Edgar Allan Poe."[1]

Poe's contemporaries recognized his genius, but they also suffered from his arrogance, brashness, and unpredictability. He was plagued by money problems and alcoholism most of his adult life. He was subject to periods of extreme depression, and while he professed to hold public acclaim and wealth in contempt, he also desperately, and unsuccessfully, sought them.

The great significance of Poe's contributions to the mystery genre is unquestioned. With the April, 1841 publication of "The Murders in the Rue Morgue" in *Graham's Magazine*, Poe gave the world a new literary form: the detective story. He introduced the model for all later fictional detectives, including Sherlock Holmes, with his creation of C. Auguste Dupin. He created the three elements which are the foundation of mystery literature: (a) a crime of sufficient interest to engage the reader; (b) a detective who ascertains the identity of the criminal; and (c) the unique method of detection which the sleuth employs. Arthur Conan Doyle imbues the great Holmes with a remarkable facility for "deduction," but Poe had given the same trait to Dupin forty years earlier and called it "analysis." When Holmes tells Watson "You see but you do not observe," he is repeating Dupin's comment to his narrator, "The necessary knowledge is of *what* to observe." Acute observation as a trait owned by the detective is yet another contribution Poe made to the literature; it is especially apparent in "The Purloined Letter." Poe utilized cryptography in "The Gold Bug," making it the rage of his day and a staple in much of the mystery literature which was to follow (e.g., Conan Doyle's "The Adventure of the Dancing Men").

Poe lived a life of personal torment and profligate waste, but in his short lifetime he also created masterpieces which continue to fascinate and entertain humanity in every part of the world, generation after generation.

Note

[1]Stuart Levine and Susan Levine, *The Short Fiction of Edgar Allan Poe* (Indianapolis, Ind.: Bobbs-Merrill, 1976): xxx.

* * *

To learn more about Poe's life and his writings, consult these resources:

Buranelli, Vincent. *Edgar Allan Poe.* Boston: Twayne, 1977.

Knapp, Bettina L. *Edgar Allan Poe.* New York: Ungar, 1984.

Levine, Stuart, and Susan Levine. *The Short Fiction of Edgar Allan Poe.* Indianapolis, Ind.: Bobbs-Merrill, 1976.

A Literary Mystery

Who was William Shakespeare and did he really pen all those magnificent plays and sonnets? For generations, literary critics and historians have debated the authenticity of the authorship of great dramatic works such as *Hamlet, King Lear*, and *Macbeth* by a somewhat obscure man named William Shakespeare. Being very much a doubter himself newspaper columnist Sydney Harris sparred journalistically for many years with readers as to Shakespeare's authenticity. He was not alone. Mark Twain (Samuel Clemens), Walt Whitman, and Henry James were also doubters. More recently, scholar Charles Ogburn challenges the attribution of the plays to William Shakespeare in his book *The Mysterious William Shakespeare*. He suggests the true playwright may have been Edward DeVere (1550-1604), the Seventeenth Earl of Oxford. The pieces of evidence critics have marshalled include the following:

Shakespeare ?

No contemporary historian mentioned Shakespeare in text and the first Shakespeare biography did not appear until a century after his death.

Despite the fact that the plays reveal a playwright well schooled in geography, history, and culture, there is no evidence that William Shakespeare ever traveled extensively or received any schooling.

Even though the plays were popular even in the lifetime of William Shakespeare, there are no known notices of his death and no printed eulogies.

There is no record or evidence that the man purported to be the greatest writer in the history of the English language ever wrote or received a single letter of correspondence.

Nowhere is there any record that William Shakespeare ever spoke or wrote of having crafted the plays attributed to him.

Here is a genuine literary mystery to be investigated! Who was this man William Shakespeare, did he write the plays, and if not, who did? Literary sleuths in the classroom can use evidence they find in library research to marshall facts and reasoning in support of a hypothesis or hunch they forward.

For further research projects and ideas involving famous real-life mysteries such as the case of Lizzy Borden, turn to the research projects section found in "The Social Studies" chapter. Topics for additional research are also suggested in the "Crime and Punishment" chapter.

Fictional Biographies

Hercule Poirot was the first fictional character ever accorded an obituary in *The New York Times* (August 4, 1975). Numerous biographies have been written on the "life" of Sherlock Holmes.

The complete story of Sherlock Holmes is colorfully and delightfully told in two books by Holmesian scholar Michael Hardwick: *Sherlock Holmes: My Life and Crimes* and *The Complete Guide to Sherlock Holmes.* Ann Hart provides a profile of Jane Marple's life in *The Life and Times of Miss Jane Marple. Detectionary*, edited by Otto Penzler is a biographical dictionary of leading characters in detective and mystery fiction both teachers and students may wish to consult. Julian Symons provides a wonderful mystery pastiche with *Great Detectives: Seven Original Investigations.* A vicar informs readers that Miss Marple was not always well liked in the village of St. Mary Mead. Holmes is viewed in his retirement years. Hercule Poirot, Ellery Queen, Nero Wolfe, Philip Marlowe, and Maigret are other great fictional detectives who come under the delightfully imaginative scrutiny of author Symons. This creative book can serve as an inspiration to older students in dealing with biographical treatments of the great sleuths. Younger students may also want to project their favorite sleuths into the future. They might write an obituary for Nancy Drew at the end of her long, illustrious career, or write a mystery story in which the Hardy *boys* are *men* in their forties still solving mysteries, perhaps working for the F.B.I.

Students may profit from researching and comparing the lives of famous fictional sleuths. Through their reading of mysteries, students may wish to keep a notebook of data relative to lives of favorite detectives in order to create biographical portraits. Another assignment stressing good thinking skills is the comparison of two famous detectives using a Venn diagram format. Figure 2.11 compares and contrasts the characters Sherlock Holmes and Hercule Poirot.

The Venn diagram can, of course, be utilized in the comparison of other fictional detectives, mystery writers, and mystery styles. One fascinating comparison might outline the similarities and differences between American and British sleuths.

Fig. 2.11. A comparison of two great detectives.

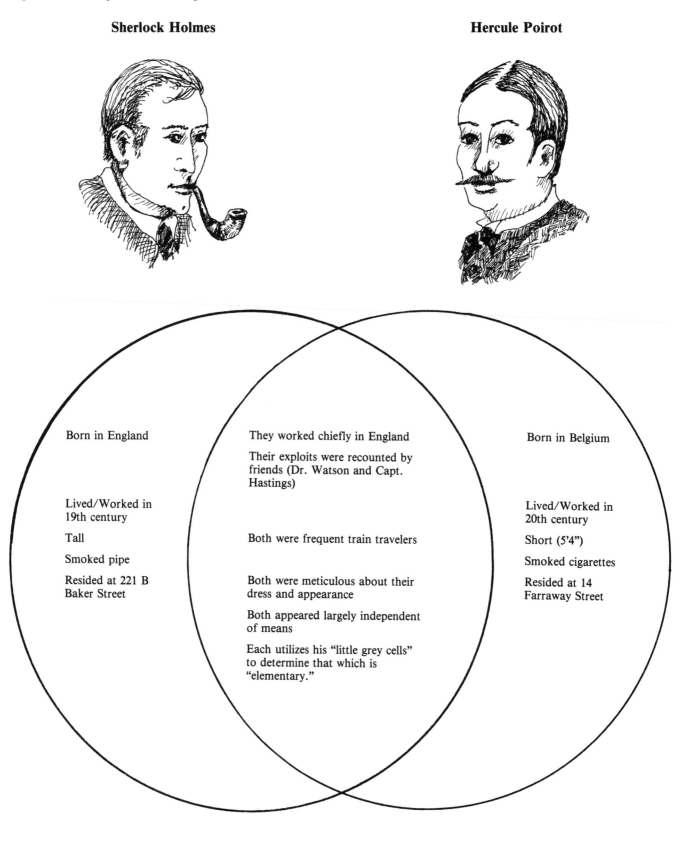

Sherlock Holmes

Hercule Poirot

Born in England

Lived/Worked in
19th century

Tall

Smoked pipe

Resided at 221 B
Baker Street

They worked chiefly in England

Their exploits were recounted by
friends (Dr. Watson and Capt.
Hastings)

Both were frequent train travelers

Both were meticulous about their
dress and appearance

Both appeared largely independent
of means

Each utilizes his "little grey cells"
to determine that which is
"elementary."

Born in Belgium

Lived/Worked in
20th century

Short (5'4")

Smoked cigarettes

Resided at 14
Farraway Street

Write a Letter to Sherlock Holmes

In 1890, a Philadelphia tobacconist wrote a letter to Sherlock Holmes requesting a copy of his monograph on tobacco ash. Ever since, Holmes has received much correspondence. Perhaps only Santa Claus and the Internal Revenue Service receive more mail annually than Holmes does. Richard Lancelyn Green has compiled the best and most unusual letters mailed to Holmes in the last century in his book *Letters to Sherlock Holmes*. People from nearly every nation in the world have written epistles to the great detective asking for his advice and assistance. Holmes has been asked to solve murders in Poland and Japan, to find a missing person in Belgium, and to become a pen pal of children around the globe.

Writing a letter to Holmes affords a wonderful by-product—student practice in the skill of writing business and friendly letters. It is a skill that even some of the most gifted students appear to be totally lacking. Students do not need to mail their letters, but they can at least draft one in their mystery notebook and write or type a final, edited copy. The combined letters of all the students would make an attractive bulletin board. Perhaps the school or local newspaper will print the best letter. It would be fun to mail one of the best letters to London and wait anxiously to see if there is a reply.

Vocabulary

A significant benefit of any mystery unit may be the vocabulary development students gain. A portion of the mystery notebook should include pages set aside for recording new vocabulary encountered. A classroom bulletin board may also be set aside for the daily addition of new words students discover in their reading. Class discussions can be opened each day with a sharing of new vocabulary found in overnight reading. The Latin derivations of many words encountered in criminology can enrich the understanding students have of the English language and its origins. Encounters with slang terms offer opportunities for discussions about the dynamic, continuously evolving nature of language. Many words found in detective fiction are spelling demons and provide many opportunities for lessons and practice. Readers can even encounter that great lexicographer, Dr. Johnson, in Lillian De La Torre's mystery, *Dr. Sam: Johnson, Detector*.

A beginning vocabulary list might include the following sampling of mystery fare terms:

accomplice	perjury	alibi
gumshoe	cyanide	disguise
modus operandi (M.O.)	belladonna	paraphernalia
assassin	collar	precinct
surveillance	villain	skullduggery
mouser	"the clink"	burglar
forgery	corpus delicti	perpetrate
malice	red herring	acquit

Gruesome Grammar

There is no need to leave grammar studies behind in planning a truly integrated English/language arts unit based upon mystery fiction. Just as spelling lessons and vocabulary development may be related to mystery fare, grammar studies can be criminal too! Using a little pedagogical larceny, teachers may adapt the old Mad*Libs® game by utilizing short passages from the Sherlock Holmes stories or the works of Poe. Or, a gifted student may be encouraged to write a mini mystery ala Mad*Libs fashion which classmates can utilize for grammar practice. Figure 2.12, a brief Mad*Libs example, follows. To utilize "Death at the 50 Yard Line," place students in teams of two. Student A, secreting the written form from Student B, asks the partner to provide words of the appropriate part of speech where there are blank lines on the document. For example, Student A will ask Student B to provide an adjective and a noun in order to fill in the first two blanks on figure 2.12. Because Student B has no idea of contextual clues, random words are given. When the blank spaces are completely filled in, the incongruous and often hilarious passage is read by Student A. Roles can then be reversed and the game continued, utilizing the same passage or a new one.

More advanced students may be encouraged to compare the grammar and syntax of authors like Poe, Doyle, and Hammett. An especially clever student might be encouraged to write a mystery with the plot turn revolving around confusion over a key word clue functioning as more than one part of speech. Or, perhaps, tongue-in-cheek, a sleuth may be created whose specialty deals with bringing to justice those who "murder" the English language.

Fig. 2.12.

Death at the 50 Yard Line

The _____ _____ had finally arrived.
     adjective   noun

_____ of football fans filled the _____.
   number greater than one   noun

_____ more fans were set to _____ the
   number greater than one   verb

Super Bowl on _____. Teams _____ on the field, youth sold
            noun   verb-past tense

_____ and _____. TV commentators predicted _____
    noun   noun   plural noun

and _____ for TV viewers. The crowd was unaware of the tragedy about to
         plural noun

happen. _____ , _____ _____ ,
       adverb ending in -ly   famous person's first and last names

the quarterback of the _____ _____
                 proper noun-city   common noun-animal

fell to the ground, apparently lifeless. Players _____ , spectators
                                       verb-past tense

_____ , and trainers and a doctor ran _____ the field. The
     verb-past tense   preposition

doctor leaned over the _____ quarterback. He rose, shaking his head, and announced,
                  adjective

"I am sorry. There is nothing I can do. He's _____ . He's
                                   predicate adjective

been _____ ."
      verb-past tense

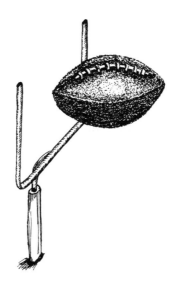

Murderous Verse

There is no need to leave poetry behind when reading and studying the mystery genre. After all, the father of the mystery story, Poe, is as famous for his poem "The Raven" as for any story he ever wrote. Many of the simple, easily mastered poetic frameworks, such as the cinquain, may be utilized by students, or more challenging forms may be attempted. The following examples may be shared with students as beginning points.

Personalized Poems

Students can create poems about their favorite detectives. Simply instruct students to write the name of a favorite sleuth on a piece of paper, vertically, one letter per line. Next, descriptions of the sleuth, words beginning with each corresponding letter of the name can be written on each line to complete the poem. Here is a personalized poem for Miss Marple.

Mild mannered

Inquisitive and

Snooping Spinster of

St.

Mary Mead

Artful,

Resourceful

Prober of mysteries—

Legendary

Englishwoman

Cinquains

The cinquain form may also be utilized effectively by students to celebrate a favorite shamus, story, author, or mystery subject. A cinquain poem consists of five lines, each containing, respectively one, two, three, four, and one words. The following cinquain speaks of one of mystery writers' favorite subjects.

Poison

Belladonna, arsenic

Lucrezia's vile ring

Tainted teas do kill

Deadly

One of the most famous examples of doggerel ever uttered was this four-line ditty chanted by school children for decades.

> Lizzie Borden took an axe
>
> And gave her mother forty whacks;
>
> When she saw what she had done
>
> She gave her father forty-one.

The verse is gruesome but its existence illustrates the power of words and how they are used. Though Lizzie Borden was judged innocent by a jury of her peers, most people associate guilt with her name because of the refusal of the verse to be forgotten.

Ask students to select people associated with crime and detection and write a verse about them. Incidentally, a criminal was famed for his verse. Onetime school teacher Charles E. Boles, alias Black Bart, routinely robbed stage coaches in the Old West. He would always leave a poem behind which identified him: Black Bart PO8 (poet). One of his verses read:

> Here I lay me down to sleep
>   To wait the coming morrow,
> Perhaps success, perhaps defeat
>   And everlasting sorrow.
> Let come what will, I'll try it on,
>   My condition can't be worse,
> And if there's money in that box
>   'Tis money in my purse.[7]

Limericks

Verbally gifted students love to write limericks. Encourage them to pen limericks about their favorite Conan Doyle story, their favorite mystery, mystery writer, or their favorite sleuth. Here is one example, a tribute to Dame Agatha Christie, which may be shared with students as an example.

> There once was a Dame name of Christie
> Penning mystr'y on mystr'y on mystr'y
>   As her sleuths dug for clues
>   And unraveled each ruse,
> The villains were vanquished to histr'y.

Isaac Asimov, a fan of Sherlock Holmes and the author of numerous mysteries, uses the limerick form to toast some of the exploits of the great detective from Baker Street in *Asimov's Sherlockian Limericks*.

Impression Poems

Impression poems are fun to write, and provide a good outlet for student creativity. There is no set form. Students simply choose a subject, brainstorm all the impressions—sights, sounds, smells, tastes, feelings—they have on the chosen subject, and then order the impressions in an eye-pleasing arrangement. The following impression poem honors great fictional detectives.

Detectives

Bloodhounds, shadows,
Private eyes,
Mousers,
Dicks, Gumshoes,
Snoops

Corpulent East Side tender of orchids,
Inspector Queen's scion,
Parisian pipe-smoking Maigret,
Father Brown,
White-haired spinster snoop

Knitted tea cosies,
Prized mustaches and spats,
Inverness cape and deerstalker cap,
Trench coats and trenchant speech,

It's Elementary!

They are our latter day knights
Righting wrongs
O, what skullduggery they unearth,
What vile plots and
Fiendish rogues
They unmask

They are our heroes—
The great detectives!

Another popular and appropriate subject for impressions poems might be the mysterious quality of a bedroom in the deep stillness of the night. Students can record all the mysterious, frightening sensations they have experienced upon suddenly awakening at say, 2 a.m. First, they think the shadow of a sweater strewn over a chair is an unknown person, or they wonder what horrible thing is creating the fearsome noise as a windblown branch scratches against a bedroom window. Ask students to list all the mysterious sights, sounds, smells, tastes ("What *does* fear taste like?" offers a provocative question), and tactile sensations they might have in the dead stillness of night. Then encourage students to put the sensations into a meaningful narrative or impressionistic poem.

Other poetic forms may also be tried. An ode may be written to Sherlock Holmes or an impression poem may be employed to describe the quiet English countryside of St. Mary Mead before a murderer strikes. Poetry may be used as an excellent supplement to the prose emphasis typically found in the reading and writing aspects of a mystery unit.

Established poets and their works may also be incorporated into the verse side of a mystery unit. An excellent starting point would be a sharing of T. S. Eliot's "Macavity: The Mystery Cat" from Eliot's *Old Possum's Book of Practical Cats*. The poem has been set to music in Andrew Lloyd Weber's phenomenally successful musical *Cats*.

Eliot calls Macavity the "Napoleon of Crime." Explain to students that this description is an example of a poetic device called a literary allusion, and then ask them to name the mystery writer from whom Eliot borrowed this descriptor. Conan Doyle has Sherlock Holmes refer to his arch enemy, Professor Moriarty, as the Napoleon of Crime in the story "The Final Problem."

As students read "Macavity," ask them to name the criminal behaviors Macavity exhibits. What heists or "jobs" does he pull off? What agencies does he baffle?

As follow-up activity, ask students to create their own animal poems. Eliot created the feline equivalent of Moriarty. Ask students to create a feline equivalent for Sherlock Holmes. What other famous criminals or sleuths can students anthropomorphize? Perhaps the collected poems of the entire class can be shaped into an anthology with a title like *Dogged Detectives* or *Catastrophic and Criminal Cats*.

Incidentally, the illustrations for the Harcourt, Brace, Jovanovich edition of Eliot's cat poems were done by Edward Gorey, whose artwork introduces and concludes the weekly Public Television series "Mystery!"

Mystery Newspapers

One way students may share what they learn in the mystery unit is through the creation of a mystery newspaper. Students can choose a name for their newspaper like the *Scotland Yard Times* (see figure 2.13), and select an editorial staff. The newspaper can serve as an outlet for the biographical sketches students write about mystery authors and sleuths, and the reports of research findings about topics like fingerprinting and wiretapping. The findings of polls conducted to determine favorite mystery writers or detectives may be published in the mystery newspaper. A real news story might include current crime statistics. Using a news story format, students can convert a Sherlock Holmes story or an adventure experienced by Nancy Drew into a hard news article. Cartoons and classified ads can further carry out the mystery theme. For example, what kind of a classified ad might attract the attention of Sherlock Holmes, or how might the Hardy Boys advertise their detection services. Contemporary computer software packages such as "The Newsroom" and "Publish It!" make the creation of a classroom mystery newspaper a relatively easy project for students to produce.[8]

Fig. 2.13.

SCOTLAND YARD TIMES

HOLMES MIDDLE SCHOOL   NOVEMBER 18, 1995

HOLMES IS ALL-TIME HOLLYWOOD FAVORITE SLEUTH

HOLLYWOOD, CA (UPI) - Sherlock Holmes out-numbers both Count Dracula and Zorro as the most often filmed fictional character. *The Baker Street Detective* reports more than 175 separate films have been made.

POLL REVEALS MYSTERIES, SCI-FIC FAVORITE READING

A poll conducted at Holmes Middle School revealed that 60% of eighth grade students prefer Conan Doyle, Agatha Christie, and Isaac Asimov to Charles Dickens, Shakespeare, and ...

Fairy Tales: They're Positively Criminal!

Have your students ever pondered the crimes committed in fairy tales? Murder, kidnapping, larceny, child abuse and abandonment, vagrancy, malicious and willful destruction of property, false identities and impersonations with intent to do great bodily harm. The list goes on and on! Why, a law school primer could be written about the crimes committed in Little Red Riding Hood alone! And, what are we to make of the legal wranglings which might emanate from the Rumplestiltskin child custody dispute?

Ask students to examine a classic fairy tale, carefully noting all the crimes for which characters could at least be under suspicion or indicted. Then, direct students to find one of the cases which begs for a trial. Allow students to have fun examining the evidence and arguments for all sides involved. Some students can be on the prosecution team and build a case against the big bad wolf, for example, while those in the legal activist society and Save the Wolf environment group can join forces to work out his defense. The remaining class members can be jurors, witnesses, and reporters covering the trial for Black Forest TV Station or the Grimm Newspaper Syndicate. A resident cartoonist can draw wonderful cartoons of a poor, pitiful wolf taking the stand in his own defense, or of a shy, frightened girl in red cloak recounting that horrible afternoon in the forest when her grandmother sprouted a hairy upper lip. Incidentally, this idea works just as well with high school seniors in honors English classes as it does with fourth-grade students. For complete details and suggestions for holding a classroom trial, see The Advocacy Trial format in the "Crime and Punishment" chapter of this book.

Crime can be fun when it is housed within the context of fairy tales, and considerable creativity and good humor can flow in the classroom.

Here is another fairy tale idea. After students have read some mysteries, and have a familiarity with the mystery genre and various styles of writing within it, ask them to rewrite a classic fairy tale as a mystery story. For example, one student might pretend to be a hard-boiled, cynical private eye investigating the slaughter of a wolf by a woodsman, while another offers a Black Forest version of Encyclopedia Brown or Cam Jansen cross-examining two children—their faces covered with frosting—who tell a preposterous story about being abandoned by their parents and subsequently threatened by an old woman who is now in an oven! Students need not limit themselves to fairy tales. Classic nursery rhymes are filled with elements of mystery and intrigue students may capitalize on in writing creative mysteries.

Literary Trivia

There will be some who stick up their noses and quickly dismiss the mystery genre and those who practice it. Initial class discussions about the form and function of mystery and detective fiction should extend to an examination of definitions of good literature. The standards arrived at from these discussions can be applied to mysteries students have read. They can then compare representative detective fiction to other literature. It will be instructive and fun to discover how many famous authors have written mysteries. According to *Murder Ink*, all of the following winners of the Nobel Prize had mystery stories published in *Ellery Queen's Mystery Magazine*.[9]

Pearl Buck	T. S. Eliot
William Faulkner	Ernest Hemingway
John Galsworthy	Rudyard Kipling
Sinclair Lewis	Bertrand Russell
George Bernard Shaw	John Steinbeck

Mark Twain jumped on the mystery bandwagon in the latter half of the nineteenth century by giving his classic characters Huckleberry Finn and Tom Sawyer a mystery to solve. *Tom Sawyer, Detective* was written by Twain in 1896 and represents the *Roman à clef* (real events turned into fictional form) school of mystery writing. The case, narrated by Huck, was based upon events brought forth in an actual Swedish trial.

For further trivia enjoyment, ask students to be "Truth Sleuths." Ask students to consider the following statements and determine the falsity or truth of each. They should verify conclusions based upon facts they unearth. (All of the statements are true.)

Presidents Abraham Lincoln and Franklin D. Roosevelt wrote mystery stories.

Detective fiction was born with the publication of Edgar Allan Poe's story "The Murders in the Rue Morgue."

The first Sherlock Holmes story was penned in 1886.

Former NFL All-Pro quarterback Fran Tarkenton penned a murder mystery set at a Super Bowl.

Margaret Truman and Elliott Roosevelt are two presidential offspring who have written successful mysteries.

Sigmund Freud was an avid mystery reader.

As a mystery unit progresses, students may be encouraged to attempt to stump the rest of the class with elements of mystery trivia they locate. A delightful class project might be the creation of a mystery trivia book or game which could be donated to the school library media center.

Class Detectives Club

Two excellent models exist for students interested in collaborations. Many of the giants of British mystery fiction belonged to a group known as the Detection Club, founded by Dorothy L. Sayers in 1928. Members met periodically in London to talk shop, discuss new plot ideas, and on occasion, to collaboratively solve a mystery. Each of several members including Agatha Christie, Dorothy Sayers, Henry Wade, G. K. Chesterson, and Edgar Jepson, received a mystery manuscript in varying stages of development. The writers constructed a plausible continuation of the story, introducing new clues to the solution they perceived. They submitted their solution to the crime, which was not to be seen by the other authors until the final chapter was written. One of the products of the Detection Club is the mystery *The Floating Admiral*.

The remarkably productive Isaac Asimov uses the idea of a detection club as a literary conceit in *Casebook of the Blackwidowers* and *The Union Club Mysteries*, both of which are anthologies of mystery stories. In the *Casebook of the Blackwidowers*, the Blackwidowers meet monthly for dinner and a mystery. In *The Union Club Mysteries*, the Union Club library is the setting where four elderly gentlemen ponder mysteries. Asimov is a member of The Trap-Door Spiders, an organization not unlike the fictionalized Black-widowers, and The Baker Street Irregulars.

Many Detection Club approaches to creating mysteries can work successfully in the classroom. A continuing story can circulate among interested students, each one furthering the plot with a page or two or even a whole chapter. The teacher can start a story for students and assign one student each day to take the story home that evening and add to it. The student brings it back to class the next day and passes it on to another student for further additions. When the story has circulated through the whole class (or interested students in the Detection Club), it can be duplicated and each student in the class can write the ending he or she perceives. Endings and reasons can be compared and a "best" ending chosen by students.

Students can also collectively attempt to problem solve mysteries posed by fellow classmates in the manner of Asimov's stories. Each member of the class Detection Club can take a turn finding or making up a problem for others to solve.

It Was a Dark and Stormy Night

The English Department of San Jose State University has sponsored the Bulwer-Lytton Contest since 1983. Entrants are asked to write a dreadful opening sentence to the worst possible novel imaginable. Bulwer-Lytton (1803-1873) was a Victorian novelist who penned a novel, *Paul Clifford* (1830) beginning with the now famous and much maligned sentence: "It was a dark and stormy night." A more recent would-be author, Snoopy of "Peanuts" cartoon strip fame, also employs Lytton's opening line as he desperately tries to achieve literary greatness. Students may recall that at least one author has used this opening with considerably more success. Madeleine L'Engle uses the same seven words to begin her hugely successful Newbery-medal winning novel *A Wrinkle in Time* (Farrar, Straus, Giroux, 1962).

More than 10,000 people from as many as fifty nations enter the Bulwer-Lytton contest each year. The "best" (meaning the most dreadful) entries have been published in a series of books compiled by Scott Rice (Penguin, 1984), the first of which is *It Was a Dark and Stormy Night*. Considerable adult humor is found in the books. Teachers should screen the use of the books in the classroom. A few selected and appropriate passages may be read aloud to give students a frame of reference as well as a laugh or two.

There is no juvenile division in the Bulwer-Lytton contest. That is the proposal here. Talented and creative young writers should have great fun creating intentionally ponderous, cliche-ridden opening lines for a class contest to pen the worst mystery story and novel openings imaginable.

By emphasizing bad writing teachers may indeed teach students good writing without appearing to be overly didactic. For example, once students have deliberately written about victims who are "dead as a door-nail," and criminals that are "thick as thieves," and sleuths who are either "sharp as a tack" or "sly like a fox," it is a reasonably safe bet that their own mystery stories will be free of cliches. The following opening sentences are examples of possible entries in the "Dark and Stormy Night" sweepstakes.

Inspector Smug looking down upon the now limp body of movie starlet Diana Drumley, who had only the day before completed filming of a new all-female version of *Mutiny on the Bounty* (she played the role of Fletcher Christian), and pronounced, "Accidental drowning." even as the erstwhile and intrepid Regina Smythe-Hayes who dabbled in sleuthing when she was not running Olympic marathons, writing best-selling adventure novels, or taking prizewinning photographs of lions in Kenya, was not so easily convinced, noting as she did, the thin red-blue circumambient line on Diana Drumley's neck, as she uttered the five words which had become both her distinctive signature and the terror of criminals and Scotland Yard incompetents alike: "I wonder about this one...."

Nosing aside his food dish, burping a deep Alpo-generated belch, and despondently scratching behind his left ear, Rex thought, "It's getting tougher and tougher to break into this detecting business nowadays, even when you have a nose for it."[10]

The humor found in *It Was a Dark and Stormy Night* is intentional. Unintentional humor may also be found in mystery writing efforts of students who are less than careful in proofreading efforts. Chris Paulis, a middle school English teacher in Maryland, shared numerous examples in the January, 1985, issue of the *English Journal*. One student wrote: "As a child, my mother died when I was thirteen and my dad died in prison." Yet another student would have profited from recalling a basic spelling rule: "Then you striped her and used Alena's clothes so you could pretend you were her."[11]

Observing the errors and miscues of other writers, intentional or not, prepares students well for the ultimate language arts assignment: writing an original mystery story.

Solving Mysteries Creatively/*The Mystery of Edwin Drood*

The creative problem solving model widely used in the business community and in many programs for gifted and talented students can be nicely incorporated into the mystery unit. Students should develop expertise in *both* critical and creative thinking and problem solving. Inventive use of the mystery genre can help achieve this goal. Charles Dickens's unfinished novel, *The Mystery of Edwin Drood* (Pantheon, 1981), offers a particularly good springboard for creative problem solving efforts by students.

There are many models of Creative Problem Solving (CPS). One model widely used in programs for the gifted was developed by Scott G. Isaksen and Donald J. Treffinger. The Isaksen-Treffinger model has six stages or steps:

> Mess-Finding
> Data-Finding
> Problem-Finding
> Idea-Finding
> Solution-Finding
> Acceptance-Finding

In the first stage, the problem-finder recognizes that there is a problem to solve and accepts the challenge of solving it. Once predisposed to solve the problem, the problem solver collects all the data needed to solve

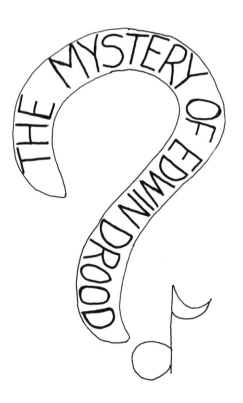

the problem. Focusing in on the real problem at hand is next. After the problem statement has been determined, the problem solver brainstorms all sorts of ideas to provide a solution. In the solution-finding stage, the problem solver establishes and utilizes criteria to assist in selecting the final, most viable solution. The problem solving process is complete when the planned solution is accepted and implemented.[12]

Late in his life, Charles Dickens began writing a mystery novel. Dickens's interest in the mystery genre may have been the result of his friendship with Wilkie Collins, author of the mystery classic *The Moonstone*. Dickens suffered a stroke and died in 1870, leaving his mystery novel *The Mystery of Edwin Drood* uncompleted. He left no notes or outline detailing the resolution of the plot. At least one creative person recognized and seized upon the opportunity this unfinished manuscript provides. Rupert Holmes in his successful Broadway musical, *The Mystery of Edwin Drood*, allows the audience to participate in the drama by choosing the ending they prefer.

The unfinished novel may also be used inventively in the classroom. Students are provided the opportunity of using creative problem solving skills to construct their own ending for the mystery. The mess is already clearly defined. The novel is unfinished; a genuine mystery remains. The lack of closure leaves potential readers unsatisfied. The data-finding occurs as students read the unfinished novel. They should collect and record in their mystery notebooks all pertinent information about the characters and plot developments. What characters are suspect? What motives do they have? What observations can they make? What inferences can they draw? One source students and teachers may wish to consult for data collection is Wendy Jacobson's *The Companion to the Mystery of Edwin Drood*, a volume of annotations to accompany the reading of Dickens's final literary effort.

Once they have collected the data, they are ready to state the key problem. What questions do readers have which go unanswered by the Dickens text? Most likely their final problem will involve creating a new ending. But, what ending will they choose? They are ready to move to the idea-finding stage of the CPS model and brainstorm ideas for possible endings. Once the students have generated several possible ideas for endings, they should move on to the solution-finding stage. Here they will establish criteria which will serve to measure the many ideas suggested. Criteria for the evaluation stage might include questions like these:

Which of the proposed ideas is the most plausible?

Which of the proposed ideas is most similar to endings typically employed by Dickens in other works?

Which of the proposed ideas is the most dramatic?

The problem solvers now use the criteria as a guide to select the best ending. The acceptance-finding occurs when the new ending is completed and tested. After students write a new ending, they may wish to share it with an English literature class or with other groups of gifted students in other schools using an electronic bulletin board.

The Mystery of Edwin Drood is not the only mystery story or novel which may be used for this activity. It is an especially provocative piece of literature to use because no one knows what ending Dickens might have chosen. Use the CPS model and exercise with any story. Simply read a mystery novel or story and have students pause in their reading halfway through the text. Ask students to apply the model to project the ending they think will take place. Once they have worked through the process and have chosen an ending, they can go back to the text and finish reading the mystery to verify their hunches and compare their ending(s) with the one the author chose.[13]

Writing a Mystery Story

The culminating project of a language arts/English unit on the mystery genre should be the writing of an original mystery story. All previous discussions, inquiries, and reading come into play as students apply what they have learned via the unit work to their story. Several authors have written books about the crafting of a mystery story. The following are particularly good resources:

Eleanor Hoomes. *Create-A-Sleuth: Writing a Detective Story*. Educational Impressions, 1983.
Hoomes provides a series of worksheets for students to use in a step-by-step approach to writing the mystery story.

Karen M. Hubert. *Teaching and Writing Popular Fiction: Horror, Adventure, Mystery, and Romance*. Virgil Books, 1976.
Hubert's chapter on the mystery genre offers many specific strategies in assisting students with writing their own story.

Barbara Norville. *Writing the Modern Mystery*. Writer's Digest Books, 1986.
Though intended for a professional audience, this book provides indispensable advice and practical writing tips teachers can easily adapt for student audiences.

Another resource teachers and library media specialists can consult is a pamphlet created by Edward Packard and R. A. Montgomery. It tells students how to create an original "Choose Your Own Adventure" story which, of course, could be a mystery. The booklet is available from Bantam Books (School & College Department, Bantam Books, 666 Fifth Avenue, New York, NY 10103).

Barbara Norville suggests the webbing technique as an especially useful prewriting technique to use with students. The crime to be featured is placed at the center of the web. The radiating lines, each fully considered, explored and developed by the writer *before writing* include: criminal, victim, sleuth, narrator, time elements, suspects, scene of the crime, background detail, and the solution. She also suggests mystery writers become thoroughly familiar with all their major characters—how they think, behave, talk, and their motives—by writing short biographies of each. That is an excellent writing tip for would-be writers in any literary genre.

There are many other writing strategies students may want to consider. Writing sequels to existing mystery stories and employing existing famous detectives can offer a safer route for some timid and unsure young authors. Countless authors have written further adventures for Doyle's classic hero, Sherlock Holmes. Excellent mystery stories can find their plot structure in classic fairy tales, mythology, or nursery rhymes. Agatha Christie based a number of her mysteries on such literary allusions.

A hostage crisis, examples of government duplicity, or other current news events may suggest further ideas for stories. Edgar Allan Poe's "The Mystery of Marie Roget" is an example of the *Roman à clef* mystery. (In *Fatal Fascination*, Phil McArdle and Karen McArdle include a copy of Poe's 1842 letter to the editor of *Notion* magazine in which he tries to sell this story. In the letter, Poe sells his story by detailing how he built it around the real death of one Mary Cecilia Rogers.)[14] The story is a fictionalized account of a real-life murder case which remains unsolved today. Agatha Christie's *Murder on the Orient Express* was inspired by the publicity surrounding the Lindbergh kidnapping case. However, students do need to realize that there is a good reason why authors use the classic disclaimer statement: "All the chracters and events in this book are imaginary." Authors can be sued if their stories invade the privacy or trample on the rights of others.

A forced association technique may also serve as a prompt for student writers. The teacher may simply suggest five or six random words (e.g., blue, scream, woods, perfume, knife, darkness) and ask students to build a mystery around the given words. Similarly, the teacher can describe a fictional event created at random and ask students to build a mystery story upon the brief description provided. The following are examples:

The school mascot, Opie, had disappeared. Where on earth could he be? There just didn't seem to be any reasonable explanation.

John wandered aimlessly in the school parking lot at 2 a.m.

Most creative and talented students will easily generate their own ideas for mystery stories. For those students who develop a writing block, the story starters in figure 2.14 may serve as the catalyst needed.

Mystery Story Starters

Fig. 2.14. Launch ideas for stories.

You are Madison High's whiz kid detective. The school bully knows it. He bumps into you in a crowded hallway during the passing of classes and whispers to you, "If you know what is good for you, you'll forget about Mrs. Andre's missing grade book." What mystery lurks behind this provocative incident?

* * * * *

" 'Why did I do it? Why did I do it?' Try as he might, he could not erase those five simple words from his conscious mind." What did the person do, and why did he do it?

* * * * *

There has been a fire at the home of famed British mystery writer Dudley Smythe-Finkel. His entire study-library burned and his whodunit, works-in-progress were destroyed. All that is left are a few charred fragments of paper. Can you come to poor Dudley's rescue? Help him reconstruct first-rate mystery stories from the singed remains:

...no weapon, no clues, no body, yet he knew a crime had been committed.

The sherds of pottery on the floor told the whole sad story of...

The light of the moon silhouetted the burglar as he....

* * * * *

Thomas Alva Edison was totally baffled. He was used to solving the mysteries of electricity, not the wily ways of criminals. He had no choice but to apply his brilliant mind to a new kind of detection. If the theft and vandalism in his laboratory were not halted soon, his entire new project would have to be scrapped. What are the specifics in the Edison mystery? Who is the criminal? What is the motive? How does Thomas Edison solve the mystery?

* * * * *

More than a few criminals have committed a second crime to cover up or destroy the evidence connected to their primary criminal act. Example: a robber becomes an arsonist when he sets fire to the store he has just robbed hoping the fire will destroy all the clues leading the police to him. Create a story with at least two crimes committed, one of which is a "red herring."

* * * * *

Your favorite rock group is in big trouble. The police have issued a warrant for the arrest of the group's leader. Your skills in sleuthing are urgently needed. What is the crime? What evidence do the police have? How can you prove the innocence of your hero? Tell the dramatic story.

* * * * *

(Fig. 2.14 continues on page 62.)

One of the cleverest ideas in recent mystery literature is Gary K. Wolf's juxtaposition of humans and cartoon characters in his novel *Who Censored Roger Rabbit?*, filmed by the Disney studios as *Who Framed Roger Rabbit?* Create a mystery with animals or fictional characters coming to life and mingling with human beings. For example, what kind of mystery story might develop if Huck Finn came to life and helped his creator Samuel Clemens solve a puzzling crime? Can you create a mystery story in which Mickey Mouse and Donald Duck assist Walt Disney in a sleuthing effort?

* * * *

How might an apparent disability turn into an asset in detective work? In Alfred Hitchcock's famous movie mystery *Rear Window*, actor James Stewart portrays a man temporarily confined to a wheelchair, who, because of his enforced confinement witnesses and solves a murder mystery no one else even suspects. Ironically, the actor portraying the villain in that film, Raymond Burr, later assumed the role of a sleuth who solved crimes from a wheelchair in the television series "Ironsides." Perhaps you can write a mystery story with a deaf detective. Because of the loss of one of the five senses the others have sharpened keenly. An acute use of the senses of vision, touch, taste, and smell all aid in trapping criminals.

Although the story should be the culminating mystery unit project, assign it early to insure that students have plenty of time to write and edit several drafts. Considerable time should be spent in prewriting efforts, creating the sleuth, plotting the crime, exploring character motivations, practicing the writing of dialogue, and devising an original resolution. One of the virtues of this writing assignment is that it forces students to organize their thinking and tighten their writing. A well-crafted mystery has a tight organizational structure with details given to readers in a systematic fashion. The writer is alert to the clues he provides and the ordering of the clues given. For students who have never exercised much control in their written work, crafting a mystery story is a highly motivating challenge and an opportunity to hone and sharpen their composition skills.

Create an Authors' League

At seventy-two Mark Twain became an exemplary mentor for a gifted girl named Dorothy Quick. Dorothy was eleven years old in 1907 when she first met Mark Twain. She told him how much she admired him and that, like him, she wished to be a writer. Twain founded an "Authors' League" for the two of them. He gave her one of his unfinished stories and told her to write a new ending for the story. For the rest of his life he gave her advice on the craft of writing. He critiqued her work and allowed her to watch him at work: writing, editing, and rewriting. He shared with Dorothy information about publishers, popular tastes, and every other aspect of writing and publishing that he knew.[15]

The "Authors' League" Mark Twain created with a gifted child provides a model for educators worthy of emulation. Is there a mystery writer in the community who would become a mentor for a highly gifted young writer? Is there a teacher in the school system who "moonlights" as a writer and could serve as a mentor? Is there a high school student who enjoys writing and would be willing to serve as a mentor for younger gifted students? Within the classroom, the most gifted writers could share their talent and agree to serve as mentors, editors, and critics for another student whose writing skills are not as highly developed.

Mark Twain not only wrote the mystery *Tom Sawyer, Detective*, he also wrote a parody of Arthur Conan Doyle's Sherlock Holmes stories entitled "The Stolen White Elephant" which is very funny.

Notes

[1]Barbara Norville, *Writing the Modern Mystery* (Cincinnati, Ohio: Writer's Digest Books, 1986), 59.

[2]Karen M. Hubert, *Teaching and Writing Popular Fiction: Horror, Adventure, Mystery, and Romance* (New York: Virgil Books, 1976), 98-100. This particular outline is based in part on Hubert's model. (Also see Norville, note 1 above, 62-63 for excellent outline of the mystery story.)

[3]John Hathaway Winslow and Alfred Meyer, "The Perpetrator at Piltdown," *Science 83* 4, no. 7 (September 1983): 32-43.

[4]Hugh Eames, *Sleuths, Inc.* (Philadelphia: J. B. Lippincott, 1978), 41-46.

[5]The unusual disappearance of the famous mystery writer is the basis for the 1979 Vanessa Redgrave-Dustin Hoffman film *Agatha* distributed by Warner Home Video.

[6]Eames, *Sleuths*, 106-107.

[7]Album notes for *The Badmen*. Columbia Records Legacy Collection produced by Goddard Lieberson. p. 15.

[8]"The Newsroom" is published by Springboard Software, Inc., 7807 Creekridge Circle, Minneapolis, MN 55435. "Publish It!" is published by Timeworks, Inc., 444 Lake Cook Road, Deerfield, IL 60015.

[9]Dilys Winn, *Murder Ink: The Mystery Reader's Companion* (New York: Workman, 1977), 36.

[10]Elizabeth Nielsen contributed this opening sentence.

[11]Chris Paulis, "A Few Blood Gurgling Screams: Accidental Humor from Student Detective Stories," *English Journal* 74, no. 1 (January 1985): 73.

[12]Scott Isaksen and Donald J. Treffinger, *Creative Problem Solving: The Basic Course* (Buffalo, N.Y.: Bearly Limited, 1985).

[13]The author wishes to acknowledge and thank Brett Carter who suggested this use of Charles Dickens's unfinished novel.

[14]See Phil McArdle and Karen McArdle, *Fatal Fascination: Where Fact Meets Fiction in Police Work* (Boston: Houghton Mifflin, 1988), 151.

[15]Dorothy Quick, *Enchantment: A Little Girl's Friendship with Mark Twain* (Norman, Okla.: University of Oklahoma Press, 1961).

Teacher Resources

Anderson, LaVere. *Allan Pinkerton: First Private Eye.* Champaign, Ill.: Garrard, 1972.

The Armchair Detective. New York: Mysterious Press.

> This quarterly publication provides information on the latest in mystery fiction as well as interviews with mystery authors, historical articles about the genre, etc. Order from The Mysterious Press, 129 West 56th Street, New York, NY 10019.

Asimov, Isaac. *Asimov's Sherlockian Limericks.* New York: Mysterious Press, 1978.

> Asimov salutes Holmes with limericks about his greatest cases.

California State Department of Education. *Literature and Story Writing: A Guide to Teaching Gifted and Talented Children in the Elementary and Middle Schools.* Sacremento, Calif.: Bureau of Publications, 1981.

> An excellent mystery bibliography for young readers, plus excellent writing tips are included.

Carr, John C. *The Craft of Crime: Conversations with Crime Writers.* Boston: Houghton Mifflin, 1983.

> Carr interviews a dozen popular purveyors of the mystery genre. Readers are allowed the opportunity to eavesdrop, as it were, to conversations between Carr and such writers as Emma Lathen, Dick Francis, Peter Lovesey, and Jane Langton.

Christie, Agatha. *Agatha Christie: An Autobiography.* New York: Ballantine Books, 1987.

Eames, Hugh. *Sleuths, Inc.* Philadelphia: J. B. Lippincott, 1978.

> A fascinating study of mystery writers as problem solvers. The real-life exploits of Doyle, Simenon, Hammett, Ambler, and Chandler are told.

Eliot, T. S. *Old Possum's Book of Cats.* Illus. by Edward Gorey. New York: Harcourt, Brace, Jovanovich, 1982.

Green, Richard Lancelyn. *Letters to Sherlock Holmes.* New York: Viking Penguin, 1985.

> Since the 1890s people around the world have been writing letters to Sherlock Holmes. Green has compiled some of the best representative letters.

Hardwick, Michael. *Sherlock Holmes: My Life and Crimes.* Garden City, N.Y.: Doubleday & Company, Inc., 1984.

> Holmes tells his own story in this "biography."

_____. *The Complete Guide to Sherlock Holmes.* New York: St. Martin's Press, 1986.

> The story of the creation of the great detective and his life and times.

Hart, Anne. *The Life and Times of Miss Jane Marple.* New York: Dodd, Mead, 1985.

> A biography of Agatha Christie's everpopular spinster sleuth.

Higham, Charles H. *The Adventures of Conan Doyle: The Life of the Creator of Sherlock Holmes.* New York: Pocket Books, 1976.

Hitchman, Janet. *Such a Strange Lady: A Biography of Dorothy L. Sayers.* New York: Harper & Row, 1975.

Hoomes, Eleanor W. *Create a Sleuth: Writing a Detective Story.* Hawthorne, N.J.: Educational Impressions, 1983.

> A resource guide especially appropriate for the elementary classroom.

Hubert, Karen M. *Teaching and Writing Popular Fiction: Horror, Romance, Adventure and Mystery in the American Classroom*. New York: Virgil Books, 1976.

Hubert provides straight-forward analysis of the mystery story and practical writing tips. Most appropriate for junior high school classrooms.

Hughes, Dorothy B. *Erle Stanley Gardner: The Case of the Real Perry Mason*. New York: William Morrow, 1978.

Jacobson, Wendy S. *The Companion to the Mystery of Edwin Drood*. London: Allen & Unwin, 1986.

A chapter by chapter annotation to accompany the reading of the mystery novel.

Johnson, Diane. *Dashiell Hammett: A Life*. New York: Random House, 1983.

Knapp, Bettina L. *Edgar Allan Poe*. New York: Frederick Ungar, 1984.

A good, scholarly, and easily read biography of the father of mystery literature.

Lambert, Gavin. *The Dangerous Edge*. New York: Grossman, 1976.

Lambert examines the lives of mystery creators like G. K. Chesterton, Alfred Hitchcock, and Graham Greene to find the roots of their fascination with criminology.

McArdle, Phil, and Karen McArdle. *Fatal Fascination: Where Fact Meets Fiction in Police Work*. Boston: Houghton Mifflin, 1988.

Norville, Barbara. *Writing the Modern Mystery*. Cincinnati, Ohio: Writer's Digest Books, 1986.

Norville is an author and editor of mysteries. She has worked with such successful writers as Emma Lathen, Ed McBain, and Dorothy Uhnak. She clearly knows her craft and offers a multitude of suggestions and easily understood advice for writers with clear application to students and professionals. This is an especially valuable tool for high school composition teachers.

Ogburn, Charles. *The Mysterious William Shakespeare: The Myth and the Reality*. New York: Dodd, Mead, 1984.

A noted scholar examines a mystery which will probably never be solved.

Osborne, Charles. *The Life and Crimes of Agatha Christie*. London: Collins, 1982.

Penzler, Otto, ed. *Detectionary*. Woodstock, N.Y.: The Overlook Press, 1977.

The leading sleuths of mystery and detective fiction are profiled.

Quick, Dorothy. *Enchantment: A Little Girl's Friendship with Mark Twain*. Norman, Okla.: University of Oklahoma Press, 1961.

This is a first-person account of a very special mentorship.

Rice, Scott, ed. *It Was a Dark and Stormy Night*. New York: Penguin Books, 1984.

A compilation of intentionally badly written opening lines to books.

Symons, Julian. *Great Detectives: Seven Criminal Investigations*. New York: Harry Abrams, 1983.

The author cleverly examines the lives of seven famous sleuths.

Winn, Dilys, ed. *Murder Ink: The Mystery Reader's Companion*. New York: Workman, 1977.

> A requisite item for any serious study of the mystery genre. Winn followed this volume with *Murderess Ink: The Better Half of Mystery* (Workman, 1979). Together, the two volumes provide teachers and students with an encyclopedic view of mysteries and their perpetrators.

Woeller, Waltraud, and Bruce Cassiday. *The Literature of Crime and Detection: An Illustrated History from Antiquity to the Present*. New York: Ungar, 1988.

> The authors chronicle the history of the mystery genre. The text is complemented with excellent illustrations.

Classic Mysteries

Christie, Agatha. *The Mysterious Affairs at Styles*. New York: Bantam Books, 1983.

> Hercule Poirot makes his debut.

Chesterton, G. K. *The Father Brown Omnibus*. New York: Dodd, Mead, 1951.

> Six Father Brown tales of mystery.

Collins, Wilkie. *The Moonstone*. New York: Dodd, Mead, 1955.

> One of the first mystery novels penned.

Doyle, A. Conan. *The Sherlock Holmes Mysteries*. New York: New American Library, 1984.

> There are numerous volumes of Arthur Conan Doyle's great stories. This version includes all the stories treated in the Public Television "Mystery!" series. Classics such as "The Adventure of the Speckled Band," "A Scandal in Bohemia," and "The Musgrave Ritual" are found in this anthology.

Hammett, Dashiell. *The Maltese Falcon*. New York: Vintage Books, 1984.

> Sam Spade is introduced.

Poe, Edgar Allan. *The Short Fiction of Edgar Allan Poe: An Annotated Edition*. Indianapolis, Inc.: Bobbs-Merrill, 1976.

> The detective story is born in Poe's great stories "The Murders in the Rue Morgue," "The Gold Bug," and "The Purloined Letter."

Sayers, Dorothy L. *The Five Red Herrings*. New York: Harper & Row, 1986.

> One of the many occasions for meeting Lord Peter Wimsey, aristocratic sleuth.

Mystery Reading List for the Language Arts

Asimov, Isaac. *Casebook of the Black Widowers*. New York: Ballantine Books, 1980.
Each month the Black Widowers meet to dine and solve a mystery.

_____. *The Union Club Mysteries*. New York: Ballantine Books, 1983.
Elderly gentlemen meet in the Union Club to discuss murder and mystery.

Barnard, Robert. *Death of a Mystery Writer*. New York: Dell, 1978.
Sir Oliver Fairleigh-Stubbs, a widely read author of whodunits suffers the same fate of some of his famous characters.

Christie, Agatha. *A Pocketful of Rye*. New York: Pocket Books, 1967.
Miss Christie once again uses literary allusion, basing her mystery on a classic nursery rhyme. See also her allusions to Greek mythology in *The Labors of Hercules* (Berkeley Books, 1984).

Christie, Agatha, et al. *The Floating Admiral*. New York: Charter Books, 1980.
Members of the British Detection Club collaborate on a mystery novel. Besides Christie, Dorothy L. Sayers, G. K. Chesterton, and others contribute.

Clemens, Samuel L. (Mark Twain). *The Complete Short Stories of Mark Twain*. Charles Neider, editor. Garden City, N.Y.: Doubleday, 1957.
Twain's spoof of detective fiction, "The Stolen White Elephant," is found in this anthology.

_____. *Tom Sawyer, Detective*. New York: New American Library, 1985.
The famous author gives Tom Sawyer further adventures in this *Roman à clef* mystery. Twain based the story on a real courtroom drama which took place in Sweden.

Cross, Amanda. *Death in a Tenured Position*. New York: Ballantine Books, 1981.

Cross has created a literary sleuth, Kate Fansler, professor of English literature who deals with mystery and mayhem in literary circles.

De La Torre, Lillian. *Dr. Sam: Johnson, Detector*. New York: International Polygonics, 1983.

A series of mystery episodes in four books is available involving Dr. Johnson and narrated by Boswell.

Estleman, Loren D. *Sherlock Holmes vs. Dracula*. New York: Doubleday, 1978.

One of the many continuations of the Sherlock Holmes chronicles by an author other than Doyle, this book is of special interest to English teachers in its pairing of two of the most famous literary creations ever penned.

Langton, Jane. *Emily Dickinson Is Dead*. New York: Penguin, 1985.

The popular author of children's books turns a deft hand in creating a murder mystery interwoven with a celebration of the Belle of Amherst. See also *The Trancendental Murder* (Penguin, 1989).

Milne, A. A. *The Red House Mystery*. New York: Dell, 1984.

Yes, the writer who gave the world *Winnie-the-Pooh* also wrote a mystery novel.

Raskin, Ellen. *The Westing Game*. New York: Avon, 1978.

Raskin's Newbery Award-winning children's novel is a mystery puzzle and story, featuring the would-be young author Theo Theodorakis.

Schier, Norma. *The Anagram Detectives*. New York: Mysterious Press, 1979.

Lovers of word puzzles will enjoy this work.

Wolf, Gary. *Who Censored Roger Rabbit?* New York: Ballantine Books, 1981.

The source for the highly original and successful film "Who Framed Roger Rabbit?"

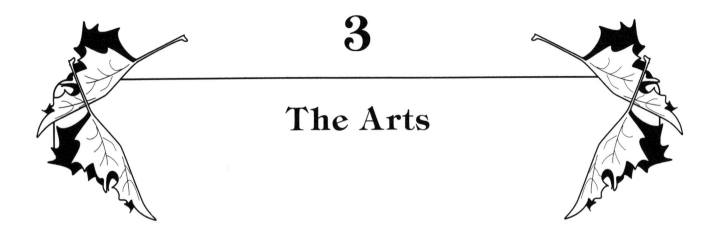

3

The Arts

Meet the Author and Meet the Illustrator
of *Mystery and Detection*

Jerry Flack is Associate Professor of Gifted Child Education at the University of Colorado in Colorado Springs, Colorado. He has received academic degrees from Michigan State University, Western Michigan University, and Purdue University. He has written numerous professional articles about curricula for gifted and talented students and is the editor of the Gifted Treasury Series for Libraries Unlimited. *Mystery and Detection* is his fifth book. Dr. Flack sits on the Board of Directors of the National Association for Gifted Children and the Board of Governors of The Association for the Gifted.

Gay Graeber Miller is a consultant for the Indiana Department of Education Shared Information Services at the Wilson Education Center in Jeffersonville, Indiana. She received a B.F.A. from the University of Mississippi and her M.Ed. from the University of Louisville. She has taught art is all the school grades. She is an active member of the National Association for Gifted Children. Ms. Miller has exhibited one-woman art shows in Louisville and Lexington, Kentucky. She is the mother of two teenage sons.

A Letter from a Professional

Fig. 3.1. A letter to students from the author and the illustrator of *Mystery and Detection.*

University of Colorado at Colorado Springs

School of Education

P.O. Box 7150
Colorado Springs, Colorado 80933-7150

From the author:

"No man is an island" wrote the seventeenth century English poet John Donne. His words speak about the collaborative problem solving process. What happens when more than one sleuth tackles a case or when two or more persons work together to solve a common problem? The results, of course, can be mixed. Joint efforts can fail for many reasons: conflicting personalities; opposing styles of sleuthing; or varying goals. Sometimes the old proverb "Too many cooks spoil the broth," holds true. But many joint efforts do succeed. When we watch a good detective film, enjoy a ballet, or applaud the performance of a symphony orchestra we are responding to a successful collaborative effort. We would like to tell you about one such collaboration.

Your teacher has probably shared with you several mystery desks from the book *Mystery and Detection.* An example of the shared problem solving process working is the story of the creation of the mystery desks. I (in this case, your author) shared with the illustrator of this book an idea I used in my classes to challenge the critical thinking skills of my students. I asked students to list objects in their desks or lockers on unsigned slips of paper. The slips of paper were collected and students used detective skills to determine the true identity of the desk a given slip of paper described. I also asked students to create a mystery game with lists of items they might find in the desks of famous people. A colleague, Dr. Elizabeth Nielsen, suggested a further idea. Why not include a mystery desk of a famous person at the beginning of each chapter of the book. The next task was to select a famous person or persons for the desks to be included in the book. Desks or work spaces for a mystery author, a detective, an artist, an anthropologist, and a futurist or science fiction writer were needed. For the literature and language arts chapter of the book, I selected a Victorian family prominent in English literature, the Bröntes: sisters Emily, Anne, Charlotte, and brother Branwell.

From the illustrator:

Jerry asked me if I would illustrate the book. I had a vision of how the desks should look. Each one should be a pen and ink drawing, complete with clues incorporated throughout the whole sketch. The literature and language arts desk illustration needed a Victorian feeling, both for the sake of accuracy, and to complement the period in which Sherlock Holmes, the great sleuth, lived and worked.

Jerry sent me the names of the famous people for whom he wanted mystery desks to be created. He suggested items for each desk which could serve as visual clues and made recommendations about time periods and settings. For the Brönte children he sent this information:

The family was very poor; parsons were not paid well in the 1830s. The children grew up in a Yorkshire (England) parsonage. They may well have had old furniture dating back to the 1700s. I enclose pictures of miniature books the children created. Items in the desk: twelve wooden soldiers, miniature books, a young person's drawing of the Glasstown Confederacy, a handwritten history of Angria, and a sketch of the Duke of Zamorna.

Now, my problem solving or sleuthing began. With the information Jerry sent, I went to the Louisville, Kentucky Public Library to pour over books on English antiques from the 1700s. I also spent time researching toy soldiers. At that point, I began a number of rough sketches while making decisions about where to "hide" clues within the drawing. The drawing had to represent a desk inside a parsonage, hence, the church and graveyard outside the window and the Bible on the desk. Also, I wanted to emphasize that the desk belonged to children, so I made the ink well and quill larger in proportion.

Each of the desks took approximately 8 to 10 hours to complete. As I got close to finishing a desk drawing, I would call together my family and have them try to guess whose desk I was working on at the moment.

There is a great deal of self-satisfaction that comes from solving problems, especially problems in personal fields of interest. We can testify that the joy multiplies itself when the correct solutions are found through a collaborative effort. May you enjoy the hunt, find the clues incorporated in the desks, avoid the red herrings, make accurate predictions, and resolve your cases successfully!

Jerry Flack   *Gary A. Miller*

Case Study

Fig. 3.2. Arts case study.

Problem solving and sleuthing do not always precisely follow the six-step pattern outlined by the author. There are notable exceptions and peculiar twists. One of the most fascinating wrinkles involves the case of Han van Meegeren, the most celebrated art forger of all time.

By May, 1945, Holland had been liberated from German occupation. Dutch police were rounding up Nazi sympathizers and collaborators as World War II came to a close. Throughout the war years the notorious Nazi Reichsmarschall, Hermann Goering, had stolen or extorted great works of art, amassing a fortune in paintings. Art experts who joined frontline Allied troops in rushing into Germany to recapture and save masterpieces by da Vinci, Titian, and van Gogh discovered a painting called *Woman Taken in Adultery* by the great seventeenth-century Dutch artist Vermeer. It was a startling discovery. None of the experts knew anything about it. It was not listed in any art registry or history. A trail of clues lead police to Amsterdam and the door of an obscure Dutch painter and art dealer, Han van Meegeren. Police took van Meegeren into custody on suspicion of collaboration with the enemy for selling one of Holland's great art treasures. After six weeks of interrogation in police custody, van Meegeren confessed. His confession is the wrinkle in this case.

On July 12, 1945 Han van Meegeren confessed art forgery, not collaboration with the enemy. No, van Meegeren asserted, he had not collaborated with the enemy. Instead, he claimed, he had duped the enemy. Goering had purchased a fake Vermeer. But van Meegeren had not completed his confession. To substantiate the claim that he was indeed capable of counterfeiting great works of art, he confessed to the forgery of some fourteen Dutch masterpieces, including several works supposedly done by Vermeer. These pieces were among the most prized possessions of famed Amsterdam and Rotterdam art museums.

The Dutch art world was in shock. Less than a decade before, one of the greatest Dutch art critics, Dr. Abraham Bredius, had proclaimed *Christ and the Disciples at Emmaus*, which hung in Rotterdam's Museum Boymans, the greatest of all Vermeer's work. Equal praise had greeted other works credited to Vermeer, Frans Hals, and other Dutch masters that entered the Dutch art market and found their way into museum collections between 1932 and 1945. All had supposedly undergone scrupulous testing to determine their authenticity.

Now here was the dilemma for the Dutch art world: In order to save their own reputations and the works of art in question (Dutch law and precedent at the time required all works of art declared as forgeries to be destroyed), the art critics had to prove that Han van Meegeren *was innocent!* Roles were reversed. The criminal in this case had to prove he was guilty and the establishment had to prove him innocent.

The motivation of each party in this unique case was critical. Collaboration with the enemy in a country which had suffered the nightmare of Nazi occupation for more than five years was a capital offense. Found guilty, van Meegeren would face the death penalty. The crime of forgery was a lesser offense. This was one instance when an accused man wanted to plead guilty and be proved correct! The art establishment had just as much at stake. Millions of dollars worth of art would be worthless if van Meegeren's assertion of guilt by forgery stood. The art community of the Netherlands joined in a unanimous chorus denying van Meegeren's claim. Han van Meegeren was merely trying to save his own neck with his preposterous claim, they argued.

The search for evidence, its organization and classification, and the formulation of predictions began. The Dutch government also entered the scene forming a special investigative commission headed by a Belgian museum laboratory director, P. B. Coremans; the commission also included chemists from the Dutch legal system and art historians. The art community made public their evidence in order to prove that the Vermeers in question, especially the *Emmaus*, were authentic. They cited the fact that the surface of the *Emmaus* had resisted alcohol and solvents. The chemistry of the paint corresponded to pigments known to be utilized in the seventeenth century, and X-ray studies demonstrated no previous paintings residing on the canvas under the *Emmaus*.

To conclusively prove his guilt, van Meegeren offered to recreate the processes used and to bring to the art world a brand new "Vermeer," *Young Christ Teaching in the Temple.* An old canvas from the seventeenth century was brought to him in prison. He scraped it clean in the same manner he had used with the earlier forgeries. He did this in order to authenticate both the age of the canvas and to eliminate the risk of X-rays revealing another painting beneath the surface. He mixed his paints using the same phenol and formaldehydes he had used earlier to create a synthetic resin which would dry rapidly and provide the aged, hardened appearance and texture of antique paintings. He also described to the commission how he had baked the canvases, rolled them to create "age" cracks, filled the cracks with India ink, and flaked away paint from parts of the painting, all to simulate the wear of centuries. While van Meegeren toiled away creating a new Vermeer, Coremans's commission employed new and perhaps more thorough techniques in examining *Emmaus* and the other questioned works. They discovered the "dirt" in the cracks of the surfaces was too uniform in depth and composition to have occurred naturally and that the surface cracks had been artificially induced. Two of the questioned paintings contained pigments not available in Vermeer's day. In one sense, van Meegeren had been too good at his art. The paint layer of his works proved to be inpenetrable whereas the surfaces of authentic seventeenth-century works were hardened but could be severely damaged by solvents.

Confirmation of van Meegeren's claim came in a Dutch court more than two years after the investigation began. His trial lasted but one day. The commission headed by Coremans backed van Meegeren's claim: he had not sold masterpieces to the enemy; he had created forgeries. The forger was sentenced to one year in prison, but he never served his term. He died of a massive heart attack less than two months following the sentencing.

The resolution of the Vermeer-van Meegeren affair was hardly complete. The Dutch art community admitted that evidence confirmed that van Meegeren was a forger of *some* of the works in question, but that two works, *Emmaus* and *The Last Supper* were authentic Vermeers. They theorized that van Meegeren discovered these two superior works and masterminded a scheme to forge others using the two pieces in question as models. The debate raged on for twenty-one more years as critics continued to attack the commission's report and remained resolutely convinced of the authenticity of the two paintings. Finally, in 1968, the Mellon Institute in the United States settled the affair conclusively. Scientists at the Mellon Institute discovered a way to measure the radioactive decay of uranium found in paint pigments containing lead used by artists for centuries. Examinations of *Emmaus* and *The Last Supper* and two genuine Vermeer paintings never in question lead to the unmistakable conclusion that the *Emmaus* and *The Last Supper* could not possibly have been painted during Vermeer's lifetime and thus were twentieth-century forgeries.

Of course, one mystery remains. Is a painting once thought by millions (including distinguished art critics) to be a masterpiece no longer a great work of art because the authentic signature should be van Meegeren rather than Vermeer?

(Fig. 3.2 continues on page 74.)

Sources:

Fleming, Stuart J. *Authenticity in Art: The Scientific Detection of Forgery.* New York: Crane, Russack, 1976.

Jeppson, Lawrence. *The Fabulous Frauds: Fascinating Tales of Great Art Forgeries.* New York: Weybright and Talley, 1970.

Werness, Hope B. "Han van Meegeren *fecit.*" In *The Forger's Art: Forgery and the Philosophy of Art*, Denis Dutton, ed., 1-57. Berkeley, Calif.: University of California Press, 1983.

Tools of the Trade

Figure 3.3 is a high school for the performing and fine arts. First, ask students to identify which art is practiced in each of the rooms in the drawing. Next, ask students to generate a list of tools which might be used by problem solvers in each of the arts represented. Encourage students to complete the arts high school scene by drawing students and teachers using the tools in the practice of their respective art.

Part of the discussion held with students may lead to the question of which arts are not represented with rooms in the drawing. Students may wish to add rooms to the school for the arts representing their favorite art form.

Fig. 3.3. Tools of the trade for arts.

Mystery Desk

Invite students to examine the desk in figure 3.4 closely. Teacher directions might be as follows:

What are the clues you have available? If the answer to the ownership of the desk or worktable is not readily apparent, how might you begin to use the clues to determine the correct answer? What inferences can you draw? Where can you locate help in interpreting the clues? What tools in the library media center would assist you in determining the ownership of this desk or table? To whom does the desk belong?

Fig. 3.4. Mystery artist's workspace.

Mystery Windows

Figure 3.5 can be used to provide students with another mystery. It is a pattern which may be used with figure 3.4. Use the pattern shown in figure 3.5 to cut four "windows" in a piece of thin cardboard. (One-half of a letter-size manila file folder works very well. The cardboard should be thin enough to allow for ease in opening and closing of the windows to be cut.) Make an overhead transparency of figure 3.4. Place the window form on top of the transparency and put both on the overhead projector. Tell students you are going to show them the work table and studio of a very famous artist and that you are first going to reveal the artist's studio through a series of mystery windows. Students may guess who the artist is at any time, but they must justify all answers by linking fact with reasoning. Begin opening the windows one at a time. After each window opening, ask students what facts or evidence they can visually determine. What inferences can they make based on the visual evidence? Open all four windows. If students still can not determine the ownership of the worktable and studio, remove figure 3.5 and reveal the entire picture.

This strategy works well with other black and white drawings. For example, teachers and library media specialists can make transparencies of some of the classic Sidney Paget drawings of Sherlock Holmes which first appeared with Arthur Conan Doyle's stories in *Strand* magazine and then create window patterns to accompany each illustration. Tease student curiosity by revealing the pictures one panel or window at a time until the subject matter, episode, or character is correctly determined. Of course, patterns can be made to accompany all the other Mystery Desks and Traces found in this book.

Fig. 3.5. Mystery window pattern.

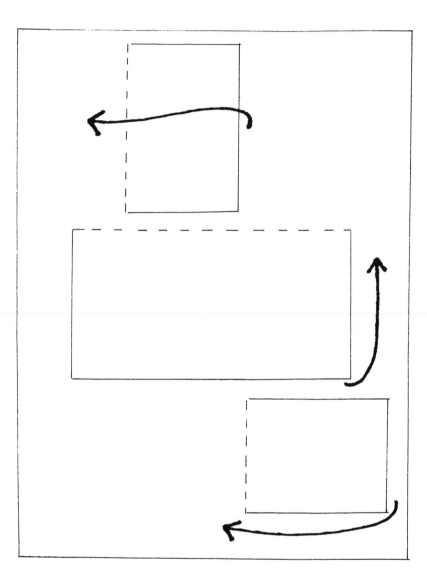

Traces

Figure 3.6 represents a scene from the arts. A particular group of characters is represented in a stage performance. Share the drawing with students. Can they determine the story that is being portrayed on stage? What clues lead them to the solution? Once students have determined the name of the play, can they also identify each one of the traces or footprints made by the characters. See the Answer Key for the identification of each trace.

Fig. 3.6.

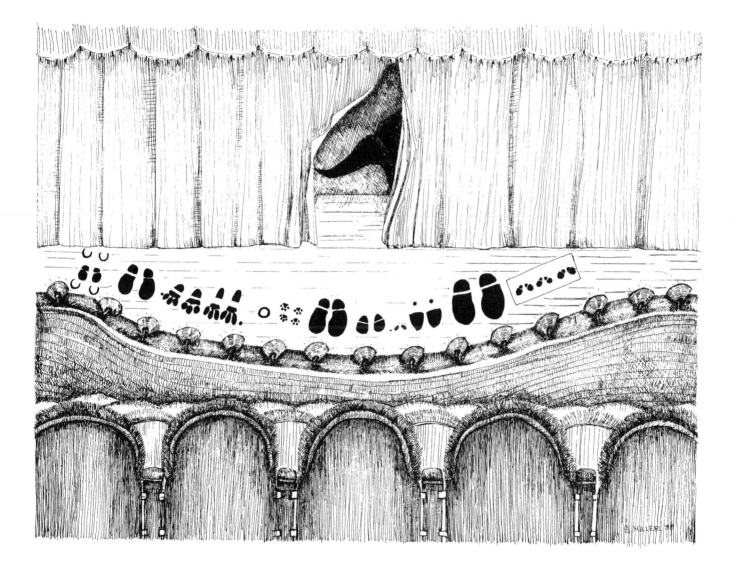

The Arts Activities

The arts encompass many separate disciplines. No attempt is made here to be encyclopedic. Rather, many of the arts are sampled to explore possible ways of developing thinking skills, creativity, and problem solving using mystery as the central theme. Hopefully, the shared ideas will serve as catalysts for library media specialists, teachers and their students wanting to go much deeper into these and other arts areas such as photography, drawing, drama, and music.

Creative Dramatics

Awareness Activities

Classic creative dramatics warm-ups are appropriate to a mystery unit or inquiry because they teach and reinforce good detection skills in natural and fun ways. The following sample activities are appropriate with any age group and in any classroom. All the activities emphasize the critical importance of utilizing *all* of one's senses in detecting any type of mystery.

1. *Who is the leader?* Send a volunteer student to the hall. Appoint a "leader" who will initiate all future actions in the classroom. Explain that the actions may include clicking fingers, changing posture, crossing the left leg over the right, etc. The other students will imitate the behavior of the leader. For example, if the leader begins to scratch his or her neck, all students in the room should soon be scratching their necks. Behavior moves and changes should obviously be subtle, so as to deceive the student volunteer who will be returning from the hall, and will have to use his or her detection skills to find the leader. Begin the game action before bringing the volunteer back into the room so that the first action or behavior is already begun when he or she re-enters the room. When the classroom Sherlock Holmes determines who the leader is, a new round can begin with the former leader becoming the next detective. Play several rounds of the game. It may be a very good idea to debrief the detectives after each round. Have them share with the class how they determined the identity of the leader. What clues were used? A stop watch may be used to determine which student volunteer is the speediest sleuth. Penalty points for wrong guesses are advisable to keep students from just making random guesses.

   For a variation on this activity have the class watch a particular sport (e.g., a tennis match). The detective is sent out of the room while the class decides which sport to observe. When the volunteer returns to the room he or she must decide what sport is being watched. Other activities could include eating certain types of foods, watching specific television shows, or reading certain books.

2. *What's the crime?* To encourage students to recognize and use all their senses in detection and problem solving, stage a mystery in the classroom depriving them of one sense. Ask all students to close their eyes and to keep them closed until signaled to open them. (Blindfolds can be used if needed.) Inform students that a crime is about to take place in the classroom. They must be absolutely silent, listening for clues that will help them detect what crime is committed. Act out a "crime." Example: The teacher may enter the room, walk to a student's desk, rifle through his notebook, take out an assignment, and secretly place it in the file cabinet. After the "crime" has been committed, advise students to open their eyes and begin solving the case at hand. Random guesses are not allowed. All statements about the crime must be accompanied with evidence and reasoning. Once the activity has been demonstrated by the teacher, students can perpetrate the crimes in future rounds of the game. Emphasize to students that while playing the game is fun, the debriefing (determining the crime) is where the real learning takes place as they use sensory facts paired with reasoning to solve a mystery.

A variation of this exercise asks students to determine what an object is from tactile sense clues. Again, ask students to close their eyes. Pass objects around the room. Use familiar (e.g., a flash light battery) and unfamiliar (e.g., an antique apple corer) objects, and ask students to identify each object. Reasons must be given with each identification. How do they know what the item is? What tactile sensations did their brain record and what did this stimulus instruct them to reason? The olfactory sense can also be used by asking blindfolded students to determine various scents. Scratch-and-sniff stickers or actual objects such as an empty pop bottle, a pipe, or an empty pizza carton can be used.

3. *What's been changed?* Direct students to form pairs and sit facing one another. Each is to carefully study the appearance of the other. Signal all players to turn away from their partners and sit back to back. Each partner should change three things about his or her appearance (e.g., untie one shoelace). Signal partners to face one another again and detect what three things have been changed in appearance. When this game is played, students quickly note the crucial importance of becoming critical observers and noting even seemingly insignificant detail.

Movement, Pantomime, and Improvisation

> *Drama comes in the door of every school with the child.*
> — Viola Spolin

Children are great natural actors; they are spontaneous and inventive in their creation of instant drama. From simple movement exercises used to reinforce vocabulary building to full blown, original mystery dramatizations, the creative talents and problem solving skills of all students can be developed and enhanced with mystery related creative dramatics activities. Such activities are appropriate whether they occur in a kindergarten classroom or in an honors English class for high school seniors. I reemphasize that the following activities are merely starting points. Creative and resourceful library media specialists, teachers, and students can use these stimuli as building blocks in more fully developed dramatic pursuits.

1. *Adverb Walk.* Want to increase students' mystery vocabularies? Ask them to line up in a circle or in a snake-like line. Instruct them to begin walking according to the adverbial prompts supplied. With younger students, the teacher may need to demonstrate adverbs such as "stealthily." Sample adverbs include:

stealthily	fiendishly
witheredly	frightenedly
stalkingly	diabolically
mysteriously	

Of course, a grammatical point is being made, too. Students will quickly realize the suffix most common to adverbs. Variations include expansions into character types through the addition of adjectives: walking like a *confident* detective, a *curious* policewoman on patrol, a *secretive* Sherlock Holmes, a *frightened* would-be victim, or a *suspicious* criminal.

2. *Pantomime Crimes.* Start out by providing students with simple, easy crimes to pantomime. Building upon early successes, the pantomimes may become increasingly elaborate, sophisticated, and longer in duration. The crimes certainly do not have to be of the violent nature, nor do they have to be real crimes. "Burglarizing" the refrigerator at 2 a.m. makes a great pantomime subject. Team pantomimes lasting no more than 30-50 seconds may be good starters. Begin with prompts like these:

A person raids the refrigerator at midnight and is caught.

Two cat burglars steal jewels from a wall safe.

Two 4-year-olds pilfer goods from the cookie jar.

Two students copy from a third student during a test.

Two bungling house burglars commit their first (and unsuccessful) robbery.

A policeman/woman catches a crook.

Sherlock Holmes snoops for clues.

A variation includes the classic mirror exercise. Again, pairs are utilized. Partner A initiates an activity such as cracking a safe. The activity is mirrored exactly by partner B who stands facing player A and pretends to be his or her mirror image. A second crime may be committed with the roles reversed; partner B initiates the action and partner A follows. Once again, stress the critical importance of very careful observation and detection if the resultant action is to truly represent a person and his or her mirror image.

Either of these activities is enhanced by adding appropriate music. Effective recordings include Henry Mancini's "Peter Gunn" and "Pink Panther" themes. Eventually, appropriate mystery music can be the chief stimulus. Play a recording and ask students to invent a mystery-based pantomime to accompany the music.

Older students can exercise considerable creativity by selecting a famous story by Edgar Allan Poe or Arthur Conan Doyle which they interpret through pantomime, with or without musical accompaniment. The rest of the students play the role of detectives trying to use the pantomime clues to determine what famous story is being reenacted.

3. *Environmental Walks.* Another creative dramatics classic is the environmental walk. The instructor or leader reads a passage rich in sensory detail. Students move about the room reacting as if they are physically experiencing the environment(s) described. The passage is read slowly enough to allow students reaction time to pantomime the feelings, behaviors, and actions narrated. This is a terrific pre-reading activity. Choose a mystery story or novel with an unusually evocative opening passage. Through the environmental walk experience, students become intellectually *and* physically involved with the story. At a natural stopping point, ask students to quietly return to their seats and finish reading the story silently. Alternately, a short discussion may be held following an environmental walk in which students are asked to predict what will happen in the story before silent reading commences. The environmental walk is an activity rich in possibilities. Once students are familiar with it, they can create their own scripts for subsequent mystery environmental walks. This becomes a particularly popular writing activity at Halloween. Students love writing descriptions of scary walks through haunted houses at midnight. The writing of sensory-rich exposition and narration assists in the development of composition skills. The completed environment scripts may be read by students for the activity or placed on audio tapes with appropriately mysterious music for accompaniment.

4. *Improvised mysteries.* Build upon the dramatic skills developed in pantomime by moving on to improvisations with dialogue. Imagination and problem solving really flourish when students are provided a few words or objects as stimuli and are directed to improvise their own original mysteries. The key to improvisation is creativity and not memorization of lines. The dialogue flows naturally out of the characterizations and situations students create.

To get improvisations rolling, try a couple of approaches. First, list four or five cue words on the chalkboard or overhead. Words (and phrases) chosen might include:

stolen	blue
scream	vase
handkerchief	child
2 a.m.	

Divide the class into groups of four or five. Assign each group the task of creating a mystery which revolves around the cue words given. After each group acts out their improvisation, discuss the wide variety of dramas resulting from the same cues.

Providing each group of four or five students with three to six real objects which they must use in an improvised mystery drama is another approach. Here all groups do not have the same objects. The props provided may include colorful old clothes and hats, costume jewelry, ordinary kitchen utensils, school supplies such as rulers or crayons, books, art objects, and other items rummaged from storage closets. Once again, the variety of responses to stimuli and the myriad problem solving approaches used will be great. Each group's dramatization should be followed by sharing the particular problem solving steps they used in creating their improvisation with the class.

Character improvisation provides another approach to creative drama. Ask each student to create a character. The character can be of any age, background, profession, or situation. Examples: a modern, inner-city private eye; a Victorian sleuth; a teen-age, student, pet detective. Each student becomes an inventive investigator. That is, students create a background of information about their character including relevant data about character traits, likes, dislikes, manner of speech, way of walking, personal quirks, etc. Since students are inventing the characters, each is free to invent all this information. Students create an F.B.I.-type dossier for their invented character complete with pictures (photos cut from magazines, or more creatively, drawings done by the student). Pictures may show the character at different ages, engaged in different hobbies, or reveal the character through his or her car, favorite room, vacation spot, etc.

When the dossiers are completed, place students in groups of four or five. Have them introduce their characters and share dossiers. Then ask them to create an improvisation, a mystery, in which all the characters are involved. They may be detectives who jointly solve a mystery. Or, one may be a detective, one a villain, and the rest suspects and/or victims. Many possibilities exist. Of course, the final dramatizations are shared with other classmates.

The idea of throwing random characters together is not new. Agatha Christie's *Ten Little Indians* (available in novel and dramatic formats) is one of many mysteries where strangers are suddenly placed together in a common setting. This activity is especially good for helping students learn how to develop believable, complete characters rather than caricatures.

5. *Games into plays*. A popular British party game is called "Murder in the Dark." The game is played using a deck of cards. The facilitator removes one jack, one ace, and as many other numbered cards from the deck as needed to ensure that each player receives one card from the deck. Each player is then given a card. The remaining cards are set aside. Only the person who receives the jack reveals his or her card. This person temporarily leaves the room, but not out of hearing range. All other players remain silent and do not reveal their cards. The person who has the ace of spades becomes the killer. Lights are turned out and players are told to silently and carefully mill about the room. At some point, the person with the ace of spades gently and furtively places his or her arm around the neck of a victim who quietly slumps to the floor. The first player who sees the crime committed or stumbles onto the body screams or yells, "Murder!" At this point, the lights are turned back on and the detective, having heard the cry of "Murder," rushes into the room and begins to solve the crime. The real fun begins as the detective tries to sort out conflicting eye witness accounts and attempts to piece together seemingly unrelated clues.

This old parlor game can serve as the catalyst for original dramatizations created by students following the game. Students can provide motives and characterizations for the persons played during the game. An infinite variety of possible victims, murderers, witnesses and detectives is possible since new roles are created by chance every time they play.

6. *Create-A-Mystery Game.* One of the most popular forms of home entertainment is the mystery game in which participants play the roles of detective and suspects in a fictious murder mystery. Packaged games are readily available in book and games stores, but talented students can more creatively and productively design their own. In an excellent article in *Writer's Digest*, author and mystery game creator Linda Melin outlines the steps one should follow in creating a mystery game:

1. Choose a theme

2. Choose a crime

3. Choose your cast

4. Choose the victim

5. Determine the motives

6. Choose method of murder/robbery/etc.

7. Select the prime suspects

8. Match players with roles created

9. Plot the crime

10. Write the game[1]

This author's gifted middle-school students often turned their best mystery stories into mystery games. The best procedure was to have teams of six to eight students take one story and translate it into a mystery game for another team to unravel and solve. Each team would develop clues and hide them in the classroom, the library media center, and throughout the school building. The teams then dramatically presented the opening scene from their mystery up to the point where the crime is discovered. They then turned the mystery over to another team of students to solve. When team A completed their turn solving the mystery team B had created, the roles were reversed and team B had to solve the mystery game generated by team A.

Radio Dramas

Listening

One of the many faults of television drama is that it robs students of the power of imagination. Students listening to "The Shadow" or "The Green Hornet" in the 1930s and 1940s could envision for themselves the appearance of the characters and settings. Today's students only take in one interpretation, one image: the one provided by the producer. The producer and/or director decides what the heroes and villains and haunted houses and mean streets should look like, hires actors accordingly, and builds sets to conform to his personal view. Students can experience mysteries in a different way, the way their grandparents did, by listening to old-time radio dramas. Many episodes of old radio mystery programs are available on inexpensive cassettes. Many Sherlock Holmes stories and episodes from radio mystery programs such as "The Green Hornet," "Suspense," and "The Shadow" are available in audio-cassette format.[2]

The use of radio mystery provides students with a brand new experience: the story stimuli is entirely auditory. Listening skills are reinforced in the classroom. Creativity can flourish. One way to overcome the idleness of this activity is to provide students with paper and colored pencils and ask them to draw their impressions of characters or scenes as they listen. When the students later compare their drawings with one another, they may be surprised to note how differently the auditory stimuli is interpreted by individual listeners. There is another bonus, too. Listening to these tapes provides students with a simulated experience of what it was like to grow up in a different age. Many tapes not only contain program content but 1930s and 1940s commercials. A young actor named Ronald Reagan may be telling listeners how good Camel cigarettes taste, or references to the World War II effort (e.g., buy war bonds) may be made during program breaks. Radio tapes of mysteries present an oral history time capsule.

Creating Radio Mystery Dramas

After students have listened to old-time radio tapes of mysteries, allow them to create their own radio broadcasts. Recreating or simulating the "Golden Age" of radio with an audio broadcast is a project which affords students great latitude and practice in the exercise of creativity and problem solving. The agenda for such a project may include the following checkpoints:

1. *Determine the subject matter.* Will the students create an original drama for the broadcast or will they use a published mystery? If the published mystery is chosen, stories for all ages abound. Elementary school children may want to use a mystery like James Howe's *The Celery Stalks at Midnight*. Middle school students might read a chapter from Ellen Raskin's *The Westing Game*, while high school students might make use of classic tales by Poe and Doyle. Of course, decisions on length will determine whether a cutting from a longer story or novel, or a short story is used.

2. *Decide how the broadcast will be made.* Will the radio drama be a live broadcast or will it be taped? Taped dramas are much more forgiving of student errors and can be listened to again and again, but live broadcasts more closely approximate the true flavor of the environment of the old-time radio days. Many of the other decisions will be affected by this one.

3. *Write a script*. Unless actual copies of a radio mystery script are used, students will have to revise existing works or create new mysteries using a radio script format. Copyright permissions may be needed. The library media specialist can be especially helpful in finding the answer to this question. Script writing involves cutting out all the "he said" and "she said" explication, eliminating unnecessary narration, frequently shortening the text, and providing cues for both actors and sound effects personnel. Students who have not previously written in the script format will find this experience another new and useful challenge.

4. *Choose roles*. The most important roles may be the sound effects persons. In addition to actors and crew, a producer is needed to supervise the total production, including time schedules and budgets. Of course, advertisers have to be contacted and commercials written as well. Incidentally, separate actors are not necessary for the commercials. In radio days actors often stepped out of character for sixty seconds to tell listeners of the joys of buying war bonds, a particular cigarette, cereal, or detergent.

The sound effects crew has some real, but fun, problem solving ahead. Remind students that no pictures will be available to their audience. If a carnival scene is called for in the script, the sound effects crew must convincingly create the impression of one via auditory stimuli. The following are just a few of the many sounds which may be called for in a script:

the creaking of stairs	the squeak of a door hinge
a ringing telephone	eerie whistling sounds
echoes	muffled cries
galloping horses	a house aflame
footsteps	a window being broken
rain on a roof	

Experimentation and problem solving occur as students try different techniques of sound effects production. One of the author's students, for example, discovered that cellophane cookie container dividers, when crinkled, emit a sound like a crackling fire. Some research in the school library media center or at the public library may aid experimentation. If students do not find books on sound effects, they may be able to locate books about radio production with chapters on sound effects.

Of course, music needs to be part of the radio play. The sound effects and engineering team need to select appropriate music carefully for the various mood passages that require a musical interlude.

A decision about advanced taping of some sound effects and music must be made. Even in the case of dramas where the rest of the broadcast is live, musical backgrounds and sound effects may be prerecorded.

5. *Rehearsal*. After the sound effects crew and the actors have rehearsed separately, at least one joint rehearsal with a complete, uninterrupted reading should be held.

6. *The audience*. Part of the producer's job is to find a listening audience. If a large class is involved there may be as many as two or three groups creating radio dramas. The groups can serve as audiences for one another. With the convenience and sophistication of tape equipment and public address systems, it is not difficult even for younger students to broadcast a radio drama into other classrooms in the school. Sixth grade students, for example, can create a radio drama of a James Howe story and become the storytelling entertainment for third grade classes. One ninth grade class can select a story by Edgar Allan Poe, found in their ninth-grade literature anthology, dramatize and broadcast it into all ninth grade English classrooms. Many larger school systems have their own radio studios and broadcast frequencies, and may be willing to publicly air the drama. If students create an unusually well-polished radio drama, teachers and the producer may want to contact a local affiliate of National Public Radio to see if a broadcast is possible there. If students know their work will ultimately be shared with many people, the levels of quality and productivity increase dramatically.

It may be profitable, during the creative process, to show students a short segment of Woody Allen's 1987 movie *Radio Days*. The film, available in VHS format, contains wonderful scenes of "live" radio broadcasts complete with sound effects technicians.

Readers Theatre

Although readers theatre involves many of the same steps and procedures as the creation of a radio drama—selection and cutting of a mystery story, drama, or novel, the rehearsal, and the presentation—it is a less ambitious and more feasible project for many classrooms to tackle. Once again, finding age-appropriate literature is not difficult. One group of gifted junior high students chose Mark Twain's classic spoof of mystery stories, "The Stolen White Elephant," for a readers theatre presentation because of its comedic value.

In readers theatre, parts are assigned, scripts are produced, and roles are rehearsed. There are no sound effects; the narrator provides all background information necessary for audience understanding. Readers sit on stools or stand in front of an audience and read the chosen, edited script interpretively. In small classes or groups, readers can assume several roles. One advantage of readers theatre is the emphasis placed on the author or playwright's words. It is not the flair of the actors, nor the sets or costumes that dominate. The full, rich flavor of the author's words are front and center stage.

Music

Creating a Mystery Theme

The value of background music in multimedia mystery presentations cannot be underestimated. Students who have listened to old-time radio mysteries understand this. To demonstrate the point, show students an action sequence from a Sherlock Holmes film or another mystery movie with the sound turned off. Students will perceive how important music is to a movie or television mystery. The following projects should help students come to appreciate the valuable contribution a musical director makes to any cinematic effort.

1. *Music composition*. Encourage musically gifted students to compose theme music for their favorite detectives or for favorite mystery stories and novels. Considerable problem solving is involved in creating an original piece of music. The support and encouragement of the school music instructor will be helpful with this project.

2. *Selecting music*. Students unable to compose music can be asked to listen to a variety of classical themes and select a piece of music to accompany the class radio drama. Their selections could work as background music for a readers' theatre presentation or for silent reading periods. One example of music suitable to accompany mystery readings is Mussorgsky's *Night on Bald Mountain*.

3. *Music criticism*. How good are some of the famous mystery/suspense/adventure themes? Listen to theme music created for old-time radio shows and more modern movie music such as John Barry's themes for the James Bond movies or Henry Mancini's *Peter Gunn* and *Pink Panther* scores. Are such themes evocative? What makes them special? Are they character appropriate? Which themes in the modern music pantheon have become so familiar that the mere hearing of a few bars of music triggers a mental image of the detective, the spy, special scenes or actions originally associated with the music?

4. *Murder at the Met, etc.* Ask students with good musical background (any music form or type) to write a mystery in which musical knowledge or a musical background is central to the plot. For example, could a rock star double as a secret agent? Could a famous conductor find deadly clues in a particular symphonic passage revealing a murderer's identity? (In Alfred Hitchcock's 1955 classic James Stewart-Doris Day movie, *The Man Who Knew Too Much*, an assassination is timed to occur in a London concert hall exactly as cymbals crash in a symphonic orchestra performance of *Storm Cloud Cantata*. In the same film, the rescue of an innocent boy is directly tied to the movie's theme song, "Que Sera Sera" as sung by Doris Day's character.)

Perhaps the plot of a mystery might revolve around this question: Why is every woman who sings the role of Carmen in a particular opera house the target of a madman? How does a backstage set designer solve the mystery? Can country music fans create a sleuth who solves crimes at the Grand Ole Opry? Infinite possibilities for mysteries set in the world of music and/or involving musical clues exist.

Teachers and library media specialists should be aware that at least two Broadway musicals are mystery-based. In 1965, *Baker Street: A Musical Adventure of Sherlock Holmes* made its Broadway debut. The musical with a book by Jerome Coopersmith and music and lyrics by Marian Grudeff and Raymond Jessel is based on the Conan Doyle story, "A Scandal in Bohemia." Because the musical premiered so many years ago, the soundtrack is difficult to find, but sleuthful library media specialists and teachers may be able to locate a copy in a used record store or in a public library record collection. The soundtrack was produced by MGM Records, a division of Metro-Goldwyn-Mayer, Inc.

More recently Rupert Holmes (no relation to Sherlock!) created the book, words, and music for the Tony award-winning musical, *The Mystery of Edwin Drood*. Billed as the "Solve-It-Yourself Broadway Musical," the contemporary work is based on Charles Dickens's unfinished mystery novel of the same name. Since the novel does not resolve the mystery (see the creative problem solving activity in the "Language Arts" chapter), contemporary audiences attending performances of the musical vote on the ending they desire, including which of the nine or ten characters will play the roles of villain and detective. Because as many as thirty-six different endings are possible, the composer painstakingly created 600 additional pages of orchestrations for the show. The soundtrack for *The Mystery of Edwin Drood* is manufactured by PolyGram Records and is available in record stores.

One of the most applauded recording effects in recent years was the EMI-Angel recording of the Jerome Kern and Oscar Hammerstein classic American musical *Show Boat*. First staged in 1927, the musical show was based on Edna Ferber's novel on life aboard a Mississippi River showboat. Most people are familiar with the story and music as presented in two Hollywood movie versions which utilized only part of the original musical score. Musical historians believed a great deal of the original music had been lost forever, but fortunately much of it was located in a New Jersey warehouse in 1982. Conductor John McGlinn engaged in a great deal of sleuthing to reconstruct the music as Kern and Hammerstein meant it to be heard. McGlinn's restoration of this classic piece of Americana is a story as fascinating as any mystery penned by Doyle or Christie. Students interested in music history may enjoy a bit of sleuthing themselves by delving into other stories of music preservation and restoration.[3]

Visual Arts

Cartooning

Some great private eyes began life in the funny pages. Many have gone on to greater fame in other media. Dick Tracy is one celebrated sleuth who graduated from his original pulp existence to radio, television, and the movies. Comic strips are not the only place where mystery may be found. Celebrated political cartoonists often make political statements via mystery allusions. A famous senator investigating supposed malfeasance in government may be shown dressed in Holmesian fashion and manner.

Many student projects can be created using the mystery cartooning connection.

1. *Funny pages sleuthing.* Ask students to reexamine the familiar newspaper comics with a fresh eye. Who are the pulp sleuths? Can they find general and political mystery references in single frame cartoons. Ask students to compile a scrapbook of such cartoons or to include examples in their mystery notebook.

2. *Creating a sleuth.* Some students will want to begin an original comic strip with a detective of their own creation as the hero or heroine. Perhaps the best examples can find a place into the school newspaper, or the class anthology, "Mystery Times." Figure 3.7 is an example of a comic strip sleuth created by Jamie Miller of Louisville, Kentucky. Students may also be interested in reading Jamie's recollection of what led him to create Brett Connor.[4]

3. *Mystery cartoons.* Other students may want to create single or multiframe cartoons rather than comic strip serials. Your author asked one 8th grade student to create a cartoon which utilized some aspect of crime or mystery as a central focus. As a test of the critical thinking/sleuthing definition, the student (who was not an avid artist and had little formal art training) was asked to trace her own thinking and problem solving as she worked on the cartoon. Figure 3.8 displays her cartoon and her account of the thinking processes she used.[5]

Fig. 3.7.

Brett Connor

Sandy blond hair
Green eyes
Thin
6'0"
Enjoys reading voraciously, writing occasionally, solving crimes. He doesn't care for socializing or politeness. He fell in love once—avoids intimacy. He toys with the idea of becoming a cop, but there's more money in cafe management.

Brett owns and runs a cafe next to a major police station. He is very intelligent, insightful, and observant, but his cafe is as far as he will go in life due to his pointed and deliberate lack of social skills. Detective Steven Brichaillese, a frequent customer of Brett's, often shares tough cases with Brett—who offers great insight, even if he doesn't solve the case (a rarity). Brichaillese sometimes takes Brett to the scene of the crime. Brett is not a good shot and rarely participates in action or gunplay.

I developed Brett Connor while trying to avoid other stereotypes such as Hercule Poirot, Sherlock Holmes, Columbo, Jessica Fletcher, or Magnum P.I. I wanted to create a character who didn't solve crimes on the side for fun, like Miss Marple, or as a lifestyle, like Holmes, or as a career, like Kinsey Millhone. I wanted a character who solved crimes because he had no other way to apply his vast intellect other than the occasional book or logic problem. I also wanted a character who was low on the social ladder, but who held a position where he could observe other people. Why not a diner? The image of a genius short-order cook discussing the latest big robbery with an aging detective over the daily blueplate special and a cup of hot, black coffee appealed to me.

Jamie Miller

Fig. 3.8.

The idea for my cartoon came to me as I was working on a science experiment using pond water. Everytime I opened the jar of pond water I was assaulted with a disgusting smell. I couldn't believe the ducks could stand to stay on the pond where I had collected the sample of water. I decided this would be a good idea to pursue in creating a cartoon. I had a general idea of what the drawing should look like, but I needed to think about the wording to go with it. I kept changing the wording until it was short enough, but still communicated the intended message.

When I began drawing, I tried to put all the activity into one scene. I also tried to show the entire house, but both things took up too much space. I decided to try the idea of three panels; each would focus on a different part of the cartoon's idea. I did a rough copy so I would know how everything was positioned, and then drew the final cartoon.

Nancy Pylypczuk

Photography

A very popular pastime for many mystery buffs involves solving photographic puzzles and mysteries. At least two types exist. The first involves unusual photographic perspectives of commonplace objects. A photograph is taken at an unusual angle, or an object is photographed at such close range that its identity is obscured. For example, a photo of a pencil may not appear to be a pencil if the only subject matter seen is the metal cylinder connecting the wood body and the eraser. Photographic mystery puzzles of this type are a regular feature of *Current Science* and *Games* magazines.[6]

The second type of photographic mystery is also occasionally found in the pages of *Games*. Several photos are shown which, if studied carefully, reveal a crime, a victim, and a criminal. It is the game player's task to visually decode the mystery. Word clues are given, but must be used in conjunction with the photographs in order for accurate detection to take place. An excellent source is *Scotland Yard Photo Crimes from the Files of Inspector Black*.

Both of these photo-mystery ideas suggest activities rich in problem solving opportunities for the photography enthusiasts in the classroom.

1. *Photo mysteries.* Allow photography buffs to mystify their classmates with photographic puzzles they create. Instruct students to photograph common objects, a woven pattern of carpeting, tire treads, or wall plaster at unusual angles or in close-ups which mask their identities. Students with darkrooms and enlargers may be able to work wonders through exaggerations and photographic distortions. A close-up photo of a fountain pen part greatly enlarged is going to require real deduction on the part of classmates if they are to correctly identify the object in question.

2. *Photo crimes.* Other students may want to use friends, teachers, and family to help them stage a photographed crime which other classmates will have to solve. There may be a dozen or more staged scenes to photograph and sequence in order. Clues need to be written. Separate "mug" shots of suspects may add humor to the exercise, especially if the principal agrees to be photographed! It is not an absolute requirement for the photographer to provide viewers with the correct action sequence. A part of the viewer's task is to determine the sequence of events in the criminal activity. Once again, as in most of the activities suggested in this book, the crime does not have to be violent. Perhaps the photos reveal the disappearance of chocolate chip cookies from the kitchen and viewers must determine the real chocoholic culprit. Creating a photo crime requires considerable critical thinking and lots of problem solving savvy, but the results are highly rewarding.

The potential for neat mystery stories utilizing photography is abundant. More than a few mysteries have involved an amateur or professional photographer suddenly discovering a visual clue which is at first unnoticed, but which ultimately becomes vital. A man or woman takes a picture of a dog resting by some shrubs. The photographer doesn't notice until the negative is enlarged that a human foot is protruding from the far edge of the shrubbery and is just slightly visible. Clever students will also want to write a mystery involving a photographer as a sleuth who uses photographic skills to catch crooks.

Arts Projects

Art figures mightily in the mystery world. A work of art is often central to a story or novel. In E. L. Konigsburg's Newbery Medal-winning novel *From the Mixed-Up Files of Mrs. Basil E. Frankweiler* the youthful protagonist, Claudia Kincaid, wants to uncover the mystery surrounding the authenticity of *Angel*, a piece of sculpture supposedly created by Michelangelo. In more adult fare, British sleuth Mark Treasure, a London banker, becomes embroiled with the KGB, British tourists in the Soviet Union, and a theft of art from the Hermitage Museum in *Treasure in Roubles*. Persis Willum is an artist sleuth in *Somebody Killed the Messenger* by Clarissa Watson. Of course, mystery sleuths and their environs have been the subjects of artists, too. Many illustrators, beginning with Sidney Paget, have given the world artistic interpretations of Sherlock Holmes. Set designers in movies and on the stage have artistically rendered his lodgings at 221 B Baker Street. Real-world art mysteries such as the 1911 theft of the "Mona Lisa" and forgeries like those of Han van Meegeren are fantastic beyond the imagination of any mystery writer. Many, many art-related activities provide puzzles and mysteries for young people to solve and provide excellent opportunities for critical thinking and problem solving. The following ideas serve as examples of art-mystery connections and activities gifted and talented students may be encouraged to explore.

1. *Rebus codes.* Younger students will delight in telling story rebus fashion. The art skills needed are minimal; even stick figures work. A combination of words, letters, and simple line drawings reveal a mystery. A story might begin like this:

The first line of the story is "I first met the nice man in Turkey." The challenge is in encoding mysteries for others to solve. A real mystery can be told, or the mystery can be found in decoding a familiar saying, tale, etc. The rebus-based mystery is a first-cousin to classic mysteries by Arthur Conan Doyle ("The Adventure of the Dancing Men") and Edgar Allan Poe ("The Gold Bug") which utilize cryptography.

2. *Draw a sleuth.* Artists and illustrators have been creating images of Sherlock Holmes for 100 years, ever since Arthur Conan Doyle's stories began appearing in the *Strand* magazine. Ask students to draw their impression of their favorite sleuths. The collected drawings will make an attractive bulletin board to accompany a mystery unit in class, or the mystery section of the library media center. One excellent source book is Julian Symons's *Great Detectives* which contains Tom Adams's wonderful illustrations of the most reknowned of sleuths: Holmes, Marple, Poirot, Maigret, Queen, Marlowe, and Wolfe.

3. *Draw a residence.* Certain homes are legend in mystery fare. Baskerville Hall in the celebrated Holmes case and Manderley of *Rebecca* fame are two very large homes which come to mind. In *Literary Homes* and *More Literary Homes*, Rosalind Ashe and her illustrators provide vivid word and artistic pictures of twenty literary landmarks, providing external and internal views of each. Encourage students to emulate Ashe's conceit by creating their own portraits of domiciles found in their readings. The illustrated houses must be drawn accurately so close reading is a must. Ask students to choose a favorite mystery and create a notebook of drawings of the house(s) featured.

4.   *Gameboards.* Another avenue of artistic pursuit is the creation of gameboards to accompany the reading of favorite mysteries. Students may create a gameboard to accompany a game of their design based upon the reading of a single work such as *The Westing Game* or *The Hound of the Baskervilles.* Or, students may create a gameboard to accompany a trivia game featuring questions and answers about Sherlock Holmes, his life, habits, hobbies, friends, and his celebrated cases.

5.   *Draw a crime.* Lawrence Treat's *Crime and Puzzlement* and *You're the Detective!* solve-them-yourself picture mysteries are great diversions for students who finish work early; for bus travel seat work on a field trip; and for a host of other times when light, yet challenging diversion for students is desired. (The author has found them to be great gifts to take to students who are in the hospital for a short stay. They challenge and entertain without tiring the patient.) Figure 3.9 is taken from *You're the Detective!* The picture mystery takes place in an art gallery and involves an art-related mystery. Teachers and library media specialists may reproduce the drawing, text, and questions as an overhead transparency to motivate students to create their own visual mysteries. Please note: Any other use of the drawing and text, including photocopying, is expressly forbidden without written permission from the publisher, David R. Godine. After solving the "Picture Gallery" mystery, clever, artistic students can create their own original picture mysteries. Their first efforts are not likely to be of the same quality as Lawrence Treat's, but the thinking and planning which go into the invented crime, the drawing, and the questions posed are what is ultimately important. Answer is found in the Answer Key.

Fig. 3.9. Picture mystery from *You're the Detective* by Lawrence Treat. (Copyright © 1983 by Lawrence Treat. Reprinted by permission of David R. Godine, publisher.)

PICTURE GALLERY

Fig. 3.9—*Continued*

Whiz McGonnigle's mother loved picture galleries, and whenever there was a local exhibit she went several times and took Whiz with her. She had hopes that someday he'd be an artist, and although he showed talent, most people thought he'd either be a policeman or a bicycle racer. There was also a possibility that he'd become a scientist and discover a quick cure for a broken leg.

In due time the traveling exhibit of 18th and 19th-century American painters came to town and was shown at the local Whistling Gallery (they'd meant to call it the Whistler Gallery, but somebody got mixed up). Because of the importance of the show, everybody who could hold a paintbrush brought paint box and easel and sat down to copy.

Sketch A shows a section of the gallery as it was on the morning that Whiz's mother brought him to see it. He studied it with interest, but the second time he went with her, right after school was out, he got excited. "Look, Mom," he said. "Look—that one got stolen!"

What did he see?

Questions

1. Can a good artist duplicate a painting with sufficient skill to fool the average viewer? Yes_____ No_____ Probably_____

2. Could an expert spot a good copy as against an original by looking at it on a gallery wall? Yes_____ No_____ Not with absolute certainty_____

3. Could an expert spot a copy by close and careful study? Yes_____ No_____ Probably_____

4. Can you tell how old a painting is by finding out the age of the canvas it's painted on? Yes_____ No_____ Probably_____

5. Are spectrographic and X-ray analyses sure proof of the age of a painting? Yes_____ No_____ Probably_____

6. Which painting did Whiz point out as false?

6. *Picture mysteries.* Waldenbooks Mystery Club has graciously given me permission to reproduce the drawing in figure 3.10 which contains ten different weapons used in crimes. Students will enjoy this modern rendition of the old picture puzzle mysteries made famous by Currier & Ives that delighted Victorian youngsters long ago. Once students have found the weapons in this drawing (stumped readers should reluctantly consult the answer key found at the back of the book), the seed of an idea is planted.

Younger students may also enjoy the mystery picture of New York's Central Park in Japanese illustrator Mitsumasa Anno's book, *Anno's U.S.A.* In one two-page illustration, Anno hides all kinds of animals, presumably escaped from the zoo, in the trees of the park.

Ask students to be good problem solvers. What items can they hide in a drawing? Can they, for example, hide some classic Agatha Christie memorabilia in Miss Marple's knitting bag or shawl? Can they combine this assignment with the literary houses assignment by creating a drawing of the house in a favorite mystery which, in turn, is a mystery itself because of the story clues hidden in the drawing?

7. *Alphabet Books.* G. B. Shaw said "Youth is wasted on the young." The same might be said of alphabet books. Or, we could at least say alphabet books have their place with older students and adults as well as with primary age students. Witness the popularity of Mike Wilks' *The Ultimate Alphabet Book.* Every page is a wonderful puzzle and mystery for the reader who must attempt to identify the hundreds of items on each lettered page. Why not use a similar idea with students? Students can make mystery alphabet books with each page representing different sleuths, the names of weapons used in mysteries, obscure poisons, or famous residences in crime fiction. An alphabet book could be made about a favorite mystery story or novel (e.g., "The Hound of the Baskervilles, A-Z"), or about the life of a famous mystery writer (e.g., "The ABC's of Agatha Christie"). Each page can be a complete drawing or a series of drawn objects. Of course, the entire alphabet book does not have to be the work of just one student. Class collaborations are appropriate; each student becoming responsible for illustrating one or more letters of the alphabet. (While Mike Wilks's *Ultimate Alphabet* book contains some nude figures and therefore may not be acceptable for use with all groups, selected pages can be used with any group. One asset of this work is the artist's introduction in which he details how he was an art sleuth in the creation of the book. It is an excellent account of artistic problem solving.)

A similar puzzle technique is found in *World of Wonders: A Trip through Numbers* by Starr Ockenga and Eileen Doolittle. Combining photography and painting, the creators provide readers with a dozen scenes in which the numbers 1-12 are used again and again. Each page provides countless mysteries to be solved in the search for hidden numbers.

An alphabet book loved by children and adults alike is *Animalia* by Graeme Base. With this wonderful alphabet book, students hunt for objects and images, learn about alliteration which is used on every page, and have the added hide-and-seek fun of finding the Australian illustrator, pictured as a small boy, in each illustration. Base's *Animalia* is an excellent example of the truth that creativity alone is not enough. It took the illustrator more than three years of painstaking work to complete all the illustrations. Hard work plus creativity is what ultimately counts.

Base also created *The Eleventh Hour: A Curious Mystery*, a picture book whodunit. Horace, an elephant, invites his animal friends to a party in celebration of his eleventh birthday. One of the guests is rude and steals all the food Horace has prepared. Readers must determine the identity of the culprit.

Base is not the only illustrator who hides himself or others in his artwork to add a note of mystery and intrigue to picture books. Millions of children—and adults—have had hours of fun trying to find "Waldo" in the delightful books *Where's Waldo?*, *Find Waldo Now*, and *The Great Waldo Search* created by British illustrator Martin Handford. In *Where's Waldo?*, Waldo is found in many busy places: a department store, a ski slope, an airport, and at the beach. In every scene there are hundreds of other people. The reader has to look very closely and carefully to locate Waldo. In *Find Waldo Now*, Waldo travels through time. First, he must be located among hundreds of ancient cave men and women. Later, he is in ancient Rome's Coliseum, in the Crusades, at the Gold Rush, and even lost somewhere out in space in a future time.

Fig. 3.10. Reprinted with permission of Waldenbooks.

HOW MANY HIDDEN WEAPONS CAN YOU FIND?

8. *Calendar art.* An exciting variation on alphabet books is the creation of original mystery calendars. Ask students to select a specific or general mystery theme, create illustrations for each of the twelve months, and research important mystery-related dates such as the anniversary of the Great Brinks Robbery or the birthdate of writer Agatha Christie as they produce their own mystery calendars.

9. *Harris Burdick puzzles.* Just as alphabet books should not be perceived as being only for primary students, neither should sophisticated picture books escape the attentions of older students. One of the great illustrators of contemporary childrens' books is artist Chris Van Allsburg, winner of two Caldecott Awards. Of special interest to art and mystery fans is his work *The Mysteries of Harris Burdick.* Mr. Van Allsburg's artistic conceit is that a mysterious man by the name of Harris Burdick one day walked into a publisher's office with a portfolio of fourteen story ideas, each represented by a single drawing and a few lines of description. He never returned. He cannot be located as he left no address. What did the drawings mean? What is the rest of the story in each of the fourteen cases? The black and white drawings are provocative. In one, a huge ocean liner is coming down a Venice canal. In another, only the corner of what is labeled as a third-floor bedroom is shown. A window has been left open and the breeze is playing with gauze-like curtains. The wallpaper is a pattern of doves. It seems at first to be an unbearably tranquil scene. Then, the viewer realizes one of the doves in the wallpaper is alive. There are many uses for this endlessly creative book with students. Each story fragment and picture provided by Van Allsburg can be used as a separate story and art stimuli to engage students in discussions, story completion writing, and/or further art explorations. Students can "discover" more drawings by Harris Burdick. They can verbally and artistically solve the mystery of Burdick's disappearance. Infinite possibilities exist. Of course, foremost, they can simply enjoy Chris Van Allsburg's wonderfully mysterious book!

No education in the subject of mystery can be complete if the students have not sampled the mysterious world of Japanese master illustrator Mitsumasa Anno. Each of his glorious works provides new mysteries and puzzlements. *Anno's Journey* is a case in point. A lone traveler arrives on the shores of northern Europe and starts down a path leading him through fields, villages, and cities. What at first appear to be simple watercolors are, in fact, marvelous mysteries, for the artist has woven into the tapestry of his pictures numerous references to the history, architecture, art, music, and literature of Europe. The lone traveler crosses bridges found in Van Gogh's paintings and encounters details from the works of Courbet, Renoir, and Seurat; he meets characters from *Don Quixote* and *Little Red Riding Hood*; he spies Beethoven sitting at a window, composing. The masterful mystery goes on and on. Hardly a book just for young children!

The pages of *Anno's Journey* can and should be taken in again and again if its mysteries are to be fully probed and appreciated. Creative young artists may want to emulate Anno's style by creating scenes and tableaus which mysteriously contain references to great works in the arts.

10. *Illustrated art mystery.* Occasionally, the world press focuses on a sensational art crime or theft. Ask students to write a mystery story involving the theft of a famous painting. Why is the work of art stolen? Who are the crooks? How do they manage the robbery? How are the crooks caught and the painting recovered? Add a dimension to the story writing. Ask students to illustrate their stories with no less than five to ten drawings.

11. *Mystery by the dozen.* Ask students to engage in a very "egghausting" and "eggsacting" task. Instruct them to choose the dozen most favorite detectives and sleuths in literature and popular entertainment media. Next, ask them to boil a dozen eggs, making sure to save the egg carton. Invite them to draw the face of each of the twelve sleuths on the eggs, returning each to the carton (which they also decorate) when it is completed and dried. When finished, the egg carton of sleuths will be very attractive. Variations include twelve different scenes from a favorite mystery, or a mixture of eggs decorated to represent sleuths, tools of crime, and mystery titles.

12. *Sculpting heroes.* If student tastes and talents are more three-dimensional in nature, try assigning some sculpting projects. Would a papier mâché bust of Hercule Poirot or Edgar Allan Poe add interest to the mystery corner of the library media center? How about life-size cardboard sculptures of Sherlock Holmes and Dr. Watson? Students can problem solve individually and in groups, to determine the subject matter for sculptures with mystery themes, and determine what kinds of materials to use.

Students may also wish to sculpt a mystery chess set. Many gifted and talented students love to play chess. The more ambitious and artistically talented students might create mystery-lover's chessboards and sets of chessmen modeled after mystery heroes or authors. For example, a king might be sculpted to represent Arthur Conan Doyle with a queen symbolizing Agatha Christie.

13. *Fingerprint art.* Fingerprints are central to mysteries and detection, so why not include them in an arts approach to mystery? Even the child (or adult!) who feels hopelessly devoid of drawing skills can succeed with fingerprint art. The only tools students need are their fingers, pencils, paper, inked rubber stamp pads, *and* their creative and critical thinking and problem solving skills. The basic drawing is simple. The student inks a finger or thumb, makes a fingerprint anywhere they choose on a clean sheet of paper, and completes his or her drawing by adding the necessary line drawings to complete a figure, object, or scene. A single fingerprint could be a man's body. The student then adds legs, arms, and a head. A fingerprint might also be an apple, needing only a stem. Single drawings of crooks and detectives can be completed, or students may choose to tell an entire mystery story in fingerprints. Critical pre-planning and layout work is essential on the part of the student if an entire story is told. There is no need for students to add the final artist's touch by signing their fingerprint art masterpieces. Since every human being's fingerprints are unique, they have already signed their works!

(A bit of mystery trivia: no two people, including identical twins, have identical fingerprints. Fingerprints were used for purposes of identification in China as far back as 782 A.D.! There is a fascinating account of the history of fingerprinting and its use in police work in *Fatal Fascination* by Phil McArdle and Karen McArdle. While students are creating their own fingerprint mystery artworks, the teacher can read this account to them.)[7]

14. *Greeting cards.* Young artists might also create an entirely new line of greeting cards for mystery enthusiasts. The mystery greeting card line may include sleuthful-appearing cards for all occasions: birthdays, weddings, get-well greetings, graduations, and holidays such as Halloween and Valentine's Day. Once the basic line is created, students can devise a marketing plan to introduce their new product to the public. Really eager entrepreneurs can manufacture their line of greeting cards and market them through local mystery book stores.

15. *Desk intrigue.* Encourage students to take a cue from the mystery desks contained in *Mystery and Detection.* First have them name current, historical, or fictional heroes. Then ask them to imagine what might be found in the desks belonging to their heroes by being enterprising sleuths. From fictional or biographical data, what predictions can they make about what might be found in George Bush's desk, or in one belonging to Helen Keller? Once they have determined all the items they might find in the desk of a hero, they can artistically represent it just as Gay Miller did with the desks of Georgia O'Keeffe, Sherlock Holmes, and others in this book.

A final art-related suggestion. Students with a love for art may also wish to write a mystery story with a plot in which art is central. When works by Van Gogh are sold at auction for $50 million, it is not hard to conjure up a tale of mystery and intrigue with very high stakes in the art world.

Dance

Students do not need to be gifted dancers any more than they need to be accomplished artists to enjoy mysteries at a level above and beyond the intellectual engagement of reading. Several years ago your author was teaching ninth grade students a newspaper unit in an English classroom. For the sake of variation as well as experimentation, he divided the class into small groups and assigned tasks. Each group was to read the morning edition of the daily newspaper, select a story from it, and use their collective imagination to dramatize the chosen story for the rest of their classmates. The stories could be found in any section of the newspaper including the sports section and the advice columns.

Most presentations involved improvised dialogue, but one group presented a startling and starkly beautiful pantomime dance. The morning newspaper had reported a tragic story of a man, the father of four children, who had been stabbed to death while coming to the rescue of an old woman who was being mugged. Her purse, the target of the thief, contained less than a dollar in loose change. The four or five students involved presented a silent pantomime, accenting the tragic and dramatic nature of the story by moving as if filmed in slow motion. The effect was haunting. Their classmates and teacher were astonished. Their "dance" was so moving that it was decided to set it to music. "Slaughter on 10th Avenue" was chosen as the background music to which the students choreographed their movements. Ultimately, they performed their ballet version of the tragic news story, set to music, on a stage flooded only in blue light, in a darkened auditorium, as part of a school talent show. Not one of the students involved had ever had any previous dramatic or dance experience.

There are many dance activities which might serve as spinoffs of the mystery genre. Many, many mysteries involve breathtaking chase scenes ("Come, Watson, come. The game's afoot!"). Younger children love to choreograph chase scenes to fast-paced music reminiscent of player pianos and Keystone Cops background music. Ask interested students to interpret a famous mystery through dance, choreographed to appropriate music. A single episode or an entire scene may be choreographed. If students need models or reference points, ask them to recall that some of the most famous ballets are treatments of famous fairy tales and other literary pieces.

Notes

[1]Linda Melin, "Creating a Mystery Game," *Writer's Digest* 68, no. 7 (July 1988): 38.

[2]Many resources exist. One repository of such tapes is the *Wireless* catalog which contains "The Baker Street Dozen," featuring Sir John Gielgud and Ralph Richardson reading twelve Sherlock Holmes stories; and, "Radio's Greatest Mysteries," featuring among others "The Shadow," "The Green Hornet," and "Suspense." For a catalog, write *Wireless*, Minnesota Public Radio, 333 Sibley Street, Suite 626, St. Paul, MN 55101. Many public libraries have collections of old-time radio recordings.

[3]For more information about conductor John McGlinn's restoration attempts see the album notes of the EMI-Angel 1988 recording of "Show Boat." See also "A Classic Reconstruction" by Katherine Ames in *Newsweek* 112, No. 19 (November 7, 1988): 112-113.

[4]The author wishes to acknowledge and thank Jamie Miller of Louisville, Kentucky for his creation of the Brett Connor cartoon.

[5]The author wishes to acknowledge and thank Nancy Pylypczuk of Colorado Springs, Colorado for the use of both her words and her cartoon.

[6]Mystery photos are found on the back cover of *Current Science*, a biweekly school publication. For subscription information contact Field Publications, 4343 Equity Drive, Columbus, OH 43228. For information about *Games* magazine, write Games Magazine, P.O. Box 10147, Des Moines, IA 50347-0147. *Games* magazine is also readily available in news stands.

[7]Phil McArdle and Karen McArdle, *Fatal Fascination: Where Fact Meets Fiction in Police Work* (Boston: Houghton Mifflin, 1988): 125-135.

Teacher Resources

Anno, Mitsumasa. *Anno's Journey*. New York: Philomel Books, 1982.
One of many picture books by perhaps the greatest book illustrator alive today.

_____. *Anno's U.S.A.* New York: Philomel Books, 1983.
American history, folklore, and legend is woven into a series of exquisite watercolor-and-ink paintings. The mystery lies in finding all the Americana the artist has hidden in the seemingly simple illustrations.

Ashe, Rosalind. *Literary Houses: Ten Famous Houses in Fiction*. New York: Facts on File, 1982.
Imaginative illustrations of homes described in classic literary works (e.g., Baskerville Hall) are found in this wonderful book.

_____. *More Literary Houses*. New York: Facts on File, 1983.
More of the above.

Base, Graeme. *Animalia*. New York: Harry N. Abrams, 1986.
A breathtakingly beautiful alphabet book with more than one mystery on every page.

_____. *The Eleventh Hour: A Curious Mystery*. New York: Harry N. Abrams, 1989.
The author/illustrator provides a visual mystery for readers. A code and the top-secret solution to the mystery are provided.

Handford, Martin. *Where's Waldo*. Boston: Little, Brown, 1987.
This is an artistic needle-in-a-haystack. Kids must be good visual detectives to find the character Waldo in a dozen different and very busy scenes.

_____. *Find Waldo Now*. Boston: Little, Brown, 1988.
Waldo's adventures continue, but this time he is a time-traveler and observers must find him hidden in scenes out of history.

_____. *The Great Waldo Search*. Boston: Little, Brown, 1989.
Still further adventures with Waldo.

Hindley, Judy, and Colin King. *Fakes and Forgeries*. Tulsa, Okla.: Hayes Books, 1979.
One of the books in the Good Detective Series, this volume deals with forgeries in the art world and is a delightful and informative treatment of the subject.

McArdle, Phil, and Karen McArdle. *Fatal Fascination: Where Fact Meets Fiction in Police Work*. Boston: Houghton Mifflin, 1988.

The account of fingerprinting is especially fascinating.

Ockenga, Starr, and Eileen Doolittle. *World of Wonders: A Trip through Numbers*. Boston: Houghton Mifflin, 1988.

The creators combine photography and painted backgrounds in a dozen imaginative picture puzzles.

Scotland Yard Photo Crimes from the Files of Inspector Black. New York: Simon and Schuster, 1981.

First published in Great Britain in 1983 by Dorling Kindersley Limited. No author is credited for these wonderful mystery diversions students can enjoy and imitate.

Symons, Julian. Illus. by Tom Adams. *Great Detectives: Seven Original Investigations*. New York: Harry N. Abrams, 1981.

Tom Adams illustrations of great sleuths such as Maigret and Queen. Their surroundings are as great as Symons' word pictures.

Treat, Lawrence. *Crime and Puzzlement*. Boston: David R. Godine, 1982.

Solve-them-yourself mystery pictures students and adults love. There are several subsequent volumes.

_____. *You're the Detective!* Boston: David R. Godine, 1983.

More of Lawrence Treat's great puzzles, this time created especially for children.

Van Allsburg, Chris. *The Mysterious of Harris Burdick*. Boston: Houghton Mifflin, 1984.

A master illustrator poses unique mysteries with fourteen sensational drawings.

Wilks, Mike. *The Ultimate Alphabet Book*. New York: Henry Holt, 1986.

There are 7,777 items to be found, alphabetically, in this splendid artistic mystery book. Wilks' introduction is a classic problem solving account.

Mystery Reading List for the Arts

Adler, David A. *Cam Jansen and the Mystery of the Monster Movie*. New York: Dell, 1984.
The youngest mystery buffs will enjoy a mystery involving the cinema.

Christie, Agatha. *Ten Little Indians*. New York: Pocket Books, 1973.
This Christie mystery is alternately titled *And Then There Were None*. The same material is presented in dramatic format in Agatha Christie's *The Mousetrap & Other Plays* (New York: Bantam Books, 1986). "The Mousetrap" is the world's longest running play. Besides "The Mousetrap," and "Ten Little Indians," this volume includes Dame Christie's excellent "Witness for the Prosecution" and five other plays.

Crispin, Edmund. *Swan Song*. New York: Avon, 1981.
Adult mystery fare of the locked-room type set against the backdrop of grand opera.

Dicks, Terrance. *The Case of the Missing Masterpiece*. New York: Elsevier/Nelson Books, 1979.
The Baker Street Irregulars become involved in a mystery surrounding a missing Constable painting.

Keene, Carolyn. *The Mysterious Image*. New York: Simon & Schuster, 1984.
Nancy Drew solves a mystery involving photography and drama.

Konigsburg, E. L. *From the Mixed-Up Files of Mrs. Basil E. Frankweiler*. New York: Atheneum, 1967.
Middle school readers will enjoy this story involving, in part, a mystery about the authenticity of a sculpture attributed to Michelangelo. The chief setting is the Metropolitan Museum of Art in New York City.

Montgomery, Ramsey A. *The Mona Lisa Is Missing*. New York: Bantam, 1988.
Montgomery's book is one of the many and popular "Choose Your Own Adventure"® books.

Page, Martin. *The Man Who Stole the Mona Lisa*. New York: Pantheon, 1984.
History and fiction meet in the Louvre Museum.

Paul, Barbara. *A Cadenza for Caruso*. New York: Signet Mystery, 1986.
Adult fare as murder stalks the Metropolitan Opera and the great Caruso plays detective.

Watson, Clarissa. *Somebody Killed the Messenger*. New York: Atheneum, 1988.
Persis Willum of the exclusive Gregor Olitsky's North Shore Galleries is the sleuth in this and other art-related mysteries by Watson.

Williams, David. *Treasure in Roubles*. New York: Avon, 1986.
A shrewd London banker becomes embroiled in the theft at the famous Hermitage Museum in the Soviet Union. Opera also figures in this mystery.

Wolf, Gary K. *Who Censored Roger Rabbit?* New York: Ballantine, 1981.
Cartoon characters and real folks mix in this original adult detective story.

4

The Social Studies

Meet an Anthropologist

James Michael Hoffman is a biological anthropologist at Colorado College in Colorado Springs, Colorado. Dr. Hoffman earned M.A. and Ph.D. degrees in anthropology from the University of Colorado. He also earned an M.D. from the University of Maryland School of Medicine. He has taught at the University of Colorado, Northern Arizona University, the University of California at Berkeley, and at Colorado College. In addition to his professional responsibilities at Colorado College, Dr. Hoffman also assists law enforcement personnel in forensic work, which he describes in his letter to students. Dr. Hoffman also works with archaeologists in the identification of Pre-Columbian human remains discovered in the American Southwest.

A Letter from a Professional

Fig. 4.1. A letter from Dr. James Michael Hoffman, biological anthropologist.

THE COLORADO COLLEGE

COLORADO SPRINGS, COLORADO 80903

21 November 1989

Dear Students,

I am a biological anthropologist, sometimes called a physical anthropologist, teaching in an undergraduate liberal arts college in Colorado. Biological anthropology is one of two major subdivisions of anthropology, the study of humankind; the other major division of anthropology is cultural anthropology. Respectively, biological and cultural anthropology study human biological and cultural variation through time and across the surface of the earth.

One of the ways I use my knowledge and understanding of human biological variation is to assist local coroners and police officers in identifying unknown human skeletal remains; then I am working as a forensic physical anthropologist and applying what I know about variation in human skeletons. These deceased individuals may be people who died accidentally while hiking or camping, or who might have been killed by someone else who then tried to hide the body. When unknown human skeletons are found, I have a number of questions I want to answer to help the authorities identify this person. The basic questions I pose to myself are: How old was the individual at the time of death? What was the sex of the individual? What was their biological heritage, or what some people would call race? How tall was the individual? What other features about this person can aid in their identification—such as old injuries, evidence of surgery, unusual bone structure, tooth variation; did you know, for instance, that the sinuses in the forehead of the skull are as unique as fingerprints? Quite often I work with a forensic dentist who can compare old dental records with the teeth of this unknown person to establish an identification.

The techniques of age estimation, sex determination, stature estimation, and race assessment are all based on large samples of individuals for whom these characteristics were known at the time of their death. Following death, the bones of these known individuals were observed and measured in a number of ways to establish standards for age, sex, stature, and race. For instance, individuals of different biological heritage [race] have, on average, different facial features which reflect, to some extent, the underlying bones of the face. If we have a good sample of whites, blacks, Asians, Indians, etc., we can determine what the common features of each group are and then apply these to an unknown skull. Also, we know the best place in the skeleton to determine sex is the pelvis or hip bone region. This results from the fact that at the time of the adolescent growth spurt, a girl's pelvis grows in a slightly different way than a boy's; this prepares her pelvis for childbirth at some time in the future if she chooses. Men and women also differ in stature as adults and we can measure the bones of their arms or legs to calculate how tall they were.

The human skeleton, particularly an unknown one, provides a great mystery for the anthropologist. If one knows how to read the clues, the bones will reveal their identity.

Sincerely,

J. Michael Hoffman, MD, PhD
Associate Professor
Department of Anthropology

Case Study

Fig. 4.2. The social studies case study.

Question: When is it better to create a mystery or problem than to solve one?

Answer: When you are at war and trying to deceive the enemy.

The motivation is obvious. During a war the very survival of one's country and the lives of its citizens are at stake. One of the great tasks of any war effort is communications. Massive war efforts can only proceed effectively if communications between all elements are in place, and a critical problem for military intelligence is to be sure communications are not infiltrated by the enemy. Telephones and radiotelephones can be wiretapped and codes can be deciphered. U.S. intelligence experts knew this in World War II. They successfully intercepted and correctly interpreted Japanese and German communications. What communications strategies could the U.S. develop for the Allied war effort which would be failsafe? The search was on.

Part of the data search and analysis led to an examination of previous U.S. intelligence practices. During WWI, in 1918, a Captain E. W. Horner of the 141st Infantry discovered that the American Indian tongue was so foreign to European ears that he could successfully use eight Choctaw Indians to transmit orders by field telephone with complete security from enemy interception or decoding. An analysis of the problem lead to the following hypothesis: find a Native American tribe with a language so unusual that it would be totally unintelligible and indecipherable to the enemy, and with a large enough military-age male population to provide ample messengers in a huge theatre of war. Find such a population and a tamperproof communications system can be established. Part of the verification of this hypothesis lead to the discovery that the Navajo tongue was one of the most unusual and difficult-to-learn languages in the world. Navajo was understood by only twenty-eight non-Navajo persons, all of whom were anthropologists and missionaries and none of whom were German or Japanese in nationality or service. Additionally, the Navajo nation was a large nation numbering at least 50,000 persons in 1941.

The resolution of the communications security problem was highly successful. The system developed utilizing over 400 Navajo U.S. Marine "codetalkers" was never cracked by the enemy and was a vital part in the ultimate Allied victory in the Pacific theatre of the war.

Source:

David Kahn, *The Codebreakers: The Story of Secret Writing*, (New York: Macmillan, 1967), 549-550.

Tools of the Trade

Figure 4.3 is a partial drawing of an archaeology site. Teachers and library media specialists should duplicate the figure and ask students to complete the drawing by adding to it the tools archaeologists would need in order to perform their work as sleuths searching for answers about the far distant past. Urge students to include tools and objects used inside the tent as well as in the out-of-doors. The library media specialist can be especially supportive in helping students locate resources to learn about the profession of archaeology. As the students determine the essential tools used by practioneers of this profession, they will have the added benefit of learning *how* such tools are used by men and women who try to unravel the mysteries of time and culture.

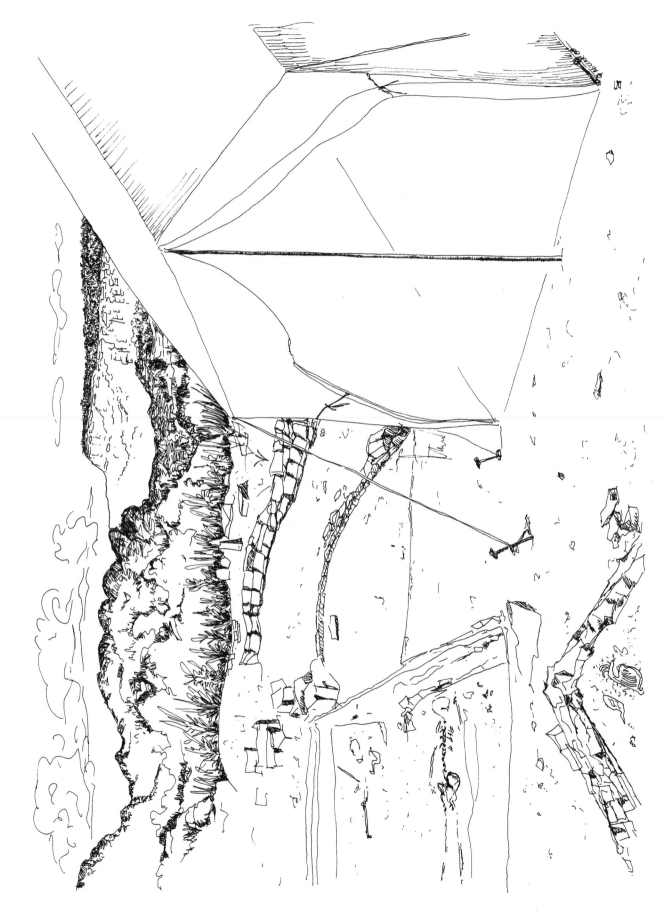

Fig. 4.3. Tools of the trade for social studies.

Mystery Desk

Figure 4.4 is the imagined desk of a very famous anthropologist. The clues in the drawing should help students who are good detectives determine the owner of the desk. Alert students to the fact that nothing has been left to chance in the drawing. The view out the window, the map on the wall, and the books on the shelves are all clues as significant as the objects on the desk.

Fig. 4.4. Desk of famous anthropologist.

Traces

Figure 4.5 may be shared with the class as a handout or an overhead transparency. The Traces mystery drawing for the social studies can be used in tandem with the Tools of the Trade drawing. Both are archaeology sites. They are drawn from differing perspectives, however. Ask students to use the visual clues in the drawing to determine what kind of detective would be able to use bones and pottery sherds to unravel a mystery.

Fig. 4.5.

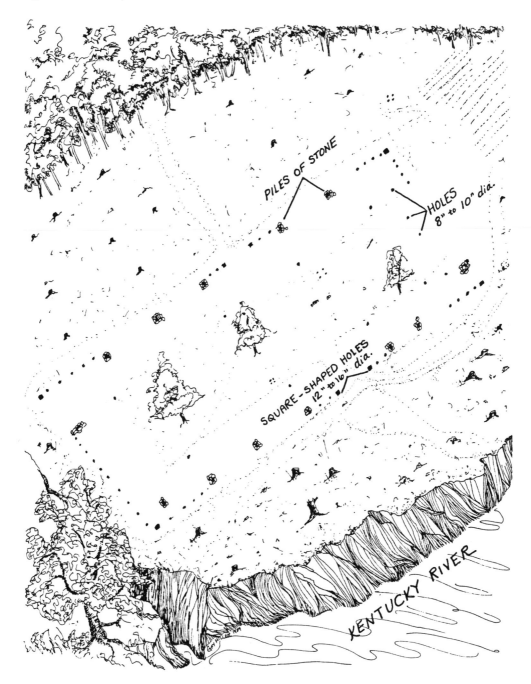

Social Studies Activities

The social studies incorporate many disciplines: archaeology, anthropology, sociology, psychology, history, government and law, economics, and geography. Each of these fields contains fascinating mysteries for students to explore. Professionals in these fields exemplify detection, critical thinking, and problem solving skills in the best Holmesian tradition. Historical and archaeological detectives unlock the riddles and mysteries of the past. Sociologists and psychologists attempt to clarify the present, hypothesizing and verifying why we behave the way we do. Geographers chart where we live. Political scientists and economists analyze the rules, ways, and means of our lives. It is impossible to address such a broad, exhaustive field comprehensively in a single chapter. Therefore, the activities herein should be viewed as beginning points to stimulate critical thinking, creativity, and problem solving on the part of students and teachers. Utilizing the webbing technique introduced in chapter one, students can generate many additional avenues of interest for further study and devise unique and creative ways to pursue such studies.

Research—Probes and Inquiries

Research is vital to any investigation. It is the very heart of the social studies. Students can emulate Sherlock Holmes by tenaciously tracking down information. They can formulate hypotheses, keep systematic notes, and distinguish between incidental and vital clues. They will assemble evidence, using reason to build a case and verify a hypothesis or thesis, and then make known the results of their investigations (Holmes frequently referred Watson to a monograph he had penned about the detection of types of pipe tobacco ash or some other obscure subject.).

Research and the subsequent publication of findings is vital to a fully functioning, literate society. It is also frequently the bane of many students' and teachers' existence. The fourth grade social studies report and the ninth grade term paper can be deadly for all concerned. The fourth grader attempts to tell the history of the United States in two pages and the ninth grader paraphrases or plagiarizes, depending upon his counterfeiting skills, an article from an encyclopedia on psychology as a career. Often the culprits in such scenarios are the boring and uninspired topics chosen for research inquiries and the limited research tools and information sources student researchers have utilized. The exciting, fascinating topics and unique research tools available in mystery units may entirely change the perceptions *both* students and teachers have about research projects.

Research is not, of course, limited to the social studies disciplines or classrooms. As suggested in chapter two, biographical research may lead students to inquiries about the mysteries found in the lives of persons like Agatha Christie and Arthur Conan Doyle. Blood typing and fingerprinting are topics of relevant research as science projects. Every discipline offers a multitude of topics and research tools. The vastness of relevant mystery topics, unsolved riddles, and sleuth-like research strategies within the social studies, make its disciplines appropriate for targeting the training and development of research and inquiry skills.

Teaching Research and Independent Inquiry Skills

Because the school library media center is so vital to student research efforts, a wise teacher shares the planning and teaching of a research skills unit with the school library media specialist. There are several aims of independent inquiry training. Educators want students to be able to:

select a researchable topic

ask appropriate questions

observe their environment

find and evaluate resources

take notes

organize and outline data

develop a plan of study

share information and knowledge gained

evaluate the success of the inquiry

There are many effective strategies teachers and library media specialists may utilize to help students achieve these goals. The following suggestions have worked successfully for many educators.

Selecting a Topic

An exceptionally clever teacher, W. Keith Kraus, outlines how he challenged students to engage in exciting research by using the subjects of mystery and intrigue in *Murder, Mischief, and Mayhem*, a National Council of Teachers of English publication.[1] Like so very many educators who teach at all levels, Dr. Kraus, a teacher of freshman English at Pennsylvania's Shippensburg State College, found his students' research papers and reports abominable. The topics were generally boring, leaving students uninspired and unmotivated. Further, the typical subject matter was already so overworked that there was virtually nothing new for students to say. At best, they learned to paraphrase with varying degrees of success; plagiarism was rife. Nothing much in the way of content or process was learned by the students. Then Kraus tried a different approach. The college library contained all *The New York Times* files on microfilm, providing a resource and a tool familiar to most students. Using the *Times Index*, students could find significant amounts of high-interest primary source material from the year 1851 onward under the subject heading "Murder." Students were off and running, fascinated by their research. Eventually they turned in the best research papers Kraus had ever received. The students felt they were doing *real* research, too, no doubt a major factor in the dedication and effort they applied to the task. Kraus cites one instance when the FBI contacted him wanting to know why a student was interested in a 1930s murder case which is still open and remains unsolved. This wise teacher's excellent text provides a long list of possible topics, his own modus operandi, and sample student papers.

It is true that Dr. Kraus has a college library equipped with microfilm collections and facilities his college freshman can use. However, even in elementary schools teachers should not ignore his success rate. The basic idea is terrific and the topics and resource tools can be varied to accommodate differing age groups and available resources.

The subject matter of "murder" may not appeal to or be an appropriate topic of investigation for some students, but there is not a community in the country devoid of some fascinating mysteries in the rich tapestry of its history. Is there an archaeological digging project in the region, a historical restoration project, or an ongoing oral history venture? Does the area have a fraudulant money scheme, an art forgery, a bank robbery, or a notorious kidnapping in its past? The local historical society or history museum is a great place to begin collecting a list of exciting, appropriate, worthwhile, and relevant topics for student inquiries. Officials in such organizations can probably suggest appropriate resources as well. They can advise teachers and library media specialists on availability and accessibility of primary sources such as newspaper files, diaries, journals, letters, and photographs, and subjects for interviews. Most historical societies are interested in building a prospective future membership and will be glad to assist school personnel in directing students to inquiries related to local and regional history. Local libraries of any size have a substantial collection of materials and resources and can assist teachers and school library media specialists in encouraging students to research local mysteries. These same libraries should have microfilm editions of area newspapers from decades past, and may have *The New York Times* on microfilm. Newspapers have their own libraries and "morgues" made accessible to students if prior arrangements are made and the purpose of the research is known. Once a search for relevant subjects and resources is begun, a networking effect will occur; the original parties contacted will suggest other valuable contacts for students.

Of course, past criminal activity, local or beyond, need not be the only focus of student research topics. As this chapter and others in *Mystery and Detection* suggest, good researchers in any field are the successors to the Holmesian tradition. Students can inquire into other local historical topics such as famous floods and other disasters, community founders and pioneers, and regional architecture. They may examine the archaeological history of their region, explore careers in the criminal justice system, and a thousand other areas.

The broad topics of mystery and crime in the community, region, and state of the school does provide, however, some common reference points for class members and their teacher. Such studies also allow students to use some significant primary sources ordinarily unfamiliar or inaccessible. Student perceptions of research methods and sources (something other than one encyclopedia) are likely to change. Opportunities for truly original research exist. Students will not just be "going through the motions" of doing research. The resulting attitudes, commitment, and the expenditure of effort will drastically improve. Student interest and motivation will be high. The degree of parent involvement will also increase due to the high interest level. Best of all, the final products will be more interesting for teachers to read and evaluate!

Before students engage in research, however, several prerequisite skills should be in place. The following skill-oriented exercises have proved useful to many teachers and library media specialists in the teaching of research units.

Asking Questions

Any good detective knows that learning to ask the *right* question is an absolute prerequisite if one is to successfully solve riddles and mysteries. The successful sleuth asks questions like these:

What was the crime?	Who was the victim?
Where was the crime committed?	How was it committed?
Who are the suspects?	What are the possible motives?
Who had opportunity?	What clues are available?
What are the suspects' alibis?	

Similarly, students engaged in research need to ask critical questions if they are to be successful investigators. They need to ask questions like these:

What do I want to learn?

What questions can I pose which will lead me to the answer(s)?

Where can I search for answers?

Who can help me in my inquiry?

Are there adequate resources to satisfactorily complete my inquiry?

The old parlor game "20 Questions" is a good way to sharpen students' questioning skills. Select the name of a person, place or thing and write it on a piece of paper. Ask the students to guess what you have written using twenty questions or less. Chart the key word in each question and the "Yes" or "No" response as shown in figure 4.6. After students have either correctly guessed the word or failed to do so, go back over the questions which were asked using the key words as prompts for the recall of each. Which questions were helpful? Which were wasted questions? Were some questions prone to yield misleading answers? This exercise, repeated often, will have the positive result of continuously sharpening students' thinking and questioning skills. For the duration of the mystery unit, the persons, places, or things used in "20 Questions" may include the names of mystery authors, sleuths, or objects related to mystery readings.

Another excellent technique which aids the teaching of questioning skills involves a common reading of a mystery story. Engage the class in the oral reading of a story up to the point where the crime is committed and discovered. Stop reading, temporarily, and ask students to ask three questions they would use as a sleuth if they happened onto the case. Allow students time to share and discuss the relevance of some of their questions. Then let the students silently read the remainder of the story. Students can then check the usefulness of their questions had they been the sleuth in the story. Did they ask useful questions which helped to solve the mystery?

Gifted students love to ask questions. Indeed, their propensity in this direction is a commonly cited characteristic. But, even gifted students need practice in the art of questioning. They need to learn how to narrow and focus questions and they also need to learn the etiquette which any researcher or interviewer should use when asking questions.

Fig. 4.6.

20 Questions Chart

KEY WORD	YES	NO
1. Animal	x	
2. Human	x	
3. Living		x
4. American	x	
5. Author		x
6. Criminal		x
7. Detective	x	
8. Local		x
9. National	x	
10. J. Edgar Hoover		x
11. Allan Pinkerton	x	
12.		
13.		
14.		
15.		
16.		
17.		
18.		
19.		
20.		

Observing the Environment

In the *Hardy Boys Detective Handbook*, Joe Hardy shares with a friend something his father has told him: "Observation is nothing more than a series of mental images to which you apply the laws of repetition, association, attraction or its opposite, repulsion."[2] Joe uses a great trick with his friend. He reminds the friend that they have spent the entire morning together, and then asks the friend to turn away from him and describe, without looking, the shirt he is wearing. Joe demonstrates to his peer how unobservant he is most of the time.

The following tool is another good activity to use with students to remind them that they need to constantly sharpen their observation skills. Place the following letter configuration on an overhead transparency.

```
S  S  A  W  S
P  U  U  I  E
R  M  T  N  A
I  M  U  T  S
N  E  M  E  O
G  R  N  R  N
```

Place the overhead on the projector, but cover it with a piece of paper. Tell the students you are going to give them an observation test. They will have only a few seconds to see a body of letters. They must look carefully. Their task will be to reproduce, in their mystery notebooks, an exact replication of the letters. Reveal the letters to the students, proceeding *horizontally*, one row at a time. Of course, the key is to read the letters in vertical columns. But many students will miss the obvious. They will approach the problem by reading left to right rather than from top to bottom, and they will try to rapidly memorize random, unrelated letters.

Another observation training exercise involves giving each student an object such as a peanut or an orange. Ask each student to observe the object thoroughly. The observation data should be noted in the student's mystery notebook. Give the students several minutes to make the observations, and then recall the items. Mix the objects well and lay them out on a table. Ask the students to use their observation data to assist them in finding their peanuts or oranges. The teacher settles custody lawsuits by measuring the claimants' observation notes against the evidence at hand. After students have completed this first part of the exercise, ask them to categorize their observations according to senses. The students will be startled by the greater number of visual clues on their lists. As Frank Hardy says, "It is a well known fact that modern man does not use his five senses to their capacity."[3] There are many other observation activities which can be employed with students. They ride or walk home from school in certain ways every day, but can they recall the houses or streets they pass by in exact order? Can they name, without looking, all the objects in their desks or lockers? If they turn away from the mystery learning center or bulletin board, can they draw a picture of either which is accurate in detail?

Students need to learn and practice good observation skills in their research just as sleuths do in their investigative work. The successful historian notes a passage in an original document that others have missed and realizes that it is the key to understanding the behavior of someone long ago. A great scientist sees not mold but the potential for penicillin. Wise teachers note a sudden look of interest on the face of a reluctant learner and know that they have finally found the subject that will "turn on" the student. Any good researcher or practitioner is also an acute observer of the environment.

Finding and Evaluating Resources

Keen observation of one's environment naturally leads to the question: What things in my environment can I use to answer the questions I have posited? The library media center is, of course, the prime repository of resources most students utilize in their inquiries. But, there are other resources the expert observer will note and consider. Some questions the student researcher has posited can best be answered by a mystery writer, a pathologist, or a police detective. Agatha Christie's redoubtable Miss Marple uses her own memory as a prime resource. She makes connections between the behavior of suspects in a criminal case she is analyzing and the past behaviors she has noted among the residents of her little English village of St. Mary Mead. There are countless other resources students may access. Ask students to brainstorm all the possible resources they can think of which would assist them in their inquiries.

One mystery the novice student-researcher faces is how to access the many resources, printed and electronic, that libraries contain. Young researchers need to realize there are many ways to look up information in the library. The obvious approach is to use a key word, say, "detective" and find out what resources are cataloged by that topic. Many students stop there. Encourage students to be better detectives and to utilize more thorough search strategies. They might find information about detectives under other, related synonyms such as "investigator" and "sleuth." They can examine resources cataloged under an antonym such as "criminal." Students might also find information about detectives under larger topics like "crime." They can explore intersecting subjects like fiction as in "fictional detectives" or careers and vocations as in "careers in law." There may be time/place/field connections. Information about Sherlock Holmes can be found in works about Victorian England. Information about art fraud detectives may lie in works primarily cataloged under the "art" subject heading.

Once students have learned to ask good questions to focus their inquiries, ask them to make a list of at least four to six key words or topics which relate to the chosen inquiry. Then, students begin a preliminary search of the library media center to determine how well its resources may serve their inquiry. In effect, the student is creating a working bibliography. When this procedure is used early in the research stages, students will be spared the problem of delving into a subject area only to find that very limited resources exist to aid them. Figure 4.7 is an example of such a worksheet. An "X" signifies that material about the key subject Sherlock Holmes may be found in the resources (listed horizontally) under the topic headings cited (vertically).

Students need to know how to evaluate resources once they are located. Not all materials are equal in quality. Not all authors and publications share equal reputations for scholarship. Figure 4.8 is an example of a library reference sheet used to assist students in evaluating the resources they find in libraries.

The following activity works well to help students become more discriminating readers. Give them newspapers and ask them to select a news story to read. As they read, ask them to circle any words, phrases, sentences, or paragraphs which are opinion rather than fact. Students are frequently surprised to find that much of what appears to be hard news is opinion rather than fact. Carrying the activity a step further, ask students to reexamine the text they have circled and decide whether the opinion given is expert opinion or lay opinion. What information leads them to make this decision? Does expertise in one area transfer to a new subject area? That is, would a great mystery writer necessarily be an expert on criminal justice? This is a revealing exercise. The average reader assumes most of what appears on the front page is fact. In reality, what appears there is a mixture of facts and opinion; moreover, the opinion comes from reporters and others without credentials or expertise in the field in question.

Fig. 4.7. Sample worksheet.

Key Words in Search   Library Resources

	Encyclopedias	Readers' Guide to Periodical Literature	Vertical Files	Card Catalog — Author-Title	Card Catalog — Subject	
Sherlock Holmes					X	
Arthur Conan Doyle	X			X		
Detectives	X	X			X	
British Literature	X				X	
Victorian England	X		X		X	

Fig. 4.8. Library reference sheet.

Resource Evaluation Form

Select one of the resources you have located in the library media center and answer, wherever possible, the following questions.

1. Name of the author(s):

2. List any pertinent information given about the author(s), especially regarding their credentials.

3. List the publisher, place of publication, and date of publication. [Note: the library media specialist may be able to answer questions about the professional reputations of authors and publishers.]

4. Is the material or information provided current and accurate as far as you can determine?

5. Are there pictures, maps, illustrations, or graphs? If so, do they add understanding to the printed material?

6. How many pages of the book, encyclopedia or magazine article, etc. are devoted to the topic you have chosen?

7. Does the resource provide answers to questions you have posed for your inquiry?

8. Carefully select and read thoroughly three to four paragraphs of the resource. In one column below list all the facts given; in the second column list all the opinions given.

FACTS   **OPINIONS**

Taking Notes

Speaking of crimes, even the gifted student will plagiarize if not taught to do otherwise. Here is a way to stress both listening *and* note-taking skills. Select a short passage from any of the reference materials being utilized in the mystery unit and are on hand to read aloud to students. Tell students that they are to listen very carefully. They are to note, and write in the mystery notebooks, key words and ideas from the passage you will read. Read the selection. Perhaps it will be about the creation of the Nancy Drew or the Hardy Boys mystery series, or a short piece about the Federal Bureau of Investigation.  When finished reading, tell the students to summarize all they have heard in not more than three sentences. The activity works wonders. Students cannot plagiarize because the only words they have in front of them are the ones they have recorded. They must learn to take good notes. The exercise needs to be repeated several times for the students to become highly proficient note takers. An alternative approach is to tape passages and place them in the learning center. Students then can use headphones and practice note-taking and summarizing, individually.

Organizing and Outlining Data

There are many methods of teaching the sorting and outlining of the information students discover in their research. Mystery stories are natural media for looking at such talent. Hercule Poirot always draws all the suspects together in the last chapter and skillfully sorts out what seems to be an unfathomable mess. He skillfully puts every fact, alibi, and clue in its proper  place. Students may not yet have learned to use their "little grey cells" quite so artfully, but they can practice organizational skills in a variety of ways. The majority of topics for inquiries fit one of two patterns used in outlines quite nicely: topical and chronological. The lives of the students can be similarly outlined. Ask students to brainstorm a list of ten to twenty things about themselves: likes, hobbies, personal experiences, events in their lives, etc. Next, ask them to organize the material they have brainstormed into an outline with no less than three to five categories. They can try both approaches. They can divide the years of their life into chronological stages, or build an outline around topical aspects of their lives such as school, religious, athletic, and service activities.

Planning the Inquiry

Many are the students, gifted and otherwise, who have crashed their ships of potential achievement on the rocks of procrastination. The complexity and demands of today's world require students to develop effective time management skills. *Backplanning* is one tool to give to students. That's correct; not backpacking, but *backplanning*.  Step one in backplanning asks students to project and list all the things they need to do to complete their inquiry. Their list may include finding resources, making appointments with experts, conducting interviews, taking photographs, reading extensively, note-taking, writing and sending letters of inquiry, outlining and writing the study. Step two asks students to decide on significant dates and time periods (e.g., How many days are required to take slides, have them processed and returned). Step three asks the students to arrange all significant dates chronologically, working backwards from the final due date for the inquiry project.

 Figure 4.9 is an example of a backplan. The student, Sherry, knew that she needed to be ready to make a final report on February 22. To create a backplan, she began with that date and worked backwards in time listing and dating all the things she needed to do in order to be prepared for the February 22 presentation.

Fig. 4.9.

A Backplan

An example of a backplanning chart might reveal Sherry's inquiry into the history and evolution of the Hardy Boy mysteries.

January 4	Check library to determine if there are ample sources to use for the topic chosen.
January 5	Begin reading some of the 100 Hardy Boy mysteries.
January 7	Turn in thesis statement.
January 12	Write letter to Grosset & Dunlap asking for information about origins of the series and information about Franklin W. Dixon.
January 20	Make appointment with library media specialist to use Kodak visualmaker to make slides of books, covers, etc. for slide presentation to class.
January 24	Use visualmaker to create slides; send film in to be processed.
January 28	Interview grandfather about his remembrances of reading the Hardy Boy mysteries as a child.
February 1	Search *The Readers' Guide* and other indexes to find a minimum of three articles about the Hardy Boys.
February 7	Complete preliminary outline for both paper and slide/tape presentation.
February 9	Begin writing rough draft of paper and script.
February 10	Finish script for narration of slide show. Contact speech teacher to find a good narrator. Reserve room in library media center to tape narration.
February 13	Pick up slides from photography store, and sort and organize the best slides.
February 14	Work with library media specialist to synchronize the audio and visual parts of the presentation.
February 16	Edit and type final draft of paper.
February 17	Rehearse slide/tape presentation.
February 21	Turn in final paper.
February 22	Present slide/tape show on the Hardy Boys to classmates.

Using the backplan, students can keep close tabs on their level of procrastination. Each day or week they can check off those things they have accomplished. Students do not need to realize too late that they are two weeks behind schedule in photographing subjects for a study. The students know on a daily basis how things are progressing; whether they are ahead, behind, or on schedule to have the final project ready for the projected due date. The student backplan is similar to an Individual Education Plan (IEP) which is a required provision for gifted students in many states. If the backplan itself does not fully meet IEP requirement, it can at least serve to complement it. Additional questions, objectives, and categories may be added. Such additions may include a record of each student's strengths and weaknesses and how each will be addressed in the inquiry project; lists of all readings and resources to be utilized; a statement of final product expectations; and the roles in the inquiry process to be played by the student, the teacher, the parents, and mentors.[4]

Sharing Information

A few words about the products resulting from student investigations. Unfortunately a majority of students have the impression—gained in elementary school and kept for life—that the end result of any research effort must be a paper report. Teachers should not overlook the possibility of student use of other media and means to communicate results. Slide shows, posters, window displays in commercial establishments, radio talks, feature stories for newspapers, speeches, dramatizations, dioramas, and a host of other creative products may, in fact, be superior ways of communicating research  about local mysteries. Students may want to enter projects in a local history fair, give speeches or slide-tape presentations to a local civic group or historical society, present historical dramatizations to groups of senior citizens, or engage in countless other individual, small group or class productions. A great amount of public interest and positive public relations might accrue from having a class project of several window displays in a mall or downtown shopping area, each high-lighting a separate, little-known but fascinating mystery from the community's past. Of course, all projects may not be of sufficient merit to warrant public sharing, but when genuinely fascinating subjects are chosen for research, primary sources are accessible, and the possibility of significant audiences exist, the quality of student works tends to dramatically increase. The following is a brief list of possible products students may create to communicate to others what they have learned in their inquiries:

Travelogue (e.g., Holmes's England)

Survey (e.g., mystery favorites of various age groups)

Learning materials for the class learning center

Original comic book or comic strip about mystery

Original video drama

Essay (e.g., "What's Wrong with TV Mysteries")

Diorama (e.g., Sherlock Holmes's rooms at 221 B Baker Street)

Board Game (e.g., a game based on knowledge of Nancy Drew and Hardy Boys mysteries)

Mobile (e.g., scenes from a real-life mystery)

Time-line (e.g., evolution of the mystery genre)

Computer mystery game

Bulletin board display (e.g., The Mystery of Genetics)

Evaluating the Inquiry Process

Sleuths know they have been successful if the perpetrator of the crime is caught and punished. Student investigators often run a more risky course. The teacher is the sole judge of student products. Justice is not always meted out equally by educators. One student gets an A on a research paper while her friend receives a B, and neither of the students understand how the grades were determined. Teachers need to evaluate student work, regardless of the media or format used, but they should always reveal to students—well in advance of the due date—the criteria used to determine grades.

Teachers should not be the only evaluators of student work no matter how fair and judicious they may be. If students are to truly become independent learners, they must learn to make critical judgments about their own processes and products. Students should complete a self-evaluation of their inquiry project that is quite independent of the teacher's evaluation of the work. The format of student evaluations may vary considerably. Students can use checklists to indicate whether their work was excellent, good, average, or poor across several dimensions. The evaluation may take the form of narratives in their Mystery Journals with comments about things that were done well; mistakes which were made that proved to be good learning experiences; and their overall satisfaction with their investigation.

Historical Research

Many historical studies exist beyond local history for students to probe. Both the Kennedy and Lincoln assassinations contain many unsolved puzzles. Of course, crime has always lurked about royalty. The history and mystery surrounding England's Richard III and the disappearance and presumed murder of the little princes is fascinating. Henry VIII was not without his problems. The case of Lizzie Borden and the tragic Lindbergh kidnapping remain as curious today as ever. The guilt or  innocence of Bruno Hauptmann is much debated. The motivation of Leopold and Loeb, two wealthy Chicago youths who planned a supposedly perfect murder remains as confounding today as it did more than a half century ago. The mysterious unsolved disappearance in the Pacific Ocean of aviatrix Amelia Earhart in 1937 is a subject of considerable fascination.

As preparation for student inquiries into historical puzzles, it may be advantageous to have an historian come to class as a guest speaker and recount the ways he or she works like a detective. Students know history is written; they have to suffer through many history books in their educational sojourn. But, do they know *how* history is written? Do they know how an historian works? Almost any community contains at least one avid student of history, if not a professional historian, who can unlock some of the secrets of how history is collected, analyzed, and recorded.

It is worth mentioning here that one of the "crimes" students might explore is the lack of attention women and minorities have too often received in history texts. Indeed, it may also be a good move to have a speaker address the issue of women's rights or perhaps even debate a historian about the portrayal of women in history. Historians and history buffs may also be able to suggest a wide array of additional reading and research topics with respect to real, unsolved historical mysteries.

Several mystery novels are based upon real historical events or reflect historical periods and may be enjoyed by teachers and older students. They include:

Agatha Christie. *Death Comes at the End*. Pocket Books, 1986.

Margaret Doddy. *Aristotle Detective*. Penguin, 1978.

Stuart Kaminsky. *The Fala Factor*. Mysterious Press, 1984.

Peter Lovesey. *Wobble to Death*. Penguin, 1980.

Ellis Peter. *The Sanctuary Sparrow*. Fawcett Crest, 1983.

Elliott Roosevelt. *Murder and the First Lady*. St. Martin's, 1984.

Zilpha Keatley Snyder. *The Egypt Game*. Dell, 1986.

Josephine Tey. *The Daughter of Time*. Pocket Books, 1983.

With a bit of sleuthing in a well-stocked mystery bookstore, teachers can find a mystery set in virtually any historical period.

Psychology

Psychological Sleuthing

How much do your students know about one another? How adept are they at psychological sleuthing? Do they know enough about each other's interests, habits, motives, and goals, that they can combine such knowledge with effective probes in order to solve classroom mysteries? Here is a game which allows students to see just how much they really do know about one another and how to practice good questioning techniques.

Choose teams of six to eight players. Provide each player with several blank slips of paper and scratch paper. Prior to playing the game, create a master list of questions which will serve as the focus of the game. There are no right or wrong questions, but fact questions such as those asking for age will allow for little differentiation or discrimination between players. Questions asking for opinion are good. To begin, write questions whose stems contain the 5 W's (who, what, when, where and why). Some sample questions are:

Who, among all the people who have ever lived, would you most like to meet?

Who is your favorite author? composer? sportswoman?

What was your most embarrassing moment?

What was the most frightening thing you have experienced?

When are you most likely to read a mystery?

When are you most likely to whistle?

Where is your favorite place to seek solitude?

Where would you most like to live as an adult?

Where would you be most likely to spend a rainy day?

Why do you like/dislike science?

Why do you like/dislike the color red?

Begin the game by reading a question and asking students to take one minute to think of an honest response. Instruct students to privately record their responses to the question on a slip of paper. Collect the slips of paper and place them in a hat or fish bowl. Select one response and read it to the group. (For the obvious reason of handwriting as a clue, the slip itself should not be seen by students.) Now, the sleuthing begins. The object of the game is to determine who authored the response. Some ground rules should be introduced to students at this time:

The author of the response should never reveal his or her identity *except* in response to the direct question "Is that your statement?" Just as a criminal would lie to keep from being detected, so too should the "guilty" party here feign innocence and lie if need be to keep from being detected. Of course, liars often trap themselves so the author of the response in question will have to be crafty to avoid detection. To prevent simple process of elimination questions, no participant may ask the question "Did you write this?" or accuse another player more than once. If such a question is asked or the accusation is made, and it is incorrect (recall the author or "guilty" party must tell the truth on this one question), that player is eliminated from the game for this round. Note: It is not illegal for the "guilty" person to accuse another player at some point in the game, therefore taking himself out of the questioning play, and perhaps removing suspicion from himself. No player may ask more than one question in succession (unless he or she is the only qualified player remaining in the game round). One player volunteers or is chosen to begin the questioning. He or she asks one question of one of the other players. The player to the right of the first questioner asks the second question of the player of his/her choice. The next player on the right asks the third question of any player. The game proceeds in this fashion. Players may not defer to another player by forfeiting their questioning turn. A player hot on the trail of clues must still wait until his/her next turn avails itself.

Students should use scratch paper to keep good notes about the responses of other players. Combining knowledge of the personalities and characteristics of classmates with their answers to the questions, the first player to detect the real author of the response wins the round. Play is continued as a new question is provided, new responses are authored, and a new statement from among the authors is selected and read to the group.

Take time to debrief after playing several rounds. How did students arrive at correct detections? What role did psychology play in detection? How successful were the "guilty" parties in the art of deception? What kinds of questions were most successful in uncovering the truth? Were students surprised at the responses some students provided? Do we really know as much about one another as we sometimes think we do? Encourage students to play the game at home with their families.

The Psychology of Mysteries

People have always liked mystery and detective stories. But, why are they more popular in some periods of history than in others? In an October 20, 1986 *Newsweek* magazine interview British mystery novelist P. D. James considered this question. She refers to mystery literature as the "reassuring genre." Men and women and governments have failed to solve many of the great problems of our time and the result is general frustration. Mystery literature, unlike much contemporary news, provides neat and tidy resolutions. The creator of Scotland Yard's poet-policeman Adam Dalgliesh  sums up the popularity of mysteries this way, "Detective stories help reassure us in the belief that the universe, underneath it all, is rational. They are small celebrations of order and reason in an increasingly disordered world."[5]

Is P. D. James correct in her observation? How does one explain in psychological terms the enormous popularity of detective fiction, of Sherlock Holmes (probably the most famous literary creation of all time), and of television shows and movies about crimes, criminals, police and detectives? Is it just accident that the Sherlock Holmes movies featuring Basil Rathbone were at the height of their popularity during the years of the Great Depression and World War II, or that the television series "Murder She Wrote" enjoyed such enormous popularity more recently? Consider inviting a local psychologist to speak to a class on the subject. Encourage debate of mystery writer P. D. James's statement. Assign students to research books about crime and detective fiction to locate other rationale statements about the popularity of the mystery genre. Or, encourage students to conduct their own poll of students and adults in an attempt to determine the *why* of why mystery fiction is so popular.

Economics

Welcome to Mysteryland

Disney World is one of the most popular entertainment and vacation attractions in the United States. Can the gifted young entrepreneurs in the classroom imagine a mystery hotel or resort which could emulate the success of Disney World? Ask students to imagine all the ways they could build upon the love people have for mysteries in the design of their resort. Using the mystery motif, ask students to describe every aspect of their imagined mystery spa. What attractions would they build? How would they dress the workers? What rides and shops would exist in the theme park? How could they make the hotel(s) unique? What kinds of souvenirs would they market? What type of advertising campaign could they mount to attract customers? Students can describe their planned resort in a written prospectus, or they can go a step further and build a scale model of the planned mystery community?[6]

The Case of Aunt Sadie's Will

Here is an activity students should love. It is a highly motivating way to introduce students to the "mysteries" of the stock market. The only tools of the trade needed are imagination, risk-taking, and daily copies of the newspaper stock market report. Describe the following scenario to students:

Poor Aunt Sadie, recently deceased, left all her fortune to you. Sort of. You see, there is a catch in Aunt Sadie's will. She was ever-vigilant about money matters and never would leave all her money to a relative who would not make the most of the inheritance. (This is no trifling matter. Aunt Sadie was a very wealthy woman. The inheritance is $1.8 million!) There are other relatives, including greedy Griselda Grinface and conniving Casper Lotsabucks, who would just love to get their mitts on Aunt Sadie's fortune. But, we digress. To determine if you have the business acumen to deserve the fortune, Aunt Sadie is giving you a test. She has set aside an amount of $1,000 and has instructed her attorney to allow you six weeks to demonstrate your investment skills. You may invest the money in any way you choose. You can simply save the money in the bank, but in six weeks time not a great deal of interest will accrue. You can invest the money in real estate, but you probably will not realize much profit in just six weeks. You can invest the money in the stock market. Obviously, good financial detectives are going to study the stock market very carefully and make educated judgments about their investments. A conservative investment may be comforting, but not realize enough profit to win you the fortune. A risky investment may promise to pay off handsomely, but may also cause you to lose everything. The choice is up to you. Oh, by the way. How much do you need to make? Aunt Sadie was not a wild gambler, but she admired some risk-taking. After six weeks of investing, you must have earned at least $500, bringing the total stake to $1,500 or greedy Griselda and conniving Casper get to split the $1.8 million. Good luck. Can you win this mystery sweepstakes?

Wall Street Crimes

Bank robbery a la Bonnie and Clyde is not the only kind of financial crime. Conspiracy on Wall Street is often less violent and bloody, but no less sensational and often far more lucrative. And, of course, what is termed "white collar" crime extends far beyond Wall Street. One avenue of possible investigation for enterprising students involves research about famous crimes committed in the financial world. What is stock market fraud and how is it perpetrated? What is a stock speculator? What is "insider trading"? What is the Securities and Exchange Commission? What kinds of laws do they enforce and what kind of criminal activity do they prosecute? Who is Ivan F. Boesky and what was the extent of his Wall Street crime in dollars? The Boesky case is relatively recent and sensational because of the dollar amounts involved, but it does not stand alone as the only Wall Street crime in history. Hardly! When and why was the Securities and Exchange Commission created originally, and who are some famous stock market criminals of the past? What are some other types of white collar crime and how are they committed *and* detected? The subject of financial crime and its detection is a fascinating world most students know very little about. Future J. P. Morgans in the classroom will find this arena of mystery detection fascinating. Of course, older readers should not miss the works of Emma Lathen and her sleuth, John Putnam Thatcher, Vice President of the Sloan Guarantee and Trust Company in New York City's financial district. Each novel reveals the inner workings of a different type of business enterprise such as the fast food, seed catalog, and automobile industry businesses.

Geography

In Holmes's Footsteps

When Sherlock Holmes and Dr. Watson first met in 1881, (*A Study in Scarlet*), the great detective's deduction that Dr. Watson had been in Afghanistan startled the good doctor. Yet, for a man who knew an amazing amount about the world, Holmes was a remarkably unworldly traveler. Aside from a trip to Norway and the ill-fated visit to Switzerland's Falls of Reichenbach, Holmes remained in London with only occasional trips into the British countryside. Ask the geography sleuths in the classroom to trace the pathways of Holmes about London and throughout the British countryside.

World atlases found in the library media center may be used by students studying the geography of Conan Doyle's stories and novels. It also may be profitable for students to send a letter of request to the British Travel Authority, John Hancock Center (Suite 3320), 875 N. Michigan Avenue, Chicago, IL 60611. Instruct students to ask for maps of the London Underground, the foggy city's famed subway system (Baker Street is an Underground station), the city of London, and of England. Other excellent sources of London and English maps include travel guide books like those by Arthur Frommer which can be located in the public library and at bookstores. There are several stellar resources which should not be missed in studying mystery geography, British fashion. These resources include:

Alzina Stone Dale and Barbara Sloan Hendershott. *Mystery Reader's Walking Guide to London.* Passport Books, 1987.

Michael Harrison. *In the Footsteps of Sherlock Holmes.* Drake, 1972.

Tsukasa Kobayashi, Akane Higashiyama, and Masaharu Uemura. *Sherlock Holmes's London: Following the Footsteps of London's Master Detective.* Chronicle Books, 1986.

Charles Viney. *Sherlock Holmes in London: A Photographic Record of Conan Doyle's Stories.* Houghton Mifflin, 1989.

"The Sherlock Holmes Mystery Map" from Aaron Blake Publishers is another valuable resource. This attractive and inexpensive map pinpoints 130 Sherlock Holmes sites and is great for bulletin board decoration. The 20" x 27" full-color map costs $4.95 and is distributed by Gibbs M. Smith, Inc., Peregrine Smith Books, P.O. Box 667, Layton, UT 84041. The same publisher also has created similar literary maps: "The Raymond Chandler Mystery Map of Los Angeles" and "The Ian Fleming Thriller Map."

The place to begin tracing the geography of Holmes's pursuits is at 221 B Baker Street. From there students may want to trace the footsteps of Holmes to the locales mentioned in some of his classic stories:

Aldersgate and Saxe-Coburg Square ("The Red-Headed League")

Charing Cross Station ("The Adventure of Abbey Grange")

Covent Garden, Bloomsbury, and Wimpole Street ("The Adventure of the Blue Carbuncle")

Pall Mall and Whitehall (where brother Mycroft lived) ("The Greek Interpreter")

Piccadilly Circus (Watson insisted upon the older name Regent Circus) ("The Greek Interpreter")

Regent Street ("A Scandal in Bohemia")

Waterloo Bridge ("The Five Orange Pips")

Montague Street and the British Museum ("The Musgrave Ritual")

Westminster ("The Adventure of the Second Stain")

Of course, the geography sleuths cannot forget Lestrade's Scotland Yard! The adventures of the great detective occasionally took him out of London into the English countryside. After students have the London scene well assayed, ask them to track down adventures chronicled by Watson which took place outside London:

Stoke Moran (probably Stoke D'Abernon according to author Harrison) ("The Speckled Band")

Herfordshire ("The Adventure of the Boscombe Valley Mystery")

Farnham ("The Adventure of the Solitary Cyclist")

Aldershot ("The Adventure of the Crooked Man")

Woking and Ripley ("The Naval Treaty")

Cambridge ("The Adventure of the Missing Three-Quarter")

Chesterfield ("The Adventure of the Priory School")

In Holmes's Footsteps

Geographical Explorations

Geographical inquiries certainly need not confine themselves to traces of fictional exploits. Accounts of real-life searches for solutions to mysteries such as Captain Speke's search for the source of the Nile, Stanley's famed search for Dr. Livingston, and Lewis and Clark's Louisiana Purchase explorations provide challenging and worthwhile reading for gifted students. Encourage students interested in geography to explore mysteries which have baffled geographical detectives and how such cases were cracked.

Another idea related to geography was suggested to the author by a Colorado Springs, Colorado high school English teacher, Jan Kawamura. Ask students to use the concept of highway map graphics to illustrate how the lives of mystery story characters intertwine. Both lines and symbols may be used. Students prepare a legend for their maps. Solid and broken map lines of varying colors, perhaps representing the moods or fates of the characters, may chart the lives of the victim, suspects, and sleuth. Intersections are noted when the paths of the characters meet. The completed maps, when displayed, add one more touch of color and mystery to the classroom during the course of the mystery unit.

"Where in the World Is Carmen Sandiego?," "Where in the USA Is Carmen Sandiego?," and "Where in Europe Is Carmen Sandiego?" are three of the most popular computer games marketed. Created by Ken Bull, Gene Portwood, and Lauren Elliot, these games allow players to learn geography while simultaneously playing an entertaining computer game. Geographic clues lead players to the crooks.[7]

Teachers can create their own original games and simulations using a similar format. The game does not necessarily have to be run as a computer program, either. State history and geography may be reviewed through the playing of a mystery game.

Create a series of geographical clues related to a given state. The following examples are drawn from Colorado history and geography.

The "criminal" was able to lay on his back and place his arms and legs in four different states. (The Four Corners)

The "criminal" hid the money just outside a famous ski town named after a tree. (Aspen)

The accomplice was a famous silver queen; an opera bears her nickname. Both lived in Leadville. (Baby Doe Tabor)

The "criminal" attempted to established an alibi which would place him at the base of a mountain named after explorer Zebulon Pike. (Pikes Peak)

One or more sets of clues can be created. Students may be divided into teams and given clues which will lead them to solve the mystery or challenge provided. Maps may be given to students and they can also be asked to follow the mystery person's path or route throughout the state. Many variations can be tried. Reveal the identity of the mystery person, and the task for students becomes locating a scene or place of critical importance to the person (e.g., determine the site of a bank robbed by Butch Cassidy). Gifted students once familiar with the basic format or concept can soon be creating their own original geography mysteries.

Archaeology

Sleuthing through the Past

Top-notch archaeologists rival, perhaps even surpass, the great Sherlock Holmes in their use of detection skills and tools. They painstakingly plumb artifacts of the past, assembling clues, piece by fragmentary piece, in order to unravel riddles and mysteries our ancient ancestors on the planet Earth left for us to solve. The motivation is self-evident: people have an urge to know their past. Some have sought to verify events mentioned in the Bible. Former astronaut James Irwin works with archaeologists searching for Noah's ark.[8] Others merely seek to reconstruct ordinary events such as the everyday life of Viking sailors and their families. Some seek to answer very real mysteries such as why the Anasazi people, who evidenced an advanced civilization for 1,600 years in the region of the Southwestern United States, appear to have suddenly vanished about 800 years ago.

In archaeology, the search for evidence is more difficult than in any case tackled by Sherlock Holmes, Hercule Poirot, or Nancy Drew. The witnesses are mute, silenced by death hundreds and even thousands of years ago. The clues have often been tampered with by ancient grave robbers and modern collectors of antiquities. The steady and relentless erosion of time is another obstacle. The analysis of the few available clues is agonizingly slow and painstaking. Sites are chosen carefully after much study and hypothesizing and sometimes even at the risk of ridicule. King Tut's tomb in Egypt's Valley of the Kings was discovered only because of English archaeologist Howard Carter's persistence and tenacity. Hordes of earlier archaeological teams had combed every inch of sand in the Valley of the Kings and determined that the tombs of the great pharaohs had all been found and plundered by ancient thieves. There was nothing left to discover. But, Carter steadfastly kept on digging until, in 1922, he discovered the greatest archaeological site and find of all time, the undisturbed tomb of the boy king Tutankhamun. The tomb with its more than 5,000 fabulous objects intact had been hidden even from ancient grave robbers by the shifting desert sands and the tomb of another, later pharaoh which had been built over it.[9]

Once a site has been chosen the evidence must be collected, analyzed, organized and classified. Dirt must sometimes be painstakingly removed with teaspoons and icepicks instead of shovels to insure that artifacts are not damaged. Seeds and bones must be scientifically examined. Every fragment of pottery must be charted and mapped, photographed, and cataloged. Records must be scrupulously kept. Only after all this is done can a hypothesis or hunch be offered. The confirmation and verification may be maddeningly slow in arriving and can come from many different sources.

The science of dendrochronology (the study of tree rings to determine age) has been one of the major pieces of evidence leading to the hypothesis that the mysterious disappearance of the Anasazi from Mesa Verde in southwestern Colorado was due to drought conditions. Analysis of tree trunks in the region shows little growth in the rings about 700 years ago. The ancient tree rings are abnormally narrow. Scientists believe this to be evidence of limited growth due to lack of water. How do we know this information about the Anasazi and the region? Because archaeologists have written about their work. In addition to being a detective and scientist, an archaeologist must also be a writer. There may not be a Doctor Watson around to chronicle his or her casework. Professional colleagues and universities expect scientific papers to document progress in the investigation and new finds. Continued popular and financial support for a dig may require the writing of mainstream books and magazine articles. And, the final sentence? It may never come, at least not in the lifetime of a given archaeologist. The archaeologist must have an unlimited reservoir of patience. A lifetime may pass without complete confirmation of his or her theory or hunch. Sherlock Holmes, often impatient when the pieces of a particular case failed to fall into place, would it have been a very content archaeologist.

Archaeological Investigations

Students may satisfy their fascination with mysteries and employ their problem solving and sleuthing skills through the study of archaeology and some of the field's greatest mysteries past and present. The following ideas and resources should serve as excellent beginning points leading to ever widening, more challenging topics and activities which good, sleuthful students will uncover:

It is not too likely that many sleuthful-minded students will participate in a criminal investigation. However, participation in the ultimate archaeological detection activity—a dig—is not so remote. Students from fourth grade to adults can participate in real archaeological excavations of Anasazi sites at Crow Canyon near Cortez, Colorado, in the Four Corners region (where Utah, Arizona, New Mexico, and Colorado borders cojoin) of the American Southwest. Students participate in classroom instruction about archaeology, the history and environment of the region, and in field work side by side with archaeologists. For complete information on the program, contact the Admissions Director, Crow Canyon Archaeological Center, 23390 County Road K, Cortez, Colorado 81321, (303) 565-8975.

For further information about digs also see:

Velma Morrison. *Going on a Dig*. Dodd, Mead, 1981.

Roberta Newman and Wendy Thompson. *Sleuthing through History*. J. Weston Walch, 1983.

Students may wish to learn more about the famous archaeological find of King Tut's tomb. Numerous sources tell the story. Perhaps the best is Thomas Hoving's *Tutankhamun: The Untold Story*. Hoving details not only the archaeological mysteries involved but the intrigue and mystery surrounding the death of King Tut, the ancient grave robbings, the strange behavior of Howard Carter and his benefactor, Lord Carnarvon (Why did they go into the tomb illicitly and then attempt to cover up their entry?), and the supposed curse of the tomb which purportedly claimed the lives of several of the principals involved in the 1920s excavations.

Many of Thor Heyerdahl's investigations bear reading and researching. The most recent Heyerdahl probe is recounted in *The Maldive Mystery* in which he attempts to explain stone faces located in the Maldive Archipelago in the Indian Ocean, 180 degrees or exactly half way around the equator from the site of his earlier investigations of the mysterious stone heads on Easter Island.

Other sites and phenomena which reek of mystery and can lure students into exciting investigations and reading include:

Stonehenge	Cave paintings of Altamira
Viking sites	Cahokia excavations in Illinois
Pompeii	Angkor in Southeast Asia
Chichen Itza	Incan Empire city of Machu Picchu
Nigeria's Benin treasures	

It was not only the grave robbers of ancient times who made the work of archaeologists difficult. Crime continues to plague the sites archaeologists excavate. Contemporary vandals hunting pots and other relics to sell to private collectors irreparably damage archaeological sites. Even casual tourists and seemingly innocent bottle hunters ruin for all time sites which could tell much about our ancestors. Many states and nations have made activities such as pot hunting illegal, but these laws have little effect. Carol Ann Bassett conducts an excellent discussion of the contemporary vandals in *Science 86* magazine under the title "The Cultural Thieves."[10] It is not just desert sites in the Southwest which are in great danger of total ruination. Revolutionary and Civil War battle fields are losing their archaeological value because souvenir collectors hunting buttons and bullets destroy the sites. Students can consult the state historical society to find out where archaeological sites in their state are located, and they can contact the sites to determine if vandalism is a problem, what state laws exist to protect such sites, and what they can do personally to avoid the inadvertant ruination of them.

Perhaps the archaeological crime of the century was the perpetration of the hoax known as the Piltdown forgery. Sir Arthur Conan Doyle, Sherlock Holmes' creator, has even been implicated by some. The highly scientific and austere profession of archaeology is, itself, not entirely free from crime. Enterprising and inquisitive students may want to investigate the Piltdown Hoax. An excellent beginning source is an article by John Winslow and Alfred Meyer, "The Perpetrator at Piltdown," found in the September issue of *Science 83*.[11]

A particularly creative source rich in spin-off ideas for students is David Macaulay's *Motel of the Mysteries*. Macaulay, famous for his informative picture books *Castle* (Houghton Mifflin, 1977) and *Pyramid* (Houghton Mifflin, 1975) takes a hilarious poke at archaeology in general and the Carter excavations of King Tut's tomb in particular. (How do we know he's joking? Take a look at the clues. Macaulay names the motel of reference "Toot and Come In"!) Among other things, the author-illustrator spoofs the idea of ascribing all things unknown to religious origins. He also delightfully pokes fun at contemporary society. His idea is ripe for imitation. Have students pretend to be future archaeologists. How will they explain plastic plants, credit cards, McDonald's golden arches, Swatches, and the host of other modern artifacts future archaeologists will puzzle over and debate?

A particularly creative idea related to the *Motel of the Mysteries* was shared with the author by an Ohio teacher. One of the school board members in her community offered to spend a weekend in a local motel room volunteered (during the off-season, no doubt) by its education-minded proprietors. The entire plan and the identity of the board member was kept secret. The board member left behind all traces of his visit (takeout food cartons, scraps of note paper, newspapers, etc.) and the motel operators purposely did not clean the room. On the Monday morning following the board member's weekend stay, the teacher's class walked to the motel and "the case of the unknown occupant" was turned over to them. What clues could they find? How should they handle items found? Collect evidence? What did the evidence tell them? A similar crime can be perpetrated with less expense and with less time committed by setting up a similar type of situation in say, the library media center, teachers' lounge, or cafeteria. For example, plan to have a colleague use the cafeteria in an hour other than the lunch period, purposely leaving papers, a coffee cup, and other items behind. Then take students into the cafeteria and turn them loose to decipher the clues and evidence and determine the identity of the mysterious occupant.

Steamboat Springs, Colorado, teacher George Gertz shared the following mystery idea with your author. Print the name of a city on a piece of posterboard in large block letters. Then cut the poster-board into a jigsaw puzzle. Without telling students, remove pieces which will eliminate key letters of the location. Instruct students to put the puzzle together. When they realize pieces are missing, compare their dilemma to that of archaeologists when sites are looted or when artifacts are in the hands of private collectors. Ask them to infer what the name of the city is despite the missing letters. Newark, for example, could be used by eliminating the "w" and/or the "a." Students will inevitably infer New York. Put the missing pieces in the puzzle and discuss the implications. Tell the students at the onset that the puzzle will reveal the location where a certain culture originated. Drawings of simple "artifacts" instead of city names may also be used. By eliminating a few drawn lines, a spear becomes a shovel, for example.

The Artifact Box Exchange Network is a relatively new project of considerable interest. The project is an interschool exchange of objects representing the locales of participating schools. Students send and receive a box of items and try to determine their "mystery" partner. The project is for grades one through twelve. For information, contact The Artifact Box Exchange Network, University of Connecticut, 231 Glenbrook Road, Room 28, U-7, Storrs Hall, Storrs, CT 06269-2007.

Political Science and Debate

The heart of politics, government, and law is debate. At the heart of debate there are two absolute fundamentals: evidence and reasoning. These are, of course, also the primary tools of a great sleuth.

Debate may be one of the most important skills a gifted student can master. Many gifted students build upon their junior and senior high school debate experiences and choose careers which lead them into court rooms as both prosecutors and defense attorneys. (Attorney Douglas Erickson who wrote the letter to students for the crime and punishment chapter of *Mystery and Detection* began debating in the author's junior high school English class.) Debate provides students with splendid opportunities to dramatically increase their research, reasoning, and communication skills. In *The Debater's Guide*, authors Jon M. Ericson and James J. Murphy identify talents and skills essential to debate. Debaters need to have the ability to collect and organize ideas, evaluate evidence, see logical connections, think and speak in outline terms, speak convincingly with clarity and impact, and be adaptable to new ideas.[12] Note the similarity to the skills needed by a good detective. The parallel sleuthing skills are obvious, and even the requisite oratory skills are needed by future Perry Masons and Horace Rumpoles.

It is not the purpose of this book to serve as a debate primer. Many excellent resources, such as *The Debater's Guide*, are available to teachers and library media specialists. Fortunately, most school systems have at least one high school which has a fine interscholastic debate program. Often high school debaters are happy and willing to go to junior high, middle, and elementary schools to present sample debates or to teach debating skills and strategies to younger students. The high school debate teacher may also be able to provide pamphlets and books about debate procedures and training.

In a typical interscholastic debate there are four speakers on two sides, the affirmative and negative, who debate a given proposition. There are first and second affirmative and negative speakers. Each gives a constructive speech and a rebuttal. In most contemporary debates, all participants also engage in cross-examinations. A typical format is as follows:

Constructive speeches are given by the first affirmative speaker, first negative, second affirmative, and second negative. There is a cross-examination period following each speech. The debate ends with rebuttals in which the order of affirmative and negative speakers is reversed: first negative, first affirmative, second negative, and second affirmative.

In a murder trial, the evidence presented may consist of things such as clothing fibers, analyses of blood stains, and fingerprints. In an interscholastic debate the evidence is more likely to consist of statistics and expert opinion. Debaters extensively research the debate topic over a period of months to collect evidence in support of and opposition to the stated proposal. Good debaters scrutinize evidence in the light of questions such as these: Is the evidence verifiable? pertinent? reliable? unbiased? recent? statistically sound? clear? The reason for asking such questions is obvious. Each debater presents or reaffirms a position during the debate, and also refutes the case or position which the opposition attempts to build. Debaters need evidence to build their case, to refute the opposition case, and to defend their position from the rebuttal.

Once debaters have collected evidence, they need to use good reasoning skills to make the best possible use of their facts, statistics, and expert opinions in building a case. At least four kinds of reasoning are used by debaters.

Sign Reasoning occurs when the thinker *infers* one fact or condition because of the presence of another fact or condition. The former does not necessarily *cause* the latter, but it is evidence of its existence. A doctor often makes a diagnosis based upon the symptoms he or she observes in a patient. The observed symptoms did not cause the illness, but they are evidence of its presence in the patient.

Casual Reasoning occurs when two or more things are related in such a way that one is the cause of the other. For many years medical scientists could not state a causal relationship between cigarette smoking and certain illnesses. They could only say that there was a very high incidence of lung cancer and heart disease among people who smoked. More recently, scientists have claimed that there is a direct link, a causal relationship, between cigarette smoking and certain diseases.

Reason by Example occurs when the thinker *generalizes* from a sampling to a larger population. A psychometrician randomly selects five students from Miss Smith's sixth grade class and gives each of the students an individual I.Q. test. The total scores of all five students fall into the gifted range. Because 100 percent of a random sampling of subjects prove to be gifted, the psychometrician then makes the *generalization* that Miss Smith's entire roll of students are gifted and talented.

Reason by Analogy occurs when someone infers that because two or more things are alike in one manner, they will be alike in other respects. Last year Miss Smith's sixth grade class loved her unit about mysteries. Because this year's sixth grade class is just as gifted, she infers that they will also enjoy the mystery unit.

It is the task of the debaters to link evidence and reasoning together to establish their own case. Simultaneously, they also must try to prove that the opposition is using either faulty evidence or flawed reasoning or both. As Hercule Poirot might say, the "little grey cells" receive good exercise when students engage in debate.

Many topics related to crime fiction and real crime find their way into interscholastic debates. Individual and societal rights, including euthanasia, gun control, and capital punishment are frequent debate topics. Students can use the debate techniques they learn in class to debate these issues and topics directly related to the mystery unit. For example, older students might debate these propositions:

Sherlock Holmes, a drug addict, is a poor role model for students.

Dame Agatha Christie is the best mystery author ever.

The U.S. Supreme Court erred in its decision in *Miranda v. Arizona*.

For additional social studies activities, research topics, and resources please see the "Crime and Punishment" chapter of *Mystery and Detection*.

Notes

[1] W. Keith Kraus, *Murder, Mischief, and Mayhem: A Process for Creative Research Papers* (Urbana, Ill.: National Council of Teachers of English, 1986).

[2] Franklin W. Dixon, *The Hardy Boys Detective Handbook* (Revised Edition) (New York: Grosset & Dunlap Publishers, 1988), 102.

[3] Ibid., 100-101.

[4] The author wishes to acknowledge and thank Joyce Juntune who originally suggested the idea of "backplanning."

[5] P. D. James, "Queen of Crime," *Newsweek* 108, no. 16 (October 20, 1986): 81-83.

[6] See Jeff Taylor, "20 Rooms with a Point of View," *The Writer's Digest* 68, no. 6 (June 1988): 8-9. There is a retreat of this sort in Newport, Oregon. The Sylvia Beach Hotel is a writer's hotel. Each hotel room is named after a famous author and accordingly decorated. The Agatha Christie room conceals eighty clues to murder mysteries.

[7]"Where in the World Is Carmen Sandiego?" and "Where in the USA Is Carmen Sandiego?" are produced by Broderbund Software, Inc., 17 Paul Drive, San Rafael, CA, 94903-2101.

[8]See James B. Irwin, *More Than an Ark on Ararat* (Nashville, Tenn.: Broadman Press, 1985).

[9]For a complete discussion see Thomas Hoving, *Tutankhamun: The Untold Story* (New York: Simon and Schuster, 1978).

[10]Carol Ann Bassett, "The Cultural Thieves," *Science 86* 7, no. 6 (September 1986): 22-29.

[11]John Winslow and Alfred Meyer, "The Perpetrator at Piltdown," *Science 83* 4, no. 7 (September 1983): 32-43.

[12]Jon M. Ericson and James J. Murphy, *The Debater's Guide*, Revised Edition (Carbondale, Ill.: Southern Illinois University Press, 1987), 127.

Teacher Resources

Bassett, Carol Ann. "The Culture Thieves," *Science 86* 7, no. 6: 22-29.
    This excellent article details how pot hunters destroy the evidence archaeologists need to reconstruct the past.

Dale, Alzina Stone, and Barbara Sloan Hendershott, with maps by John Babcock. *Mystery Reader's Walking Guide to London.* Lincolnwood, Ill.: Passport Books, 1987.
    The mystery lover does not have to physically travel to London to enjoy this informative book.

Ericson, Jon M., and James J. Murphy. *The Debater's Guide*, Revised Edition. Carbondale, Ill.: Southern Illinois University, 1987.
    An excellent debate primer.

Harrison, Michael. *In the Footsteps of Sherlock Holmes.* New York: Drake, 1972.
    Harrison recreates the background in which the great detective and Dr. Watson operated.

Heyerdahl, Thor. *The Maldive Mystery.* Bethesda, Md.: Adler & Adler, 1986.
    Another grand adventure of Norway's modern explorer is detailed.

Hoving, Thomas. *Tutankhamun: The Untold Story.* New York: Simon & Schuster, 1978.

Irwin, James B. *More Than an Ark on Ararat.* Nashville, Tenn.: Broadman Press, 1985.
    A former astronaut details his search in the mountains of Turkey for Noah's Ark.

Kobayashi, Tsukasa, Akane Higashiyama, and Masaharu Uemura. *Sherlock Holmes's London: Following the Footsteps of London's Master Detective.* San Francisco, Calif.: Chronicle Books, 1986.
    This wonderful book of pictures by Japanese photographers is proof that Sherlock Holmes's fans truly span the globe.

Kraus, W. Keith. *Murder, Mischief, and Mayhem: A Process for Creative Research Papers*. Urbana, Ill.: National Council of Teachers of English, 1978.

One teacher's creative use of real mysteries as subjects for research papers.

Macaulay, David. *Motel of the Mysteries*. Boston: Houghton Mifflin, 1979.

A talented illustrator demonstrates that he also has a great sense of humor with this spoof of archaeology.

Morrison, Velma. *Going on a Dig*. New York: Dodd, Mead, 1981.

Archaeology lessons for students.

Neuman, Roberta G., and Wendy W. Thompson. *Sleuthing through History*. Portland, Maine: J. Weston Walch, 1983.

A teacher's guide to archaeology and history.

Viney, Charles. *Sherlock Holmes in London: A Photographic Record of Conan Doyle's Stories*. Boston: Houghton Mifflin, 1989.

Beautiful sepia tone photographs of Holmes's homebase.

Winslow, John, and Alfred Meyer. "The Perpetrator at Piltdown." *Science 83* 4, no. 7 (September 1983): 32-43.

Fascinating conjecture about Arthur Conan Doyle's possible role in the famous archaeological hoax.

Mystery Reading List for the Social Studies

There are mysteries with background themes for any of the various disciplines within the social studies. There are many historical mystery novels. There are also a number of good mysteries with unique geographical settings dealing with politics, economics, anthropology, and archaeology. Many are adult novels and should be carefully screened by teachers before sharing with students even though few are unsuitable for students of junior high age and older. For easy reference, mysteries are grouped here by subject category rather than placed in alphabetical order.

History

Christie, Agatha. *Death Comes at the End*. New York: Pocket Books, 1986.
> Murder and intrigue in ancient Egypt.

Doddy, Margaret. *Aristotle Detective*. New York: Penguin, 1978.
> Murder in ancient Greece. Aristotle unmasks the villain.

Kaminsky, Stuart M. *The Fala Factor*. New York: Mysterious Press, 1984.
> FDR's pet Scotty is kidnapped. The first lady asks Toby Peters, detective, to tackle the case.

Lovesey, Peter. *Wobble to Death*. New York: Penguin, 1980.
> Victorian England is the millieu in which inspector Cribbs works.

Peters, Ellis. *The Sanctuary Sparrow*. New York: Fawcett Crest, 1983.
> One of many Ellis mystery novels in which Brother Cadfael solves murders committed in medieval surroundings.

Price, Anthony. *Our Man in Camelot*. Garden City, N.Y.: Doubleday, 1976.
> The CIA, The Russians, King Arthur, and the Battle of Badon in sixth century England make up the unusual mixture in this mystery.

Roosevelt, Elliott. *Murder and the First Lady*. New York: St. Martin's Press, 1984.
> Eleanor Roosevelt works to save an innocent girl from the electric chair.

Snyder, Zilpha Keatley. *The Egypt Game*. New York: Dell, 1986.
> This one is for younger readers and lovers of the intrigue ancient Egypt conjures in the mind.

Tey, Josephine. *The Daughter of Time*. New York: Pocket Books, 1983.
> The case against Richard III and his portrayal by Shakespeare and Sir Thomas More is reexamined by a contemporary Scotland Yard detective.

Tourney, Leonard D. *Old Saxon Blood*. New York: St. Martin's Press, 1988.
> Husband and wife team, Matthew and Joan Stock, attempt to solve a murder mystery at the request of Queen Elizabeth I. See also Tourney's *The Bartholomew Fair Murders*, for more Elizabethan era intrigue.

Economics

Lathen, Emma. *By Hook or by Crook*. New York: Pocket Books, 1975.

John Putnam Thatcher, an executive in Wall Street's Sloan Guaranty Trust Company, becomes involved in the Oriental rug import business in this adventure. Each of the many Emma Lathen (a pseudonym for Mary Jane Latsis and Martha Henissart) books presents a neat whodunit to solve *plus* a business education in a particular avenue of free enterprise.

Anthropology and Archaeology

Hillerman, Tony. *Dance Hall of the Dead*. New York: Avon, 1973.

Hillerman not only crafts superbly written thrillers, but also provides an education through his background information about the Navajo and Hopi peoples. The chief problem confronting teachers is that the crimes perpetrated are often extremely gory. In the novel cited here, archaeology plays a major role in the murder case. More recently Hillerman has written *A Thief of Time* (Harper & Row, 1988) in which archaeology also plays a major role.

McHargue, Georgess. *The Turquoise Toad Mystery*. New York: Dell, 1982.

This mystery centers on an archaeology dig and is written for younger readers.

Geography

Gilman, Dorothy. *Mrs. Pollifax on the China Station*. New York: Ballantine, 1983.

Perhaps more appropriately placed in the spy novel genre, a close cousin of the mystery novel, this fun book chronicles another of Mrs. Pollifax's adventures. She is the grandmother who travels worldwide for the CIA. There are numerous Mrs. Pollifax mysteries, and all of them are set in exotic foreign locales. Gifted students as young as ten or twelve love the Mrs. Pollifax mysteries.

Melville, James. *A Sort of Samurai*. New York: Ballantine, 1981.

A Superintendent Otani mystery set in Japan.

Upfield, Arthur. *Murder Down Under*. New York: Charles Scribner's Sons, 1983.

Upfield's Inspector Napoleon Bonaparte ("Bony") investigates crime in Australia in this and other entries in the popular series.

van de Wetering, Janwillem. *The Corpse on the Dyke*. New York: Pocket Books, 1976.

Detective Grijpstra and Sergeant de Gier solve crimes in the Netherlands.

Politics

Dominic, R. B. *Epitaph for a Lobbyist*. New York: Paper Jacks, 1986.

"Emma Lathen" (Mary Jane Latsis and Martha Henissart) is the real author of this mystery in which a Washington Lobbyist who pushes too far is murdered.

Truman, Margaret. *Murder on Embassy Row*. New York: Ballantine, 1985.

President Truman's daughter has become a popular mystery writer and uses Washington, D.C. as the scene of the crimes she poses and solves.

5

Future Studies

Meet a Science Fiction Author

John E. Stith is a science fiction author who lives in Colorado Springs, Colorado. He also works as a data and instrumentation engineering manager for Kaman Sciences Corporation. He received a B.A. degree in physics from the University of Minnesota. He served with the United States Air Force in Alaska and in the NORAD Cheyenne Mountain Complex near Colorado Springs, Colorado. He has written several science fiction novels. Many are highly successful efforts to fuse the mystery and science fiction genres. His published novels include: *Scapescope* (Ace, 1984), *Memory Blank* (Ace, 1986), *Death Tolls* (Ace, 1987), *Deep Quarry* (Ace, 1989), and *Redshift Rendezvous* (Ace, 1990). Mr. Stith was honored with the Colorado Authors' League 1988 Top Hand Award for best adult fiction original paperback for his novel *Death Tolls*. He has also written mystery and science fiction short stories and authors a column about the intersection of science fiction and mystery for *Mystery Scene Magazine*. In addition to many speaking appearances, Mr. Stith was also a featured panelist in the 1987 Public Television program "Science Fiction/Science Fact: (SF²)."

A Letter from a Professional

Fig. 5.1. A letter from a science fiction writer.

| **John E. Stith** | 1242 Amsterdam Drive, Colorado Springs, CO 80907-4004 |

25 January 1987

Dear Sleuths:

Some people might say writing science fiction doesn't require much detection skill; after all, a writer just makes it up along the way, right?

Actually, a writer has to be a good detective in several ways. In the course of writing novels, I frequently maneuver a character into a tough situation. Once I've painted him or her into a corner, I'm faced with the same problem the character is; I have to find a logical and believable way out. If I cheat and suddenly change the rules by giving my character the ability to fly, then instantly the reader sees me cheating. At that moment, suspense evaporates, and any trust in the writer dissolves. The reader realizes that the outcome no longer matters; the hero or heroine will always find a contrived way out.

Figuring out how to get that character free of a predicament is similar to trying to figure out what a criminal—say a kidnapper—would do in a certain set of circumstances. The writer and the detective both start from known facts and then backtrack to fill in the missing information that explains the crime or makes a scene convincing. The process is a little like constructing a jigsaw puzzle rather than just putting one together. All the pieces of the puzzle must fit: characters, emotion, technology, background, and plot.

Not all detective work is glamorous and exciting; a lot of fact-gathering must be done even if it's not the favorite part of the job. The writer must research the background for the story, even if only five percent of the research winds up in print. Too, the detective and the writer have to be persistent; they must keep going until they finish.

Where the detective looks for hidden connections between seemingly unrelated events, so does the writer. The writer searches for unusual connections in language and different views of everyday occurrences. Add two elements and see what you get. The sum may be Conan the Librarian. Think beyond the obvious and the traditional. If an apple a day keeps the doctor away, what can you eat to keep the lawyer away?

The writer and the detective dig deep, to understand how and why things happen the way they do, and why people act the way they do. If the *hows* and *whys* of people are understood, then maybe the *whos, whens*, and *whats* will be more obvious.

I welcome your letters, but you may have to be something of a detective to contact me. As of the date on this letter, the letterhead address is correct. But most people don't live in one house forever, and I'm no exception. If I move, the post office will forward mail for a year. After that, my home address may not be much help. If you get a letter returned marked *Addressee Unknown*, there are other alternatives you can try. You can write to me in care of my publisher, currently The Berkley Publishing Group. As competitive as publishing is, and as often as publishers are bought and sold, you can check *Books in Print* to find out who publishes me in the future. Letters can also be sent in care of my agent, Curtis Brown, Ltd. *Literary Market Place* contains current addresses for agents and publishers. If you want to write to other authors, your local librarian should be able to help you find a starting point; research librarians are detectives in their own right, and they assist detectives in many professions.

There is something you can do to make it convenient for a writer to respond. Including a self-addressed, stamped envelope is a courtesy that will always improve your chances of a speedy reply. But remember that letters that follow the chain from publisher to author don't always go as fast as the monthly bills.

Happy Detecting,

John E. Stith

Case Study

Fig. 5.2. Future studies case study.

A reliable study of the future begins with a sound understanding of the past.
— Jerry Flack

In 1787, while the founding fathers of America were drafting the Constitution of the United States, a British fleet with 736 convicts on board set sail for Australia. The two events were not unrelated. However, the British decision to solve its penal problems by deporting criminals to an alien continent may have been portentous for events in our own future.

The same British King, George III, against whom the American colonists had revolted in 1776, presided over the government which began the establishment of Australia as a penal colony in 1788. Georgian England was a society of distinct class differences with an enormous gulf separating the rich and poor. The contrast was so great between the "haves" and "have-nots" that the wealthy feared the "criminal class" more than they feared foreign invasion. The Industrial Revolution was in full force, displacing persons, enslaving children, and wreaking havoc among the poor. Children of the poor were horribly exploited, many were sent to workhouses at the age of six years. A population explosion coupled with inadequate housing created crowded conditions in the growing industrial cities where workers were ill fed. There was no such thing as a central police force. The conditions for crime were ripe. Public hangings were frequent yet failed to deter crime, and the few jails which did exist were grossly overcrowded. Many jails were privately owned and convicts were required to pay for their keep. Obviously, the poor suffered even more under such conditions. As many as 200 offenses, including poaching a rabbit, cutting down shrubbery, and murder could result in a sentence of public hanging without the benefit of a trial. What could be done?

As early as the reign of Elizabeth I, the idea of transport of prisoners beyond British shores had been suggested. Beginning in 1611, 300 convict laborers were shipped to Virginia. In the years from 1700 to 1775, perhaps as many as 40,000 men, women, and children were shipped to British colonies in the new world. Prisoners convicted of minor offenses were transported for seven years, while those convicted of capital offenses received sentences of fourteen years. Jailers sold the convicted to shipping contractors who in turn sold them in the Carribbean and in America. Deportation helped to keep the walls of British jails from bursting.

The American Revolution brought a halt to this practice. England suddenly had no place to ship its convicts. The crisis occurred at the same time that the convict population was rising at home due, in part, to the displacement of persons caused by the Industrial Revolution. Jails became so congested that many convicts, in irons, were housed on ships in harbors. The threat to internal security was motivation enough to force the hand of the government, and to cause government officials to begin the search for a new place to transport criminals. In 1786, Lord Sydney, the home and colonial secretary, announced that a penal colony would be established at Botany Bay in New South Wales which the great English explorer Captain James Cook had claimed for the crown in 1770.

On May 13, 1787, the flagship *Sirius* captained by Arthur Phillips set sail for Australia. In all, 736 convicts were aboard eleven ships in the British fleet. Who were the convicts? There were no known murderers. There were men, women and children. The oldest known passenger was a woman of seventy whose crime had been the theft of 12 pounds of cheese. An eleven-year-old boy had been convicted of stealing 10 yards of ribbon. One man had been found guilty of the theft of 12 cucumber plants. All had been sentenced to a minimum of seven years convict labor and were being sent in exile to a land that had never been charted or colonized. None of the prisoners possessed the agricultural or laboring skills necessary for pioneering and survival in a harsh environment.

In the rush to solve their perceived problem, Lord Sydney and his advisers short-circuited the problem solving process. Little in the way of analysis of data or hypothesis testing was done. There was also no apparent concern as to how the prisoners would fare in a barren, alien space. For Lord Sydney, the problem was resolved the moment the prisoners left England's shores. For the prisoners, the resolution of the problem was as yet unknown.

The flagship *Sirius* anchored in Botany Bay on the morning of January 20, 1788, after a voyage of 252 days. The colony was yet to begin, however. The land about Botany Bay proved to be barren and inhospitable, completely unsuitable for colonization. For a week or more the captain explored the coastline for a more favorable port. He found a far more suitable harbor to the north. Captain Cook had called it Port Jackson. Captain Phillip renamed it Sydney Cove. He redirected his ships, unloaded his prisoners, and it was there that the history of modern Australia began.

And what is the connection to 2088? Consider this scenario:

It is the year 2086. A world-wide depression causes mass unemployment in the United States of America. A massive drought, which began in 2078, and the swelling population, which has reached one billion, bring food and housing shortages. The rising crime rate has pushed the capacity of the prison system beyond safe limits. Last year 25,000 people died in a prison riot in the Coltah desert (formerly the Colorado-Utah border region). President Suzanne Martinez is being pressured to reduce the critical threat the prisoners pose to the general populace. Transportation of criminals into space is not new. Since 2027, those citizens convicted of serious violations against the state have been assigned to tours of convict duty in orbiting space stations and on U.S. Moon Base *Bush*. However, the cost is great and the present financial crisis makes it impossible to continue such efforts. One possibility exists: the colonization of the hostile and barren neighboring planet of Mars. President Martinez makes a decision and addresses the nation. A United States fleet of eleven space ships carrying 7,306 prisoners from American jails will leave Earth late in the year and arrive on the surface of Mars in the year 2087.

Ask students to be good detectives. Examine the ethical issues at hand in this hypothesized scenario. Ask them to explore the scientific possibilities suggested. What equipment would the prisoners require to survive on Mars, as we now know its environment to be? (The British government felt so pressed for time that no time was allowed for any initial exploration of Australia. The ships were sent in 1786 with no guarantee at all that those on board could survive in the land for which they set sail.) Do students foresee a time when our nation would ever need to result to such measures?

Source:

Hughes, Robert. *The Fatal Shore: The Epic of Australia's Founding* (New York: Alfred A. Knopf, 1987).

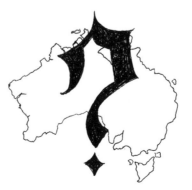

Tools of the Trade

Figure 5.3 is the office of a future sleuth who plies her trade in the ocean depths. The name of her detective agency is "Neptune's Daughter." In what future year did she create her business? Why is the office under the seas? In which ocean is it located? What types of cases does she handle? What tools does she need to successfully pursue cases?

Fig. 5.3. Office of future sleuth.

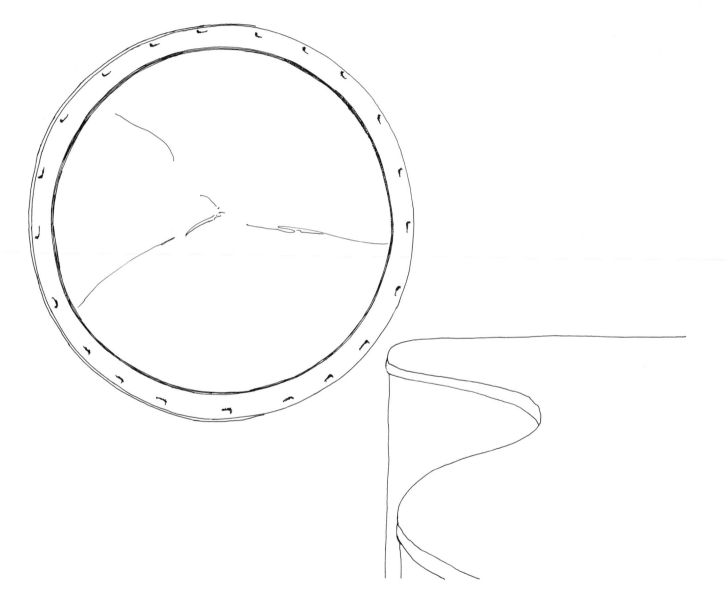

Mystery Desk

Figure 5.4 is an illustration of a desk which might be used by a very famous science fiction author. Ask students to examine the desk carefully in order to determine its owner. The illustration is filled with clues to the author's identity.

Fig. 5.4. Desk of science fiction author.

Traces

Figure 5.5 represents famous footprints. Though they are from the past, they are definitely associated with students' images of the future. Teachers and library media specialists may suggest to students that these footprints will probably become a featured part of the first United States National Park in space which the students may visit with their children on a future vacation. Just as people today follow the trail of Lewis and Clark across the western United States, in the future people will travel to a distant place to see these footprints.

Fig. 5.5.

Futures Activities

The future is, of course, one gigantic mystery. We can examine the past and observe the present, but tomorrow is unknown. Where are the clues, for example, a contemporary Sherlock Holmes could use to deduce what tomorrow will bring? Seem impossible? Well, actually it is not as difficult to predict the future as it might appear at first. Holmes does have modern-day counterparts who work just as diligently as the world's first consulting detective. Some work for the government while others are employed by private business "think tanks." Some write science fiction while still others work as Holmes did as free-lance investigators. They are called futurists and they seek to rationally and scientifically predict what will happen in the future. They seek to unravel mysteries which have not even occurred—they attempt to forecast the future. Their tools may include sophisticated computers and cross impact matrices. Their methods may include trend extrapolation and scenario writing. Like Holmes, their services are of great value.

For the national security and defense, the military must be able to predict accurately where and how the Soviets are deploying weapons, and where international terrorists are likely to strike next; businesses must be able to forecast with some accuracy the future appetites of consumers in order to have the right kinds and amounts of products in the market place; school systems must be able to anticipate the growth of their student populations in order to have enough teachers, classrooms and textbooks available to meet the demand for services. Sherlock Holmes never engaged in guesswork. He always read the facts accurately. But Holmes had only the past to read and the present to observe. Futurists also engage in as little guess work as possible. They seek to find out as much as possible by reading the past and present in order to predict the future.

The ideas in this chapter hopefully serve at least three functions:

1. To introduce students to some of the many concepts, tools, and methodologies utilized by futurists

2. To note the similarities between the work of futurists and detectives

3. To suggest future thinking about crime and mystery.

The 3 P's—The Tools of Futurist Detectives

Detectives who examine the future are called futurists. One of the ways they examine the future is through the utilization of three questions: What's possible? What's probable? What's preferable? Futurists often refer to these three questions as the 3 P's. Almost anything is possible in the future, but some things have a greater probability or likelihood of occurring than others. Not all things which have a strong likelihood of occurring are desirable. Increased pollution and crime in urban areas are strong probabilities, but they are not conditions many people will welcome. Conversely, there are many other circumstances the public may desire which are not highly probable. A free college education for all citizens is one example.

Ask students to think like futurists. Using a time frame of the next fifty years, which of the statements in figure 5.6 seem possible, probable, preferable? Keep in mind that virtually anything is possible. The reaction to the descriptors found in the first column would most likely be affirmative, unless students can defend the position that such a "possibility" is impossible. The most likely centers of discussions are the probabilities and preferabilities.

The use of this futures technique is especially useful to emphasize to students that they do have choices about the future. When students see futures which seem preferable, but also appear unlikely, they can explore ways to use problem solving skills and strategies to improve the likelihood of positive future results. Conversely, students can explore ways to halt a negative trend which appears to be gaining momentum.

Fig. 5.6.

Possible	**Probable**	**Preferable**
Crimes committed against the environment (e.g., pollution) will be considered capital offenses.	_____	_____
Laws will be authored to provide immunity from prosecution for citizens whose clones, unknown to them, commit crimes.	_____	_____
Human beings will be held legally accountable for crimes as well as civil damage committed by their robots.	_____	_____
Scientists will isolate the chromosome responsible for criminal behavior and will be able to employ genetic engineering to alter genes to insure no individual is born predisposed to crime.	_____	_____
Cryogenics will be used by police to solve mysteries and prosecute known criminal parties. Crime victims who are critically injured to the degree that they cannot supply testimony or testify on their own behalf in a trial of their assailants will be cryogenically "frozen" until such time as medical science develops the means to successfully repair their injuries.	_____	_____
Robots will replace the sidekicks/partners (e.g., Dr. Watson) fictional detectives of the future will have.	_____	_____
Machines called "Thought-detectors" will replace lie-detectors in police work, allowing the police to "read" the thoughts in the minds of criminal suspects.	_____	_____

Based on the research, mystery and science fiction reading students have done, other future possibilities will be suggested. The likelihood and desirability of each item will provoke exciting research and excellent debates. Students should be required to couple reasoning skills with documentation they uncover to support their various contentions.

Trending

Trending is another tool utilized by future-thinking detectives. Futurists look at past trends and analyze current ones in order to make predictions about where a trend may be going or to anticipate future trends. What is a trend? It is any evident phenomenon which appears to be prevailing over a period of time. Trends can be short or long. Fashion trends can be ridiculously short-lived, while a natural trend such as the gradual cooling of a geographic region could occur over thousands of years. Detectives of the future are especially concerned with trends because they try to *extrapolate* from trends in order to make predictions of future events and conditions. For example, criminologists may study the current rise in computer crime in order to predict future needs in law enforcement personnel and training. If computer crime is rising rapidly at, say, a rate of 2.3 percent a year in terms of the total number of crimes committed, then law enforcement officials will want to hire and train more personnel or make other appropriate adjustments in order to combat the projected rise over time in computer crime.

Trending is very definitely related to another tool utilized by futurists, the Cross-Impact Matrix. Like the 3 P's, this tool is not intended to bring about a finite or absolute answer. Rather, it is utilized as a means of examining possible and probable interaction effects among and between variables that might escape attention without the use of such a tool. Three to five variables are listed. Each is written, in order, on the vertical and horizontal axis of a grid. Each variable is analyzed first in terms of the probability or likelihood of positive and negative effects or trends. For example, what trends can one observe in contemporary American society with regard to cultural pluralism? We are one nation made up of many races and ethnic groups. Minority groups seek harmony with the oneness of America without giving up their distinct cultural, racial, or ethnic identity. In some areas this creates conflict within the majority culture and between separate minority groups.

After all variables are independently examined, they are examined in terms of the impact they are likely to have on all the *other* variables, again, both positively and negatively. For example, in the example provided in figure 5.7, note that changing society value systems might be judged to have little or no probable impact on computer crime, but a drastic rise in computer crime with its accompanying damage and threat to society, could very definitely alter societal values about computer crime and criminals. Actions which are today treated by society as "adolescent pranks" and "white collar" crime, might be considered particularly heinous crimes in the future.

Instruct students to combine the tools of Trending and the Cross-Impact Matrix using the matrix in figure 5.7. First, ask students to consider each of the variables separately. What possible and probable trends do they foresee in terms of each variable and its impact, preferable or not, on crime and punishment? For example, regarding the variable of value systems, students should note that society's values are continually changing. A century ago public hangings were common and starving children were sent to prison for "criminal" offenses such as stealing a loaf of bread. Today, we view such behavior as barbaric. In the 1960s American society was generally more tolerant of "deviant" behavior than it is today. Now, a more conservative trend pervades society; people are generally demanding tougher sentences for law breakers. Concern for the criminal's rights has been replaced with greater concern for the rights of the victims of crime. (It should be noted, however, that this trend is in conflict with another trend or condition: overcrowded jails and prisons.) What values and attitudes are likely to characterize American society in the future?

Fig. 5.7.

Cross-Impact Matrix

Cross-Impact Matrix

	Changing Societal Values	Increasing Tech. Change	Growth of Cultural Pluralism	Changing Family Roles	Aging of American Population
Changing Societal Values	X				
Increasing Technological Change		X			
Growth of Cultural Pluralism			X		
Changing Family Roles/ Dynamics				X	
The Aging of the American Population					X

Each of the variables should be similarly discussed and recognized trends analyzed. Then, the discussion should move to an examination of possible interactions. What impact will hypothesized changes in American values and attitudes have upon technological change or upon our culturally diverse population? In turn, what effect will hypothesized changes and developments in each of these variables have upon societal values? Examine all possible interactions.

Teachers and library media specialists should recognize that the resultant discussions and hypotheses may serve as catalysts to ignite gifted students' interest in sophisticated research topics and strategies.

Other topics and variables to consider might include the growth of international terrorism, changes in first amendment rights, increasing conservatism of the Supreme Court, and crimes involving the environment and habitat of Earth.

For a particularly good discussion of the Cross-Impact Matrix, see Draper L. Kauffman, Jr.'s *Teaching the Future.*[1]

Futures Wheel

Like Sherlock Holmes, futurists try not to miss any detail or effect in a situation which might possibly have impact on future events. One tool that helps them accomplish this is the Futures Wheel. A Futures Wheel is like the mystery web created in the "Language Arts" chapter of this book. A central event, topic, theme, issue, or trend is noted. It is written in the hub or center of a wheel. All direct or immediate consequences of the central issue or event are listed on "spokes" or cells extending from  the hub. In turn, all conceivable indirect and secondary consequences are next considered. If ... then reasoning, central to critical thinking, is employed. Consideration and listing of all possible and probable events is continued until the futurist is satisfied all reasonable scenarios have been considered. An example of a Futures Wheel is displayed in figure 5.8. Students complete the Futures Wheel by considering all the possible ramifications of the proposal to begin creating penal colonies in space. Figure 5.9 is a blank futures wheel that may be used with the following suggested exercise.

The following list of issues and possible events can be used to generate Futures Wheels. Students should see that this handy tool is extremely helpful in considering future courses of action. Actions and reactions can be anticipated and the wise user can project the future rather than being shocked by it.

Consider these "events":

Soviets break U.S. computer protection codes and access all U.S. defense plans.

A modern-day Professor Moriarty forms a gang made up of some of the most exceptional minds and talents working in the computer and artificial intelligence fields today.

The tools for mercy killing and euthanasia become more readily accessible to the general public as new drugs are discovered and made available.

Medical scientists uncover a way to immobilize the area of the brain which predisposes an individual to commit crimes.

The proportion of elderly people and the percent of crime committed by elderly citizens increases significantly.

People convicted of capital crimes and sentenced to die are offered an alternative: transport to a penal space colony.

Personal privacy becomes increasingly difficult to maintain due to the combined effects of widespread use of computers for information storage and unauthorized entries into computers.

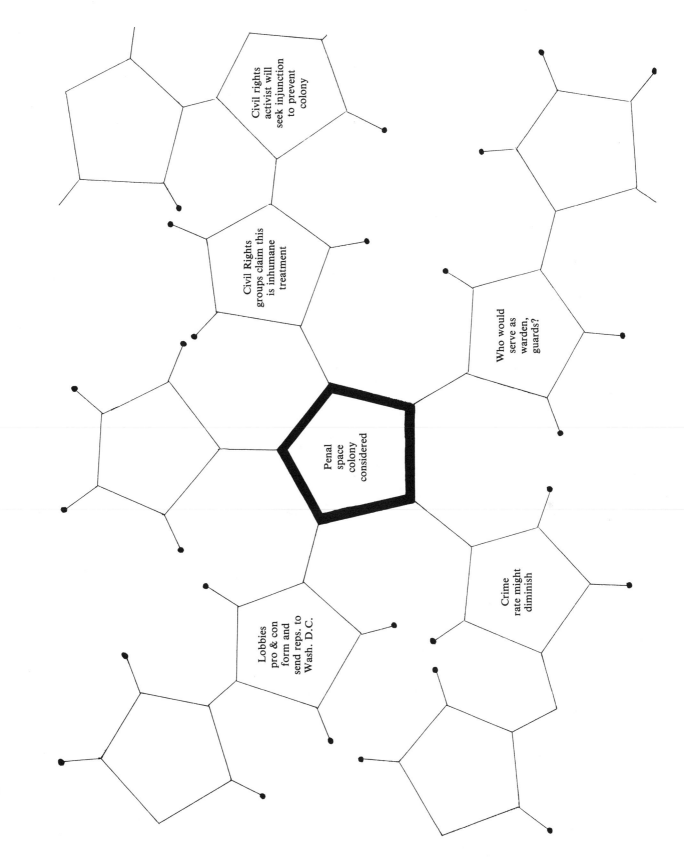

Fig. 5.8.

Civil rights activist will seek injunction to prevent colony

Civil Rights groups claim this is inhumane treatment

Who would serve as warden, guards?

Penal space colony considered

Lobbies pro & con form and send reps. to Wash. D.C.

Crime rate might diminish

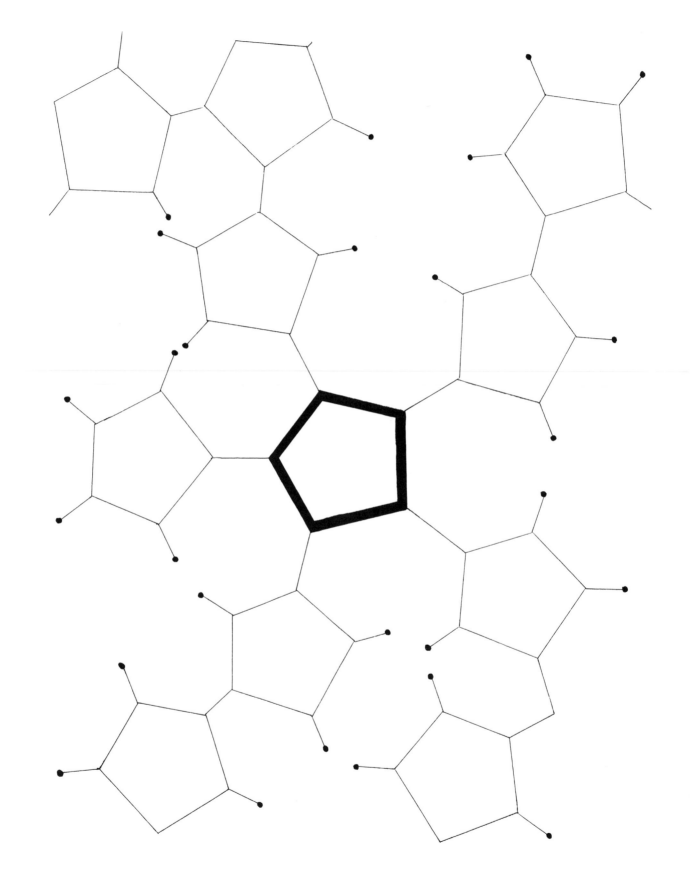

Fig. 5.9.

Computer Crime

THE COMPUTER DIDN'T DO IT.
— IBM advertisement

In 1981, IBM ran an advertisement in a number of newspapers and magazines graphically showing a computer mixed in with a number of humans in a police lineup. The accompanying caption is reprinted above. The point made is salient. When one thinks of mysteries and the future, one of the first phrases which comes to mind is "computer crime." But computers do not commit crimes any more than guns do. *People* (criminals) use computers to commit crimes just as *people* (forensic specialists) use computers to solve crimes. These two conditions offer fascinating areas of interest for bright and inquisitive students to investigate regarding the use of computers, mysteries, and crimes in the future.

One of the avenues used in computer crime is a procedure called a Trojan Horse Attack. Instructions originally programmed into a computer are modified or new instructions are added by a computer criminal. Both procedures alter the final output. Because of the complex structure of computer programs a Trojan Horse is not always easily spotted, especially when the victimized parties involved are not looking for errors or criminal computer invasions. In one real case a computer programmer working as a subcontractor for a money order firm committed a Trojan Horse Attack by writing secret commands into the company's massive program for issuing and recording payments. Put simply, he instructed the program to make payments to him, but to show no record of such payments. Because he was in a position of trust, the "attack" in this case was not discovered until after the man had embezzled over $100,000.

The entire area of crime related to computers or use of computers is now and will likely continue to be a dramatic area of interest. Estimates of monetary losses from computer-related crimes run into the billions of dollars annually. Not only is society faced with new kinds of crimes due to the criminal use of computer technology, but psychologists and law enforcement officials state that there are new kinds of criminals on the scene. Youths who would never think of stealing hubcaps off of cars, let alone cars, often do not hesitate to pirate software. Adults who would never think of committing armed robbery at their local convenience store at 2 a.m., may be up at the same time of night stealing information from a university or company computer program they have illegally entered.

A second area of great fascination is the current and probable future use of computer technology by law enforcement and government agencies concerned with our national defense. For example, computers can scan fingerprints far more efficiently and rapidly than human beings can. In some cities data such as crime frequencies and police-assistance requests are fed into computers which then draw the areas police need to patrol in order to be most effective. Computers are also utilized in the forensic side of police work assisting in the analysis of evidence. In prisons, computers are used to keep track of parole and release dates.

In March 1989 international headlines broke the story of an unlikely modern day Sherlock Holmes, Clifford Stoll. Stoll is an astronomer by profession who became a computer security expert and national hero by accident. Working at the Lawrence Berkeley Laboratory in Berkeley, California Stoll discovered an unauthorized user on his system. Stoll spent the next year stalking the intruder. He was tracking a criminal that had baffled both the CIA and FBI. Stoll set a trap that snared a spy ring in West Germany with an operative in Pittsburg which sold stolen computer secrets to the KGB in the Soviet Union. Stoll's account of his real-life adventure that would seem incredible as a science fiction plot is found in the autobiographical *The Cuckoo's Egg: Tracing a Spy through the Maze of Computer Espionage.*

So rapid has been the onset of computer technology in the perpetrating and solving of mysteries that most citizens—including some of the criminal element—are shocked to learn that much of what they thought was future technology or science fiction actually exists today.

What are the so-called computer crimes and criminals and how are others using computers to stop crime? Invite a computer specialist to the classroom to talk about crimes committed with the help of computers. Ask the specialist to talk about ethics as well as crimes and laws. Another excellent guest would be a speaker from the state or local police department who might talk about the use of computers in all phases of police detective work. Youth who may never have previously considered career work in police science may find an exciting, challenging field to enter. Students should locate and examine through their research statements of ethics and current state and national laws regarding the use of computers. There are many bright and talented young people who know only the technological aspects of computers and do not realize that some usage of computers may be illegal.

Some of the key words students may investigate include:

hackers	hardware theft, sabotage, and piracy	software piracy
Trojan Horses	trapdoors or backdoors	technological trespassers
electronic embezzlement	computer fraud	computer espionage
information theft	electronic viruses	copy protection

There are many excellent books on computer crime. For younger readers Robert L. Sperry's *Computer Crime* is part of Franklin Watts Computer Awareness First Book Series. Older readers will find Donn B. Parker's *Fighting Computer Crime* very thorough and informative. Parker's text contains especially fascinating case studies about "whiz kids" and hackers. J. Van Duyn's *The Human Factor in Computer Crime* also offers case studies of computer misuse.

Student projects may take the form of debates about the ethics of computer use by amateurs and professionals engaged in security and detection. Inventive students can consider ways to build security systems into computers so they cannot be misused. Others may compare police procedures in detection in the past and present and project future methods for a given type of crime such as burglary. Science fiction/mystery stories certainly remain an option. A creative student may want to write a story about a contemporary or future Sherlock Holmes whose forte is electronic detection.

Figure 5.10 is a futures simulation which asks students to think about the future and some of the decisions they might have to make then. For ease of use in the classroom, the directions are written directly to the students.

Fig. 5.10. Futures simulation.

The *Mayflower III*, circa 2090:
A Matter of Survival

Picture yourself in the role of a "futures sleuth" working for NASA. It is the year 2090. The United Nations Earth Settlement Act of 2021 balanced the distribution of population and the distribution of resources on the planet Earth to protect humans, animals and natural resources from the twin disasters of overpopulation and depletion of natural resources. Due to an unforeseen and unexplained natural disturbance in the atmosphere, 10,000 citizens must be moved from the upper pennisula of Michigan to somewhere off planet. Resettlement must occur within fourteen days.

These are the facts in this mystery:

1. The present disaster could not be foreseen.

2. The rapid movement of 10,000 people into any part of Earth would create a serious imbalance threatening the welfare of all living things.

3. Transportation means exist to move 10,000 people to another place in space.

4. During the last century, massive data about space, gathered by both human and mechanical exploration of space, has been placed in the super computer "Opus."

5. "Opus" can suggest 100 different possible locales in space for resettlement of the 10,000 citizens if the correct questions are asked.

Your task is to determine the questions that must be asked if the computer is to select the best locale for relocation of the settlers. What are the first ten questions you must ask?

1.

2.

3.

4.

5.

6.

7.

8.

9.

10.

* * * * *

Based on the questions asked and answered, decisions have been made, a destination site chosen, and the long journey into space has begun for you and the other modern pilgrims.

On board the *Mayflower III* you have the materials and resources to establish a new life in space. You have the following life-support items:

construction materials to create living quarters

food supplies and food growing plants and cultures

air and water supplies, plus filtration, purification, and recycling tools

heating and cooling devices

solar power resources

communications facilities to maintain contact with Earth

When the original Pilgrims were en route to the new land of America in 1620 to found Plymouth Colony, they took time during their voyage to set forth the laws governing their behavior in the new world. That document is the Mayflower Compact. Your new colony will also need a constitution or set of laws for governance. What behaviors will be considered intolerable and/or a threat to the survival of the colony and therefore illegal? What rights will people have? Take time now, on your long journey, to consider your future lives in a remote, isolated, and primitive settlement. Write a new Mayflower Compact. Write the constitution and laws which will be the basis for government, law and order in your new homeland.

* * * * *

You have arrived in your new homeland. Shelters are constructed, water, air and temperature control systems are set up and running successfully. Food production is beginning. Food production is a hopeful sign for the future because the food supplies brought aboard *Mayflower III* are significantly diminished. Indeed, they appear to be the source of the first major problem your colony must face and solve. The captain of the food stores has reported that food supplies are lower than they should be. There is evidence that some person (or persons) must be stealing and hoarding food. Now you have a potentially life-threatening mystery to solve.

Who is stealing the food? How is the theft occurring? How does the colony's sleuth catch the thief? Does the thief admit guilt, or is a trial needed? How is the thief punished? Imagine that you are the historian for the pilgrims of *Mayflower III*. Write a story recounting for future generations the events and people involved in the colony's first crime.

*   *   *   *   *

Time passes and the colony grows rapidly, first doubling, then tripling, and now quadrupling in size to more than 40,000 inhabitants. Life in the colony has become more sophisticated, complex and impersonal. As the sense of community lessens, criminal activity becomes more of a threat to your colony. You have a newly created position. You are the chief inspector for security for the colony. Describe your job. What kinds of crimes occur? What tools do you need to do your job? What does your office or laboratory look like? What has been your most frustrating case so far? How did you solve it? Back on Earth there is great interest in your colony. As chief inspector, you have been requested to author an article for a law journal published in the United States of America. They have asked you to use this title: "A Day in the Life and Crime of the *Mayflower III* Pilgrims." Write your article and fax it back to Earth.

*   *   *   *   *

Still more years have passed. You are near the end of your life, but you are not sad. After all, you have had a full and active 150 years. You spent many of those years as the chief inspector of the detective branch of security forces in a colony deep in space. Now, you have returned to Earth, your birthplace, to retire and write your memoirs. Survey the many years of being a sleuth in outer space. What was your most puzzling case? What was the most dangerous assignment? Who was the most villainous or deceptive foe you faced? Begin your memoirs by writing about your most interesting case.

Are We Alone?

Are we alone? No other question arouses as much fascination. Is there life elsewhere in the universe? If so, are "they" interested in us? Millions of people appear to believe both these questions can be answered affirmatively. In the 1930s, Orson Welles's Mercury Theatre caused a national sensation when H. G. Wells's "War of the Worlds" was broadcast on Halloween night. Despite prior announcements that the program was only fiction, large numbers of citizens believed Martians had invaded New Jersey. In the 1950s, Unidentified Flying Object (UFO) sightings were so frequent they almost became the norm. In the 1970s and 1980s, Steven Spielberg produced two of the most popular motion pictures of all time by tapping modern mythology with the production of *Close Encounters of the Third Kind* and *E.T.: The Extraterrestrial*.

How would Sherlock Holmes approach the mystery presented by reported sightings of UFO's and encounters with alien beings? Ask students to approach the enigmas of UFO's and extraterrestrials with Holmesian skepticism. What evidence exists to support the notion of UFO's? What are the facts? Which reported sightings have been hoaxes? Which sightings turned out to be marsh gasses or weather balloons? Is there any support for theories that governments have suppressed information about some sightings or investigations? Ask students to be good critical thinkers. Instruct them to establish rigorous standards for examining various theories, explanations and some of the so-called evidence offered as support. Require students to examine some of the psychological and sociological explanations of popular beliefs in such enigmas.

Possible results of investigations into the riddles of UFO's and extraterrestrials might take the form of classroom debates, a UFO Quiz, a research paper, an article for the school or local newspaper, or a slide-tape presentation for audiences which might include science classes, patients in a nursing home, or a current issues seminar.

Robots as Criminals

Isaac Asimov formulated the three laws of robotics as far back as 1941 in his science fiction story "Reason." They became especially well known after the publication of his 1950 novel *I, Robot*.[2] In Asimov's science fiction world robots cannot harm humans or disobey their commands. It is not a matter of ethics or values. They simply cannot do so because their programs forbid such actions. Ask students to imagine, however, what might result if a real-life modern-day Professor Moriarty used his great technological know-how to program robots for criminal activity. What might the results be? This is not mere science fiction conjecture. One currently marketed sentinel robot is outfitted with life-threatening equipment, but it cannot be sold in the United States when so equipped. It is, however, marketed and sold outside the United States.

Ask students to locate Asimov's three laws of robotics and share them with the class. Challenge students to investigate the many moral issues involved with real-life robotics. If current robots can be equipped with life-threatening devices, can the programming of robots to harm human beings, rob banks, museums, or stores be far behind? How might such crimes be prevented? Is there a need to require people who build robots to sign ethics and security oaths and undergo security checks? Ask students to also consider the potential impact advanced prosthetic devices may have on both criminal activity and law enforcement work in the future (discuss characters with these devices in "Six-Million Dollar Man," and *Robocop*). Students can utilize the information derived from their investigations and discussions to write science fiction/mystery stories, or perhaps propose ways that robots can be utilized in the future as crime fighters.

Mystery Catalogs Circa 2090

Share Dilys Winn's catalogs of mystery, *Murder Ink* and *Murderess Ink*, with students. Brainstorm all the things that readers might expect to find in catalogs about mysteries. Then project what might be included in a mystery catalog created for the year 2090. Questions to stimulate student thinking might include these:

What tools do detectives use today? How might they evolve and change in the next century?

Hard-boiled private eyes once represented sleuths. What traits may characterize sleuths in the 21st century?

International terrorism and computer crimes are two areas of police detective work that concern contemporary detectives that did not exist a century ago. What new forms of crimes may be of great interest to police a century from now?

If the Hardy Boys and Nancy Drew Series enjoy continued popularity into the next century, what are some of the plots likely to involve?

Literature Studies

When people think of mystery literature in the future tense, they immediately begin to mix the science fiction and mystery genres. One of the common themes of science fiction is concern for the preservation of rights, justice, and law and order. Criminals exist, but they do not triumph. Morality is as much as aspect of science fiction as it is in detective fiction.

There are many reading resources available. The novels of the distinguished author of the letter for this chapter, John E. Stith, is one of those resources. In *Scapescope*, for example, set in the 2150s, a tool called the scapescope allows law enforcement personnel to see into the future, or more precisely *futures*, to identify and observe criminals. The protagonist, Mike Cavantalo, looks into the future and finds himself projected to be a political criminal on the run. It makes no sense. He is not a criminal. Has someone rigged the scapescope? Can he prevent the future from happening?

Isaac Asimov teamed with Harry Greenberg and Charles G. Waugh to edit *Sherlock Holmes through Time and Space*, a collection of fifteen Sherlockian tales set in the future. The editors selected only those stories that best portrayed the spirit and quality of Holmes. Most are set far in the future.

Time travel is one of the favorite themes of science fiction. But one of the inviolate rules of science fiction is that the past must be left alone, for to alter the past would create unimagined havoc in the present and future.

Everything might be different in the present, if only one thing had been different in the past.
—Ashleigh Brilliant

This theme is given powerful explication in Ray Bradbury's short story "A Sound of Thunder." In Bradbury's story a hunter utilizes the services of Time Safari, Inc. to travel back in time 60 million years and go on a safari in search of a *Tyrannosaurus rex*. Altering the environment could have catastrophic implications on the future, so hunters must stay on a specially constructed path. Bradbury dramatically reveals what could happen should humans ever develop the ability to travel backwards in time.[3]

Engage students in reading some of these suggested titles and discuss the similarities and differences between the science fiction and mystery genres, as well as crossovers. Ask students to generate ideas for possible science fiction/mysteries. A few idea starters might include the following:

Explore the theme Bradbury uses in "The Sound of Thunder." A political figure hates his chief adversary. Can he go back in time and destroy the adversary's grandfather in order to "erase" his enemy? Can a detective prevent his intended action?

Murder is planned to occur at the 2028 Olympics. How does a great sleuth learn of the plot? How does she prevent the catastrophe?

Consider this scenario: Holmes did not die. In the early years of the twentieth century, Sherlock Holmes submitted himself to cryogenic science. His skills are needed in the year 2015. Why? What is the case? Who chronicles the case if Watson is no longer at his side? Or, does Watson submit himself to the same process?

Scenarios of the Future

Futurists who work in business, industry, government and education use scenarios to help their colleagues and others glimpse what the future may hold. In a sense, scenarios provide concrete examples which make abstract notions of the future comprehensible. They are future focused, but less concerned with matters of plot and characterization than science fiction stories. A point in the future is selected by the writer. This point of reference is described using the present tense. Although most events have not yet occurred in real time, the writer refers to all preceding events in the past tense.

The following scenario (figure 5.11) was written by Scott Davis, a student at Palmer High School in Colorado Springs, Colorado.[4] It is a good example of student scenario writing. It is particularly appropriate in a unit about mysteries because the narrator assumes a tough guy, Sam Spade, posture. His hero, typical of the classic American cynical private eye, must not only battle lady luck but also deal with bureaucratic feds.

Share "The Indestructible Man" with students and discuss what they find appealing (or appalling) about the scenario. What kind of an image of the future is projected? Next, ask students to write their own scenarios detailing some aspect of life in the future. How will crime be fought? Can they describe a typical day in the life of an FBI officer in the year 2030, or a day in the life of a secret service officer protecting the first woman president of the U.S.?

Student examples of scenario writing from around the globe may be found in *Save Tomorrow for the Children* by E. Paul Torrance. Gerard K. O'Neill also provides scenarios with positive future images in *2081: A Hopeful View of the Human Future*.

Fig. 5.11. A scenario.

"The Indestructible Man"
by Scott Davis

Let me tell you something before I start. Back in the 1980s when everyone was toying with the idea of the almighty superconductor, there was a rather large crater made in Arizona when the Big Boys started up their new nuke plant. It blew up a large portion of the southwest and somehow managed to contaminate the super-conductor lab. The end result was the megaconductor. This little gadget somehow managed to put out twice as much power as was put in. So now the world is run by little electronic circuits and five gallons of oil a year.

One of the Big Boys thought it would be neat if a man could be powered up with a megaconductor thereby eliminating the need for food. When the Big Boys figured out what their new toy might do, they started seeing what they could do with it. This is where I came in.

When they first contacted me, I was twenty-three. I was sitting home watching the 2037 World Series when this Suit walks right into my apartment. He points his gun on me and asks nice and polite if I would please come with him. So I tell this guy where he could put his gun because I wasn't going anywhere and besides, the Denver Dodgers were up by two. So then he says he'd make it worth my while by letting me keep the legs I was born with. I got up and followed him to his car.

He drove me to meet some doctor while explaining that I was going to become one of the country's bravest heroes. I told him that a hero was just a sandwich and asked if the car had a radio so I could follow the game.

When we got where he was taking me, some men offered me a drink while I waited. I gulped it before I could taste what they had put in it. When I woke up they had done what they wanted to do, and I never had any say about it.

What they did to me was this. Previously mentioned Big Boy got some other Big Boys to believe his crackpot idea about putting a megaconductor into a man. He said it could solve the world's hunger problems. So the gold ol' U.S. of A. chose me to see if this was true.

Then the geniuses decided that they would load me with enough raw power to supply me for the rest of my natural life, times two. Somebody somewhere decided that it would make me live twice as long. Wrongo! What it did do is make me impervious to injury.

When the Big Boys found that out, I was subjected to every possible way to kill a man they could think of. When none of the traditional ways worked, they shipped me out to one of their little comm satellites with a pressure suit and nuked me. The pressure suit melted away and I fell to Earth. I made a good sized crater in some small town in Kansas.

I decided that after that fall I was a little tired of all the Big Boy's guff about one of America's greatest heroes. I was indestructible by human standards, but that doesn't mean that all they did to me didn't hurt. So I decided that I was going to take a trip to Washington and tell them all about my gripes. I hitched a ride outside of the now demolished town and headed east.

Now I'm laying in a hospital telling this tale to a machine that is powered by nothing less than a small megaconductor. These things are only allowed in machines now, after the Big Boys found out what a human could do with one inside them. I have to admit that they really are good. No, that's wrong. A thing is only good or bad depending on how it is used. The megaconductor is a tool to be used by mankind and it is only good if it is used for good purposes. Nothing is truly good if used the wrong way.

When I made the government realize that megaconductors weren't meant for humans, they left me alone for a while to let me try to get my life back together. That little gadget inside me did help sometimes because I had some pretty lean times when I got back home. After all, I had very little money when the government first contacted me, and I had no money after I got back. I found a job as a diver for an ocean-going salvage team.

Shortly after I got my first job, Congress passed a law limiting megaconductors to mechanical uses only. My secret was kept from public knowledge until my accident with a decompressing mini-sub. When my team got be back to the surface, I had experienced more pressure than any other man had ever experienced before. Anyway, the press was notified and everyone found out. It's not too bad though. The doctors say I don't have long to live and I'm kind of looking forward to seeing what death is like.

The world is now, like I said earlier, powered by electricity supplied by five major megaconductors. Just last year, all the countries in the Middle East got together and signed a treaty because they suddenly realized that their on-going war was pointless now that oil isn't used for much anymore. The price of oil is now a mere ten cents a barrel. It's going to be hard times for a while, but I think they'll make it.

Oh yeah, one last thing. The first mission to the moons of Jupiter left last week. Maybe if I make it through this death thing I'll head out there. Maybe not. See ya.

Notes

[1]Draper Kauffman, Jr., *Teaching the Future* (Palm Springs, Calif.: ETC Publications, 1976), 177-204.

[2]Isaac Asimov, "Reason," in Eric S. Rabkin, ed., *Science Fiction: A Historical Anthology* (New York: Oxford University Press, 1983), 318-338. See also Isaac Asimov, *I, Robot* (New York: Fawcett Crest, 1950), 7. For an especially interesting first-person account of how Asimov evolved the laws of robotics, see the "Introduction" to Isaac Asimov's *Caves of Steel* (New York: Ballantine, 1983), vii-xvi.

[3]Ray Bradbury, "A Sound of Thunder," in Sylvia Z. Brodkin and Elizabeth J. Pearson, *Science Fiction* (Evanston, Ill.: McDougal, Littel, 1973), 47-58.

[4]The author wishes to acknowledge and thank Scott Davis for the use of his story.

Teacher Resources

Asimov, Isaac, Henry Greenberg, and Charles G. Waugh. *Sherlock Holmes through Time and Space*. New York: Bluejay Books, 1984.

Flack, Jerry D. *Hey! It's My Future*. O'Fallon, Mo.: Book Lures, 1986.
Future studies strategies plus recommended science fiction.

Kauffman, Draper, Jr. *Teaching the Future*. Palm Springs, Calif.: ETC Publications, 1976.
Easily one of the definitive books about future studies.

Nicholls, Peter. *The Science in Science Fiction*. New York: Alfred A. Knopf, 1983.
Nicholls work is must reading for gifted students who take their science and science fiction seriously.

O'Neill, Gerard K. *2081: A Hopeful View of the Human Future*. New York: Simon & Schuster, 1981.
A positive and illuminating look at the future by a noted physicist.

Parker, Donn B. *Fighting Computer Crime*. New York: Charles Scribner's Sons, 1983.
Excellent discussions, explanations, and case studies.

Perry, Robert L. *Computer Crime*. New York: Franklin Watts, 1986.
Perry writes for younger readers about many topics related to the title subject.

Rabkin, Eric S., Ed. *Science Fiction: A History Anthology*. New York: Oxford University Press, 1983.
This anthology looks at the evolution of science fiction.

Stoll, Clifford. *The Cuckoo's Egg: Tracking a Spy through the Maze of Computer Espionage*. New York: Doubleday, 1989.

Torrance, E. Paul, Deborah Weiner, Jack H. Presbury, and Morgan Henderson. *Save Tomorrow for the Children*. Buffalo, N.Y.: Bearly Limited, 1987.
Scenarios written by gifted students around the world.

Van Duyn, J. *The Human Factor in Computer Crime*. Princeton, N.J.: Petrocelli Books, 1985.
Excellent information and case studies of computer crimes.

Winn, Dilys. *Murder Ink: The Mystery Reader's Companion*. New York: Workman Publishing, 1977.
This volume is sort of the Sears, Roebuck catalog of mysteries. Just about everything anyone would want to know about famous mystery writers, their sleuths, and their stories may be found within the covers of this book.

_____. *Murderess Ink: The Better Half of the Mystery*. New York: Workman Publishing, 1979.
Winn more than makes up for any oversight of the feminine side of crime and detection in his first volume by creating this second volume exclusively devoted to notable women.

Mystery Reading List for Future Studies

Asimov, Isaac. *Caves of Steel*. New York: Ballantine, 1983.

Readers meet Lije Baley, a plainclothes cop who is forced to solve a case with a new partner—a robot named R. Daneel Olivaw. The adventures continue in two more books, *The Naked Sun* (Ballantine, 1983) and *The Robots of Dawn* (Ballantine, 1984). Students should not miss the introduction to *Caves* in which Asimov tells how he came to write this trilogy and evolve the laws of robotics.

Asimov, Isaac, Martin Harry Greenberg, and Charles G. Waugh. *Sherlock Holmes through Time and Space*. New York: Bluejay Books, 1984.

Mystery and science fiction meet and the spirit of Holmes is celebrated in the fifteen stories found in this anthology.

Dvorkin, David. *Time for Sherlock Holmes*. New York: Dodd, Mead, 1983.

Sherlock Holmes must go into the future to combat the evil Moriarty who has stolen H. G. Wells' time machine.

Packard, Edward. *America: Why Is There an Eye on the Pyramid on the One-dollar Bill?* New York: McGraw Hill, 1988.

The creator of the *Choose Your Own Adventure*® series is back with a new series called *Earth Inspectors*™ Creatures from the planet Turoc come to Earth to learn about its history and customs. Other books in the series include *Where Do Elephants Live Underground?* (McGraw-Hill, 1989) and *Russia: What Is the Golden Horde?* (McGraw-Hill, 1990).

Stith, John E. *Scapescope*. New York: Ace Science Fiction Books, 1984.

Mystery, detection, and the future are woven into an exciting, well-written novel. See also *Death Tolls* (Ace SF Books, 1987), *Deep Quarry* (Ace SF Books, 1989), and *Memory Blank* (Ace SF Books, 1986) by John E. Stith. Students may well want to read the fiction of the author who addresses them in the letter at the outset of this chapter.

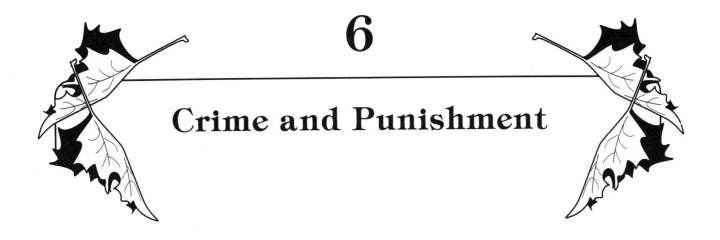

6

Crime and Punishment

Meet an Attorney

Douglas Erickson is an attorney who practices law with the firm of Winston & Strawn which has offices in Chicago; Washington, D.C.; Irvine, California; and Phoenix. Attorney Erickson works out of the Phoenix office. He is a graduate of the University of Michigan and the Arizona State University Law School. He is the author of "Undermining the Arizona Constitution: Recent Developments in Dramshop Law" which appeared in the *Arizona State Law Journal*.

A Letter from a Professional

Fig. 6.1. A letter from an attorney.

WINSTON & STRAWN

FREDERICK H. WINSTON (1853-1886)   SILAS H. STRAWN (1891-1946)

ORANGE COUNTY OFFICE
19000 MacARTHUR BOULEVARD
SUITE 620
IRVINE, CALIFORNIA 92715
714·955·2720
TELECOPIER 714·955·2507

PLEASE REPLY TO
PHOENIX OFFICE

WRITER'S DIRECT NUMBER

2300 GREAT AMERICAN TOWER
3200 NORTH CENTRAL AVENUE
PHOENIX, ARIZONA 85012
602·279·8500
TELECOPIER 602·263·8185

February 10, 1989

CHICAGO OFFICE
ONE FIRST NATIONAL PLAZA
CHICAGO, ILLINOIS 60603
312·558·5600
—
WASHINGTON, D.C. OFFICE
2550 M STREET, N.W.
WASHINGTON, D.C. 20037
202·828·8400

Dear Students:

The practice of law involves many types of work, from putting together business transactions to representing professional athletes in contract negotiations to litigating cases. In many ways, the job of a trial lawyer, also known as a litigator, is the final step in unraveling a mystery—proving what actually happened. Police officers, investigators, and to some extent, lawyers may spend months attempting to piece together evidence and figure out how a particular event or crime happened. Then the task becomes proving it.

One of the most important areas of trial practice involves the criminal law. Lawyers who practice criminal law are either prosecutors or defense attorneys. In a criminal trial, it is the prosecutor who must present evidence and prove that the defendant committed an act in violation of the law. The prosecutor must prove his case beyond a reasonable doubt.

Perhaps the most critical phase of the entire trial process occurs before the lawyers even enter the courtroom. Preparation is the key to proving a case. A frequently arising type of case in Arizona courtrooms involves people charged with driving under the influence of alcohol (DUI). Once a person has been arrested for DUI, the prosecuting attorney gets involved quickly. The first step is evaluating the evidence put together by the police department. The prosecutor reads the police report, and may also view a video tape of the arrestee, which was taken at the time of arrest, and check his or her blood alcohol level as measured by a breathalyzer. If the evidence is strong, the prosecutor files charges against the arrestee, who then appears before a judge (in serious cases, some states require a grand jury to charge the arrestee). If the judge finds that there is sufficient evidence to believe the arrestee has violated the law and if the arrestee pleads not guilty, a date for trial is set. Once formally charged, the arrestee is referred to as a defendant.

During the time between the "arraignment" and trial, both the prosecutor and the defendant's attorney prepare their cases. Both attorneys may question witnesses, search for evidence or send investigators to find evidence, and research legal issues that may arise. This part of the process is called "discovery." Either lawyer may take depositions to develop his or her case. A deposition is a formal interview of a witness that is given under oath, in the presence of both attorneys and a court reporter. The purpose of deposing witnesses is two-fold. First, to find out what happened and what the witness knows. Second, to try to prevent the witness from changing his or her story when testifying at trial. When the lawyers believe they know all the facts, they outline their cases. Before the trial starts, either lawyer may ask the court to limit or prevent the other side from presenting evidence which is questionable or inappropriate pursuant to rules of law. Once such procedural matters are finished, the case is ready to be tried.

By the time they get to trial, both sides have a good idea of what evidence will be presented, how witnesses will testify, and which evidence the lawyers can use to refute what the other side attempts to prove. Their jobs are far from over, but once discovery is finished, the lawyers can predict the outcome of the case fairly accurately.

Very truly yours,

Douglas C. Erickson

DCE/sb

Case Study

Fig. 6.2. Crime and punishment case study.

The Crime of the Century

On the evening of January 17, 1950, shortly after 7 p.m., seven men walked into the Boston headquarters of Brinks, Incorporated and stole $1,219,000 in cash and at least an equal amount in checks, money orders, and securities. It was the biggest robbery in the history of the United States. The fact that the robbers succeeded in stealing so much was not the only reason that the crime was sensational news—it was not a bank that was robbed. The target of the crime was the supposedly impregnable Brinks, Incorporated, the nation's major armored car money mover. The Brinks robbery was headline news for weeks and months. Many called it the "crime of the century."

The motivation for the crime was probably twofold. The appeal of $1 million in cash to a group of men with criminal backgrounds is obvious. The possibility of pulling off the "perfect crime" may also have appealed to the eleven men who planned and carried out the robbery. The motivation to catch the robbers is also apparent. Up to $3 million in cash and checks and securities was missing. The Brinks reputation was at stake. Law enforcement officials from the Boston police to the FBI wanted to catch the criminals and bring them to justice.

The Brinks robbery was a crime more than two years in active planning. All of the perpetrators were Boston underworld figures. The chief architects of the heist were Joe McGinnis and Tony Pino. McGinnis apparently planned, but did not participate in, the robbery. He was busy establishing an alibi for himself at the actual time of the robbery. Another perpetrator, "Specs" O'Keefe, was to figure prominently in the case, proving the truth of the axiom "there is no honor among thieves."

Once the decision to rob Brinks had been made, the search for and analysis of the ways and means of committing the robbery were underway. Incredibly, the men stealthily infiltrated the Brinks building numerous times in their two years of planning the crime. On more than one occasion, members of the gang spent an entire evening secreted inside the building. They made keys to fit five locked doors they needed to pass through to reach the vault where the cash was stored. They came to know the inside of the Brinks building so well that some of them could, from memory alone, draw plans of every room in the building, including the position of furniture in each room. The one thing that baffled the crooks was their inability to figure out how to cut the alarm system they assumed (correctly) would be activated as soon as they opened the door of the vault.

After much surveillance of the activities at the Brinks offices, the criminals came up with information that led them to decide upon their major hypothesis. Each working day, the Brinks armored trucks delivered their final loads of money to the company headquarters at 6 p.m. Cash, checks, securities, and money orders were transferred from the trucks to the vault room. Armed guards would then count the money and place it in the vault. Since the guards carried sacks of money into the vault from 6:30 p.m. to 7:45 p.m., the steel plated door of the vault was left open. (The vault was also open for a period of time in the early morning when the money was once again taken out of the vault and loaded into Brinks vehicles. However, the robbers reasoned there was considerably more activity in the vicinity in the morning hours, including heavy traffic on the streets.) The crooks hypothesized that the best time to rob Brinks would be about 7 p.m. in the evening, when the vault would be open and the alarm system temporarily disconnected.

On the night of January 17, 1950 the men pulled off their fantastic robbery. Seven of the crooks entered the building and worked their way through locked doors with keys they had made until they reached the vault room. They were all dressed identically in Navy pea jackets, grotesque rubber masks, and dark caps with visors. Each carried a handgun. They made the Brinks employees lay on the floor. The employees were bound with short lengths of rope. Their mouths were covered with adhesive tape. Within twenty minutes the robbers had stuffed sacks full of money. They left the building. Shortly thereafter, one of the Brinks guards freed himself and set off the alarm.

Now the search for clues and analysis of the evidence was the task facing the police. One of the most massive manhunts in the history of the country began as the FBI, the Boston police, and the Massachusetts State Police entered the investigation. But the clues were scarce. The only evidence left behind was a visored cap worn by a robber and the tape and rope used on the guards. None of these clues led police to the robbers.

In the beginning, when the robbers appeared to have pulled off the perfect crime, there was the suspicion that the robbery was an "inside" job. This hypothesis proved false. The guards never waivered from their accounts and all passed lie detector tests. Other hypotheses had to be considered and examined. Several members of the gang were considered as suspects. They were questioned and watched, but not a trace of the crime could be linked to them. Prior to the crime, all the culprits had agreed that they would take no action that might draw attention to themselves. This included a ban on the spending of any of the money on expensive homes, automobiles, jewelry, and so forth.

Occasional leads proved unfruitful, and for nearly six years the criminals could not be identified. Three years after the crime, the federal statute of limitations expired, meaning that the robbers could not be tried in federal court even if they were caught. But, the statute of limitations in Massachusetts was six years rather than three. Five days prior to its expiration, "Specs" O'Keefe, a habitual criminal in the Boston area and a member of the robbery gang, talked. He was deeply in debt over legal fees, in jail in Massachusetts, and wanted by Pennsylvania law enforcers. He had been shot at twice in the preceding years, and believed he had been cheated by other members of the gang who had not come to his rescue when he was in jail.

Eleven men in all were charged with the planning and/or execution of the robbery. Eight came to trial on August 6, 1956. "Specs" O'Keefe was the chief witness against the defendants. None of the defendants ever stood in the witness stand or broke their silence. The trial lasted forty-two days and resulted in the conviction of the eight men. All were sentenced to life in prison. O'Keefe served time under heavy guard in another Massachusetts prison.

The case was resolved. The criminals were found, prosecuted, and punished. Brinks reexamined its security procedures and made significant changes. The FBI and state and local police officials were jubilant that the robbery was not, in fact, the perfect crime. but there was not total resolution. Of the nearly $3 million stolen, no more than $56,000 was ever recovered. That mystery is yet to be solved!

Sources:

Behn, Noel. *Big Stick-Up at Brinks!* New York: G. P. Putnam's Sons, 1977.

Feder, Sid, and Joseph F. Dinneen. *The Great Brink's Holdup.* Garden City, N.Y.: Doubleday, 1961.

Seng, R. A., and J. V. Gilmour. *Brinks the Money Movers.* Darien, Conn.: Lakeside Press (R. R. Donnelley & Sons), 1959.

Williams, Roger M. *The Super Crooks: A Rogues' Gallery of Famous Hustlers, Swindlers and Thieves.* Chicago, Ill.: Playboy Press, 1973.

Tools of the Trade

If Sherlock Holmes is the greatest fictional detective of all time, then Moriarty, whom Holmes dubbed the "Napoleon of Crime," is one of the most infamous literary villains of all time. In *The Valley of Fear* Holmes tells Dr. Watson that Moriarty is "The greatest schemer of all time, the organizer of every devilry, the controlling brain of the underworld—a brain which might have made or marred the destiny of nations."[1]

What tools would we find in Moriarty's den of iniquity? Figure 6.3 is a sketch of his den. Ask students to fill in the room with the tools of Moriarty's criminal trade. The completed picture should be suggestive of both the Victorian period and the sinister nature of its owner. If students wish to learn more about Professor Moriarty, teachers may suggest they read *The Valley of Fear* and "The Final Problem."

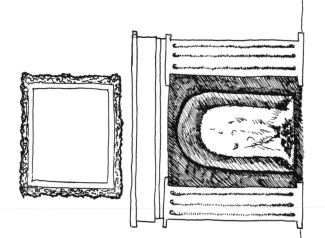

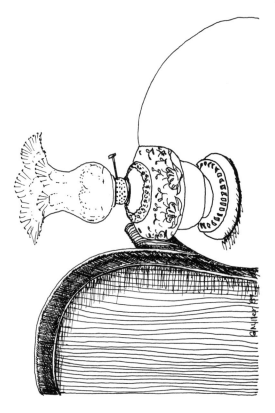

Fig. 6.3. Moriarity's den.

Mystery Desk

Figure 6.4 should be a familiar desk to students of mystery literature. The true mystery here may not be in the mere identification of the desk's owner, but in the detection of all the clues hidden in the drawing. Ask students to name the detective *and* correctly note all the references to the owner and his famous exploits.

Fig. 6.4. Famous detective's desk.

Traces

Figure 6.5 is a Traces exercise to challenge the deductive thinking skills of gifted students. In this Traces puzzle, the view is not a bird's-eye view. Rather, it may be seen as a stage setting theatregoers might witness if a famous mystery story were dramatized. The interiors of two separate rooms in a house are shown. Ask students to piece together the clues found in the Traces drawing and name the famous story from the literature of detection, crime, and punishment it represents. Incidentally, one verbal clue teachers might share with students is that the crime is particularly heinous in its perpetration, and the punishment quite unique.

Fig. 6.5.

Crime and Punishment

There are many avenues of reading and research students can pursue as they study the topics of crime and punishment. They can investigate criminology, learn how the legal system works, and explore careers in law and law enforcement. The daily work of policemen and policewomen may be investigated. The statistics of crime, the unique vocabulary of the law and law enforcement professions, and the argot of the law breakers may be studied. There are also rich historical traditions to be examined through studies of institutions such as the Federal Bureau of Investigation and Scotland Yard. There are notorious criminals, famous crimes, and trials from the past to whet the appetites of students' study of history. There are infinite possibilities of inquiry related to the broad interdisciplinary topics addressed in this chapter on crime and punishment.

Human Resources

When possible topics of study related to crime and punishment are considered, many, many resources come to mind which may be profitably pursued and examined for their potential to enhance classroom instruction. The library media specialist and the classroom teacher can work together in accessing community resource files to locate experts who can share with students information about the law, police procedures, and the criminal justice system. Parents of students who work in the legal professions may be willing to share career experiences, information and resources. Many police departments have officers who specialize in talking to student groups about law and law enforcement procedures, especially as they relate to juvenile crime and juvenile rights. Police laboratory specialists in ballistics and forensic science may also be willing to give talks and explain the very sophisticated procedures they utilize in their work. The local chapter of the American Bar Association can provide the names of local attorneys who will lend insight into such complex issues as plea bargaining and the Miranda Ruling. Similarly, the office of the city or county prosecutor may be able to supply speakers and printed materials to help students understand the law and court procedures. In larger cities, the yellow pages of the telephone book have the names of detective and investigative agencies willing to provide speakers. If there is a local or regional branch of the FBI, the agency may also provide either speakers or printed materials about federal law enforcement. Among the school staff, there may be an expert to invite to class. Teachers of civics and government can provide useful information and resources and serve as guides to help the classroom teacher design a mystery unit. They can also serve as mentors to students who wish to better understand the law, legal terminology, and court systems and procedures.

An excellent field trip to accompany the study of crime and punishment is a trip to a courtroom. A visit to a local court can be extremely instructive for students. Students see first-hand how the justice system works. They leave the courtroom with a fixed and indelible impression of what happens to people who break laws. More than a few times I have seen students on a field trip to the city courts shaken by what they witnessed. A typical response is: "Wow! I will never think about shoplifting or anything else illegal after seeing those people in court today."

The Vocabulary of Crime and Punishment

An excellent place to begin the study of crime and punishment is with a glossary or list of the terminology students will encounter. The average citizen does not always fully understand legal terms or use them correctly. For example, murders are homicides, but homicides are not necessarily murders, nor even criminal. A homicide occurs when one person takes the life of another. Murder is the willful and planned taking of another life. A bank guard could shoot and kill a bank robber who had threatened the lives of many people. The death of the bank robber would be a homicide, not a murder, and the bank guard would not be guilty of a criminal act. When most people hear the Latin phrase *corpus delicti* they think it refers to the corpse of a murder victim. It does not. The true definition refers to the body of facts and evidence that establish that the crime of murder has been committed. Civics texts and books about crime and law typically provide glossaries of criminal terminology. One excellent resource is Ralph De Sola's *Crime Dictionary*. The local police department or the local chapter of the American Bar Association may also be able to supply pamphlets which explain criminal and legal terms. For younger students, *The Hardy Boys Detective Handbook* has an especially good section called a "Dictionary for Detectives." It has an extensive glossary of criminal and police terminology. The following are some of the terms students should be able to define:

Crimes:

misdemeanor	felony	homicide	manslaughter
murder	extortion	arson	assault
battery	burglary	theft	property crime
child abuse	drug offenses	accessory	larceny

Arrests and Prosecutions:

Once a crime has been committed and detected there is terminology which covers arrest and prosecution procedures.

arrest	warrant of arrest	*habeus corpus*
bail	bondsman	indictment
duress	defendant	accomplice
prosecutor	judge	preliminary hearing
evidence	plea bargain	witness
bailiff	oath	testimony
perjury	contempt of court	acquit
appeal	grand jury	counsel

Cops and Crooks:

The good guys and the bad guys have their own special jargon or vocabulary, too. Police terminology may include:

APB	book	bug
bust	frisk	stakeout
tail	rap sheet	swoop
trolling	line-up	squeal

The argot of the criminal class may include:

box man	bag	bull
contract	fingerman	fix
heist	moonlighter	paperhanger
pigeon	stool pigeon	

Catching Crooks

In the world of mystery literature, the citizen investigator or consulting detective, be it Sherlock Holmes or Nancy Drew, solves crimes and rights wrong. In truth, crimes are solved by law enforcement personnel. Students may enjoy and profit from researching the procedures today's law enforcement personnel use to catch criminals. Since modern police work relies so much on science and computer technology, police procedures will be a topic of great interest to many scientifically and mathematically gifted students. For example, students may be fascinated to learn that police can photograph evidence and criminal activities, such as drug exchanges, in near total darkness. The film and cameras operate with light from stars in the night sky. No electronic flash is needed; criminals can be photographed without even realizing it. Ask students to investigate how the following aspects of police work operate. Each student may select or be assigned a topic to research and become the classroom expert on such topics as fingerprinting, interrogations, or ballistics:

patrolman/woman's notebook	fingerprints	lineup
pathology	forensic science	police blotter
autopsy	wiretapping	confessions
search warrants	polygraph tests	

For younger readers, a particularly fine resource about the detection of crimes is the *KnowHow Book of Detection* by Judy Hindley and Donald Rumbelow. William Butler's *The Young Detective's Handbook* will also appeal to elementary students.

The Statistics of Crime

Students can use mathematics and research skills through a study of crime statistics in our nation. Many school library media centers will have *The Statistical Abstracts of the United States* in the reference section. Published each year by the Department of Commerce and available from the U.S. Government Printing Office (Washington, D.C. 20402), this informative resource provides statistical data on a wide range of topics within the larger heading of "crime." One entire section of the annual report of statistics is devoted to "Law Enforcement, Courts, and Prisons." It includes these subtopics:

arrests	arson	assault
costs of criminal behavior	burglary	child abuse and neglect
crime prevention measures	drug abuse	homicide
juvenile crime	larceny and theft	motor vehicle theft
robbery	shoplifting	violent crime

From this resource, students can determine the incidence of various types of crime in each region of the country, how much their own state spends on law enforcement, the costs of keeping prisoners, and much more interesting information.

The Statistical Abstracts of the United States has been published since 1878 as the standard summary of statistics on the economic, political, and social organization of the nation. The U.S. Department of Commerce publishes an additional resource, *Historical Statistics of the United States: Colonial Times to 1970*, that students may wish to consult for research data. A reading of these two documents reveals the appalling rise of homicides in the U.S.:

Year —	**1900**	**1970**	**1988**
No. of homicides	230	16,848	19,527[2]

What crimes will be prevalent in the future? A futures detective would approach the problematic question by analyzing past and current trends, extrapolate from known trends, and suggest a hypothesis. Ask students to examine a particular crime (e.g., robbery) and note its incidence in the population of the United States over a period of several years, or even decades. Is the incidence of the crime growing? If so, at what rate? What is the percentage of growth (or decline)? Based upon the figures determined, what predictions about the growth (or decline) and rate of incidence can be made?

Students can use the same sources to determine the three crimes most likely to have occurred in society in the 1930s. Then, they should note the three most common crimes committed during each of the succeeding decades. From these data, can they predict the three most common crimes likely to be committed in the coming decades? For example, students may wish to predict which three crimes will be most prevalent in the year 2020. They can buttress this prediction by conducting their own surveys, asking people to predict the most likely crimes of occurrence in coming years. The school library media specialist will be an especially important ally in helping students locate the *Statistical Abstracts* and other government documents.

Famous Criminals and Famous Crimes

From Robin Hood to Bonnie and Clyde, folks who have broken the law have captured the public's attention. A few crooks have even become heroic figures. Students are generally not immune to this fascination. Adolescents may be fascinated by the rebelliousness and bravado of celebrated criminals like Black Bart and Jesse James. Students can become truth-sleuths and determine the real history behind the legends of famous crooks and criminals. One way to increase students knowledge is to have each student in class select one famous criminal they want to learn more about. Each student becomes the class expert on the villainy of his or her criminal. The sharing of information can be creative. They can dress and speak in the character of their respective outlaws; share information they have learned using wanted posters; or perhaps a *National Enquirer*-style newspaper can tell the truth people want to know about their criminals. Working together, perhaps several students could create a "Hall of Shame" bulletin board. Some of history's more infamous perpetrators of crime and con games include:

Jesse James	Billy the Kid	Al Capone
Bonnie and Clyde	Belle Starr	Wild Bill Hickok
Charles Manson	John Wilkes Booth	John Dillinger
Willie Sutton	Jack the Ripper	"Legs" Diamond
Charles "Pretty Boy" Floyd	"Baby Face" Nelson	Betsey Bigley (a.k.a., Cassie Chadwick)

An especially good resource for topics related to American criminals is Jay Robert Nash's *Bloodletters and Badmen: A Narrative Encyclopedia of American Criminals from the Pilgrims to the Present*. The same author also created the *Almanac of World Crime*. Roger M. Williams' *The Super Crooks* is also a source of information about well-known criminals. *Great True Stories of Crime, Mystery & Detection from the Reader's Digest* provides information about both infamous criminals and nefarious crimes.

Sensational crimes and misdemeanors have fascinated people for generations. The criminal activity in the 1920 "Black Socks" scandal was one of the most shocking sports stories ever to emerge in this country. Baseball, the Great American Sport, was dramatically impacted by the affair. Further back in time, students can read about the questionable exploits of Aaron Burr. While still vice-president of the United States, Burr was indicted for the murder of Alexander Hamilton and, as a result, became a fugitive from justice. Later in American history, the transgressions of Tammany Hall's Victorian-era Boss Tweed and the culprits of the 1920s Teapot Dome scandal fascinated Americans.

Trials of individuals, innocent and otherwise, have also figured prominently in American history. The Salem witch trials remain a topic of considerable fascination. As suggested in chapter 4, the trials of Lizzie Borden and Bruno Hauptmann remain firmly etched in America's historical consciousness. So, too, are the trials of Nicola Sacco and Bartolomeo Vanzetti and Dr. Samuel Sheppard. A clue to examining famous trials may be taken from the Venn diagram exercise used in chapter 2 to compare and contrast the sleuths Sherlock Holmes and Hercule Poirot. Using Venn diagrams (figure 6.5), ask students to study a famous trial and to compare and contrast the respective cases made by the prosecution and the defense in that trial. The intersection becomes the facts common to both arguments.

Americans are not the only people to have a history filled with colorful and sensational crimes and criminals. In Paris, in 1911, the most famous art theft in history occurred when Leonardo da Vinci's *Mona Lisa* was stolen from the famed Louvre Museum. Seymour V. Reit recounts the details of this shocking crime in *The Day They Stole the Mona Lisa*. In England, Jonathan Wild and Moll Cutpurse are two infamous figures from the past. In the twentieth-century annals of crime, the Great Train Robbery probably ranks as the most celebrated example of British villainy. In August, 1963, a gang of thieves stole $7,368,715 from a train carrying bank notes from Scottish banks to London.

Students can share the information they learn about crime and punishment in a wide variety of ways. A student could identify one crime—say, theft—and research the way the crime has been punished in different nations throughout history. At one time in history, thieves had their hands cut off. There were times in England's past when stealing a loaf of bread could result in imprisonment for seven to fourteen years and/or deportation (see the case study in chapter 5 about the crimes of the "convicts" sent to Australia). In some places and times, theft has been a hanging offense. Even today, concerned officials in the United States are attempting to codify penalties for certain crimes so that justice may be more equitably distributed to all citizens regardless of where their crimes are committed. From such a research project, a student could create a timeline to share the facts of their research with others. Another student could research the history of a famous trial and write and deliver a summation speech that either the defense or prosecuting attorney *should* have given.

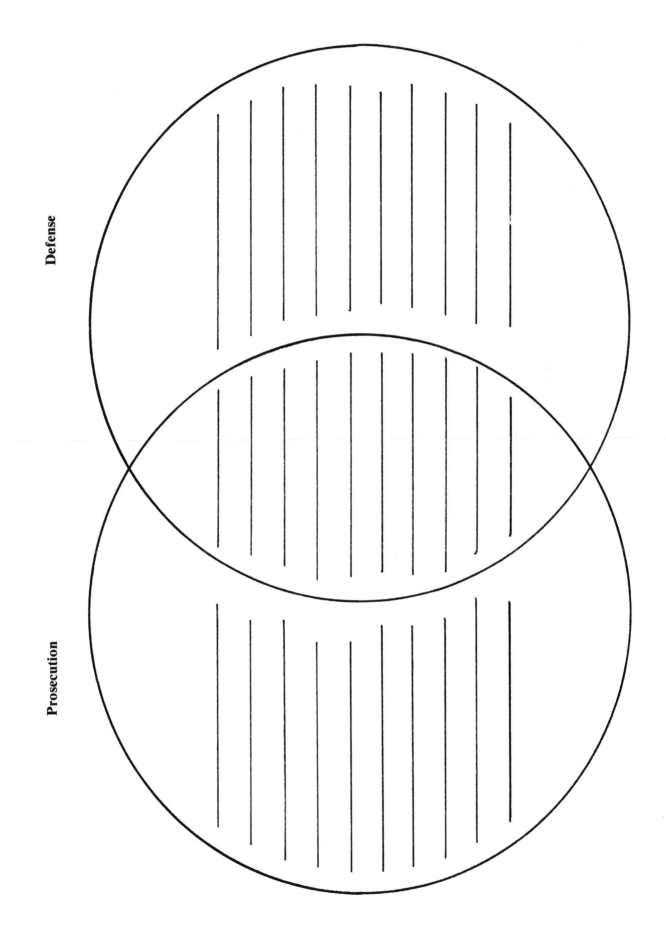

Fig. 6.5.

Crimes and criminal trials seem to fascinate people. There are enough celebrated ones in history to satiate the appetites of any class of gifted students. Another approach to trials is found in this chapter under the heading "Advocacy Trials."

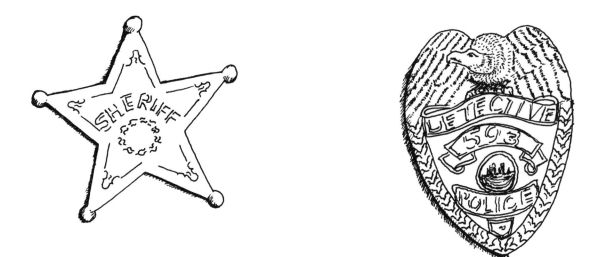

Crimebusters and Other Heroes

Students should also learn about those people who have made a significant impact on society by their work on the *right* side of the law. The following are names of investigators, police officers, lawyers, and judges who have made significant contributions to justice:

Allan Pinkerton	Sandra Day O'Connor	Eliot Ness
Robert Kennedy	Earl Warren	William O. Douglas
August Vollmer	William J. Burns	Thurgood Marshall
Sheriff Pat Garrett	Clarence Darrow	Sir Robert Peel
Louis Brandeis	William H. Rehnquist	Warren Burger
Edward Oscar Heinrich	Raymond Schindler	

One good source of information about exceptional detectives is Eugene B. Block's *Famous Detectives: True Stories of Great Crime Detection*.

Scotland Yard

Although Dr. Watson often refers to Sherlock Holmes relations with Scotland Yard, the world's first consulting detective apparently traveled there infrequently (see "The Engineer's Thumb" in *The Complete Sherlock Holmes*, Doubleday, 1930). Police Inspector Lestrade was more likely to visit the great Holmes at 221 B Baker Street.

Of course, Holmes is not the only detective ever to work with Scotland Yard. Other famous literary sleuths who worked for or frequented the Yard include Mrs. Pym, Lady Molly, and Adam Dalgliesh.

What is now referred to as Great Scotland Yard was chosen as the site for Metropolitan Police Headquarters in 1842 in Whitehall. In 1891 New Scotland Yard was built on the Embankment. These are the quarters Holmes would have visited. Today's "new" Scotland Yard offices were built in 1967. Ask students to explore the connection between past, present, and future by examining the architecture of the past and present Scotland Yard buildings and then project what Scotland Yard may look like in a new century. The following are some questions which may guide student investigations:

How did Scotland Yard receive its name?

Who was the architect who designed the building used in Holmes's day?

How does the present-day Scotland Yard differ from the one Holmes knew? When was it built?

What architectural styles do the various Scotland Yard buildings represent?

What changes have occurred over the past century in the kinds of investigative laboratories, security devices, and equipment one would find in the various Scotland Yard buildings?

What changes are likely to occur in the next century at Scotland Yard?

Books to assist student investigations include:

Alzina Stone Dale and Barbara Sloan Hendershott. *Mystery Reader's Walking Guide to London*. Passport Books, 1987.

Michael Harrison. *In the Footsteps of Sherlock Holmes*. Drake, 1972.

Tsukasa Kobayashi, Akane Higashiyama, and Masaharu Uemura. *Sherlock Holmes's London: Following the Footsteps of London's Master Detective*. Chronicle Books, 1986.

Peter Laurie. *Scotland Yard: A Study of the Metropolitan Police*. Holt, Rinehart and Winston, 1970.

Charles Viney. *Sherlock Holmes in London: A Photographic Record of Conan Doyle's Stories*. Houghton Mifflin, 1989.

Students can translate their research findings into a wide variety of projects such as:

Creating blueprints and other schematics of past, present, and projected future Scotland Yard buildings and laboratories.

Presenting a slide show of the architecture of London over the past 200 years with projections for the next century.

Drawing sketches of a future Scotland Yard crime laboratory.

Creating a catalog of famous fictional detectives whose base of operations has included Scotland Yard, then projecting descriptions of twenty-first-century fictional detectives working there.

Similar studies of the Federal Bureau of Investigation and the Royal Canadian Mounted Police will be of interest to students and may be profitably pursued. Each of these institutions, like Scotland Yard, has a rich history.

"Scotland Yard" is an excellent and challenging board game to share with students. In the game the dastardly "Mr. X" calls Scotland Yard and dares the detectives there to track him down. Two to six players take turns traveling London's city streets and the Underground in hot pursuit of "Mr. X." The game may be found in game stores, mystery bookstores, or it may be ordered from the *Games* magazine catalog (Games, Catalog Division, 800 Morse Avenue, Elk Grove, IL 60007).

So You Want to Be a Detective

For those students who decide to forego a career with Scotland Yard or the FBI, a great lesson in practical economics can be taught as they research the costs and requirements involved in planning and creating their own detective agency. What kinds of detective work do they want to do? Do they want to investigate juvenile runaways? Industrial accidents? Missing persons? Business fraud? Accident compensation claims? Wrongful deaths? Conduct background checks? Administer polygraph tests? What names will they give their agencies? Those are the easy parts. Tougher questions await them. Where will they locate? How much does it cost to rent building space in various parts of town? How much money needs to be budgeted for utilities? How much for secretarial services, an answering service, or an answering machine? If they use a car in their work, how much will the car, gasoline, insurance, and so forth cost? What percentage of their work costs are tax deductible as business expenses? What special types of surveillance equipment will they need? Is a private investigator's license called for in their state of residence? Is any kind of special business license required? What kinds of weapons will they be allowed to own and carry? What is the cost of a weapon's permit?

If possible, invite a police detective or private investigator into the class to talk about all the rudimentary necessities involved in starting a private investigation business. If such persons are not available, ask a businessperson in another line of work to talk about routine expenses common to establishing any type of business. The local prosecutor's office may answer questions regarding licensing requirements and fees.

The yellow pages of the telephone book are useful as an investigative tool for students engaged in the project. They will list existing agencies. While investigators are busy earning a living, you may find one sympathetic to the interest of students who has time to answer some of their questions. A perusal of the yellow pages will indicate how crowded the detective field is in a community and whether or not there is room for a new private detective agency, and if so, in what specialty area. (One detective suggested to the author that the "hottest" area of detective work today involves computer security.) The classified ads section of the local paper will also be useful in determining the costs of secretarial help, office space, office furniture, and so forth.

A telephone call to a public utilities company will provide answers about average rates for utilities per square foot of office space.

Students need to recognize that people do not go into business to lose money. Bills have to be paid. Once students have answers to these questions, they can determine how much they will have to charge clients per hour, per day, or per case in order to cover their expenses and overhead and make a reasonable profit. An economist from a local college or university or a member of Junior Achievement may be willing to share with students the basics of creating a business.

Incidentally, the clients of the detective agencies students create do not have to be human. A delightful book which will tickle the fancy of all animal lovers is John Keane's *Sherlock Bones: Tracer of Missing Pets.* Keane, who houses his detective agency in San Francisco, refers to himself as "the country's first and only professional pet detective." In his joyful book, Sherlock Bones (a.k.a. John Keane) tells how he became a pet detective, recalls some of his most interesting cases, and offers readers advice on how to find their own lost pets.

Solving Mysteries

Students can practice their detection skills by attempting to catch the criminal in the following fictional murder case. The activity has many bonuses. Students must learn to work cooperatively. They must operate as one unit and discuss the facts they have. It is impossible to solve the case unless all work together. Students must also use reasoning and problem solving skills. They must listen carefully. They must gather the facts of the case and link fact with reason to reach satisfactory conclusions.

In this simulation, each student has a vital clue in a murder case. The case may be solved only when all clues are heard, and critical thinking skills are used to deduce the solution from the facts of the case. The game originally appeared in *Learning Discussion Skills through Games* by Gene Stanford and Barbara Dodds Stanford. Your author has used it for at least a dozen years with students of nearly all ages. It has never failed to excite and challenge students.

Here is how the game works. Ask students to sit in a circle. Standing outside the circle, explain the activity as follows:

I am holding twenty-seven clues which will help you solve a murder mystery. You must determine five facts: the murderer, the weapon, the place and time of the murder, and the motive behind the crime. When you think you know all five facts, you may tell me. I will tell you if you are right or wrong. I will only tell you that you are right if you correctly deduce *all* five facts. If parts of the answer you give are incorrect, I will not tell you which parts are correct. You may organize yourselves in any way you like. You may not pass your clues around or show them to anyone else, and you may not leave your seats. All sharing must be done verbally. I will allow one student, whom you choose, to leave his or her seat in order to write vital information on the chalkboard.

As soon as I have passed all the clues out, you may begin. Remember, you are on your own. I will only answer "correct" or "incorrect" when you give me your group response to the five facts needed.

The clues in figure 6.6 may be cut into strips of paper and affixed to index cards for easy distribution and collection. If there are not twenty-seven students in the class, distribute additional clues to some students. The authors of this simulation do not make provisions for the one student who is allowed to leave his or her seat and serve as a recorder at the chalkboard for the group. However, your author has found this to be an important addition to the simulation for younger students. It also helps students who are predominantly visual learners participate more fully in the simulation by lowering the frustration level they may otherwise experience. It is certainly an optional part of the simulation.

Several observations will be made by the teacher and the students. The more quickly students realize that they need to organize and work cooperatively, the sooner they will solve the mystery. Confusion and bedlam reign if everyone talks at the same time or if students talk only to some of their nearest neighbors. There are red herrings included in this mystery, such as the gunshot wound Mr. Kelley sustains at the hands of Mr. Jones. The exercise is often particularly frustrating for those gifted students who are used to solving problems by themselves and who are used to having all the facts of a problem laid before them at the start. The shy, retiring student who does not participate impedes the process of solving the problem in this simulation as much as the student who typically monopolizes class discussions. Every student has a clue only he or she sees. The clue a shy student fails to share just may be the critical clue needed to solve the mystery. It is the task of all students to make sure that every student feels included and important in the problem solving process.

A debriefing of the simulation is critical. Students should discover for themselves and share the points and issues raised in the preceding paragraph. They should note the reasoning skills they utilized by tracing their deliberations backwards from the final solution. That way they note how they accumulated and discarded various pieces of information and how they linked fact to reason to deduce the correct solution. Which clues proved important? How did they piece the evidence together to solve the crime?

Normally, the teacher or facilitator remains totally out of the picture as the simulation is played. No clues or hints should be given. The only verbal teacher input comes when the students propose their solution and the teacher tells them if they are correct or incorrect. However, one incident the author experienced is worth mentioning. One of the students misread her clue and said "Mrs. Kelley was bleeding slightly," when she should have said Mr. Kelley. This completely threw the class off and sent them off on a tangent which could not possibly be successful. In that one case, the author intervened and quietly told the girl to reread her clue. She quickly informed her fellow problem solvers of the error. The incident illustrates that while the teacher should not normally intrude in the proceedings, he or she should closely monitor the discussion to be sure the clues are correctly read.

The bank robbery simulation in figure 6.7 offers students a second opportunity to test their problem solving skills and demonstrate what they have learned about group cooperation, discussion skills, and critical thinking. It may also be used in place of the murder mystery simulation by teachers and library media specialists who feel the murder mystery is inappropriate for their students.

Read the following description of a bank robbery to students. Then pass out the individual clues students need to solve the crime. The same rules will be in effect as with the murder mystery: no passing of clues, all sharing must be verbal, the facilitator responds "yes" or "no" when students are ready to state the identity of the guilty person(s).

(Text continues on page 190.)

Fig. 6.6. A murder mystery.

Clues:

When he was discovered dead, Mr. Kelley had a bullet hole in his thigh and a knife wound in his back.

Mr. Jones shot an intruder in his apartment building at 12:00 midnight.

The elevator operator reported to police that he saw Mr. Kelley at 12:15 a.m.

The bullet taken from Mr. Kelley's thigh matched the gun owned by Mr. Jones.

Only one bullet had been fired from Mr. Jones's gun.

When the elevator man saw Mr. Kelley, Mr. Kelley was bleeding slightly, but he did not seem too badly hurt.

A knife with Mr. Kelley's blood on it was found in Miss Smith's yard.

The knife found in Miss Smith's yard had Mr. Scott's fingerprints on it.

Mr. Kelley had destroyed Mr. Jones's business by stealing all his customers.

The elevator man saw Mr. Kelley's wife go to Mr. Scott's apartment at 11:30 p.m.

The elevator operator said that Mr. Kelley's wife frequently left the building with Mr. Scott.

Mr. Kelley's body was found in the park.

Mr. Kelley's body was found at 1:30 a.m.

Mr. Kelley had been dead for one hour when his body was found, according to a medical expert working for the police.

The elevator man saw Mr. Kelley go to Mr. Scott's room at 12:25 a.m.

The elevator man went off duty at 12:30 a.m.

It was obvious from the condition of Mr. Kelley's body that it had been dragged a long distance.

Miss Smith saw Mr. Kelley go to Mr. Jones's apartment building at 11:55 p.m.

Mr. Kelley's wife disappeared after the murder.

Police were unable to locate Mr. Scott after the murder.

When police tried to locate Mr. Jones after the murder, they discovered that he had disappeared.

The elevator man said that Miss Smith was in the lobby of the apartment building when he went off duty.

Miss Smith often followed Mr. Kelley.

Mr. Jones had told Mr. Kelley that he was going to kill him.

Miss Smith said that nobody left the apartment building between 12:25 and 12:45 a.m.

Mr. Kelley's blood stains were found in Mr. Scott's car.

Mr. Kelley's blood stains were found on the carpet in the hall outside Mr. Jones's apartment.

ANSWER: After receiving a superficial gunshot wound from Mr. Jones, Mr. Kelly went to *Mr. Scott's apartment* where he was killed by *Mr. Scott* with a *knife* at *12:30 a.m.* because *Mr. Scott was in love with Mr. Kelley's wife.*

From *Learning Discussion Skills through Games* by Gene Stanford and Barbara Dodds Stanford (New York: Citation Press, 1969). Used with permission of the authors.

Fig. 6.7. The First National Bank robbery.

The First National Bank of Minnetonka, Minnesota was robbed of $1 million. Using the clues I am now going to give you, you must determine who perpetrated the robbery.

Clues:

The robbery was discovered at 8:00 a.m. on Friday, November 12. The bank had closed at 5:00 p.m. the previous day.

Miss Margaret Ellington, a teller at the bank, discovered the robbery.

The vault of the bank had been blasted open by dynamite.

The president of the bank, Mr. Albert Greenbags, left before the robbery was discovered. He was arrested by authorities at the Mexico City airport at noon on Friday, November 12.

The president of the bank had been having trouble with his wife, who spent all of his money. He had frequently talked of leaving her.

The front door of the bank had been opened with a key.

The only keys to the bank were held by the janitor and the president of the bank.

Miss Ellington often borrowed the president's key to open the bank early when she had an extra amount of work to do.

A strange, hippie-type person had been hanging around the bank on Thursday, November 11, watching employees and customers.

A substantial amount of dynamite had been stolen from the Acme Construction Company on Wednesday, November 10.

An Acme employee, Howard Ellington, said that a hippie had been hanging around the construction company on Wednesday afternoon.

The hippie-type character, whose name was Dirsey Flowers and who had recently dropped out of Southwest Arkansas State Teachers College, was found by police in East Birdwatch, about ten miles from Minnetonka.

Dirsey Flowers was carrying $500 when police apprehended him and had thrown a package into the river as the police approached.

Anastasia Wallflower of East Birdwatch, Wisconsin, said that she had bought $500 worth of genuine Indian love beads from Dirsey Flowers for resale in her boutique in downtown East Birdwatch.

Anastasia said that Dirsey had spent the night of November 11 at the home of her parents and left after a pleasant breakfast on the morning of the 12th.

When police tried to locate the janitor of the bank, Elwood Smith, he had apparently disappeared.

Miss Ellington stated that her brother Howard, when strolling to Taylor's Diner for coffee about 11:00 p.m. on Thursday, November 11, had seen Mr. Smith running from the bank.

Mr. Smith was found by the F.B.I. in Dogwalk, Georgia, on November 12. He had arrived there via Southern Airlines Flight 414 at 5:00 p.m. on the 11th.

The airline clerk confirmed the time of Smith's arrival.

Mr. Greenbags was the only person who had a key to the vault.

There were no planes out of Dogwalk between 4:00 p.m. and 7:00 a.m.

In addition to keeping the payroll records, Mr. Ellington was in charge of the dynamite supplies of the Acme Construction Company.

Mr. Greenbags's half-brother, Arthur Nodough, had always been jealous of his brother.

Nodough always got drunk on Friday nights.

Arthur Nodough appeared in Chicago on Monday, November 8, waving a lot of money.

Arthur wanted to marry Camelia Smith.

Mr. Smith's father, a gold prospector in Alaska, had died in September.

Miss Ellington said that Smith had often flirted with her.

Mr. Greenbags waited in the terminal of O'Hare Field in Chicago for 16 hours because of engine trouble on the plane he was to take to Mexico City.

ANSWER: The Ellingtons collaborated to rob the bank, Miss Ellington supplying the front door key (borrowed from Mr. Greenbags) and Howard supplying the dynamite. Greenbags had already left for Brazil when the robbery took place. Mr. Smith was in Dogwalk on the night of the robbery. Dirsey Flowers was at the home of Anastasia's parents. The Ellingtons were lying when they tried to implicate Smith. There was no evidence that Arthur Nodough was connected with the robbery in any way.

From *Learning Discussion Skills through Games* by Gene Stanford and Barbara Dodds Stanford (Citation Press, 1969).

Two creative teachers, Betty Jett and Peggy Grossman, have created similar kinds of mysteries for students to solve in their books *Mysteries for Group Detectives, Collection No. 1* and *Collection No. 2*. These mysteries are suitable for students in grades four through eight.

Teachers may design similar mysteries for students to solve, or better still, encourage gifted students to create them. The creation of mysteries requires at least as much creativity, critical thinking, and problem solving as finding the solution does. Two key points to remember are to have lots of clues, and make sure that every clue is important. Red herring clues may be created, but should be contradicted by other clues.

The Search for Clues: A Forensics Simulation

Another simulation for students to try offers them the hands-on challenge of using tangible clues in working as police detectives and specialists to solve a crime. This simulation was developed by one of the author's colleagues from Great Britain. Dr. David George, Dean of the Faculty of Science at Nene College in Northampton, England, uses this forensic science activity with gifted students in middle school.

Ask students to brainstorm possible situations where a crime is committed. They must choose a crime (e.g., murder, theft) and describe the general facts involved in it such as the time, setting, and so forth.

Next, the teacher collects from each student a packet of clues including: a few strands of hair, a broken or cut fingernail, fingerprints, a few threads or a piece of clothing, and any other relevant pieces of evidence. Dr. George even collects blood samples from each student.

By secret draw a culprit is chosen, and, if necessary, a victim. The victim announces his or her selection, but only the teacher and the culprit know who the criminal is.

Participants are given time to learn how to analyze evidence and investigate a crime. It is particularly effective at this time to bring into class a forensic specialist. If a guest expert is not available, one of the school's science teachers will make a worthy substitute. In this phase of the simulation, students learn how to investigate a crime using a microscope, analyzing fingerprints, strands of hair, clothing fibers, and blood samples.

In the interim, the teacher and the culprit have worked together hiding the collected clues from the original packets. Once the clues are hidden, the students are ready to begin acting out their roles as detectives and forensic specialists. In their attempt to identify the culprit they must locate the clues. Then they must compare fingerprints, hair fragments, and the other clues.

Participation in the simulation generally serves as a strong motivating force for students to engage in further independent and small group investigations of the science side of police work. Once the culprit is identified, students can conduct a mock trial. The final verdict in the trial will not necessarily be a foregone conclusion. The culprit has, like their classmates, learned much about forensic science and evidence. The wrongdoer can point out major flaws in the evidence used by the prosecution.

Computer Crime and Punishment Simulations

Law enforcement officials use computers extensively to catch crooks. (Unfortunately, computers are also used frequently by the crooks. See chapter 5 for specific examples.) Fun and challenging computer games and simulations let mystery lovers go solo or assist the great Sherlock Holmes in catching fictional crooks.

A trip to the local computer software store is a wise investment in time for teachers and library media specialists involved in a mystery unit. Four of the most popular software packages available are "Where in the World Is Carmen Sandiego?" "Where in the USA Is Carmen Sandiego?" "Where in Europe Is Carmen Sandiego?" and "Where in Time Is Carmen Sandiego?" In these interactive programs, players must learn geography as they catch the crooks. Players assist Sherlock Holmes in his battle with Moriarty in the interactive software package "Sherlock: The Riddle of the Crown Jewels." Tom Snyder productions offers two excellent mysteries for students in grades four and up to solve. "The Granite Point Ghost" and "The Disappearing Dolphin" are two software packages in the Snooper Troops® series. In addition to solving mysteries, computer games teach students how to take notes, classify and organize information, draw maps, and analyze clues.

The Funny (and Far) Side of Crime and Punishment

Students can be inspired to create cartoons about trials, crimes, and punishments just as they were with detectives and mysteries (see chapter 3). Figure 6.8 is a product of the fantastic imagination of Gary Larson, creator of the celebrated cartoon serial "The Far Side." Teachers and library media specialists may reproduce the cartoon as an overhead transparency for classroom use to motivate students. (Please note: Any other use of the cartoon, including any photocopying, is expressly forbidden without the written permission of Chronicle Features.) Share the cartoon with students and ask them to brainstorm other examples of humor they might derive from the elements of crimes, policework, trials, and various forms of punishments. With the Gary Larson example and subsequent class discussion, the teacher has planted a few seeds. Students can incubate them for awhile then try out different concepts in their mystery notebooks. The final products will make great bulletin board material for the mystery unit and embellish the class mystery newspaper.

Fig. 6.8. *The Far Side* cartoon by Gary Larson is reprinted by permission of Chronicle Features, San Francisco, Calif.

"Well, of COURSE I did it in cold blood, you idiot!
I'm a reptile!"

The Crime Beat: Reporting Crime

Creative dramatics and reporting skills can both be emphasized in the following "Whodunit" activity. Begin by selecting six students to portray a crime reporter, a police officer, and various citizens in a neighborhood where a crime has taken place. Place the role descriptions from figure 6.9 on notecards and give them to the selected students in advance. The students may use their own names. They may dress in character if they choose. They should be instructed not to share their role card information with anyone else prior to the actual class reenactment of the crime scene.

When the six students are ready to play their roles, set the stage for the rest of the class. Tell them that a crime has been committed and that the principals involved will soon reveal, through their words, the nature of the crime.

The scene opens in the front yard of a suburban home. People are milling about outside the home. One man seems to be interviewing several of the people gathered there. Tell students they are reporters and need

reporter's notebook

to copy in their mystery notebooks all relevant information they hear in the interchanges between the interviewer and other people at the scene of the crime. As reporters, they will have to write a news story when the simulation is completed. They face the same deadline that the reporter does. Hence, their stories may be no longer than 400 words. Unlike the interviewer, however, they will not be able to ask questions of the police officer and witnesses. They must write their news stories entirely from their notes.

When the simulation is completed, students can begin writing their stories. Group sharing of news stories will prove interesting. This sharing will demonstrate that not all witnesses recall what they see and hear in the same way. The malleable memory of witnesses introduces another interesting area for discussion and research. Students will not use identical quotations from the witnesses. It is interesting to observe which testimony different reporters choose to emphasize.[3]

Fig. 6.9. Reporting a crime.

Role descriptions:

Reporter: As a crime reporter, you have been asked to write a story for the evening edition of the newspaper. You have a 12:00 noon deadline. It is now 10:20 a.m. You need to get the facts of the crime and write the best and most accurate story possible in the time you have. Due to the deadline you face, you will only have time to write a short news story (300-400 words) for today's edition.

Police officer: You were called to the scene of the crime at 8:30 a.m. You have no authorization to tell the press anything, except the minimal *facts* of the case: A man was shot. There will be an investigation. You are not at liberty to disclose any further information at this time.

Wife of the victim: Your husband has been shot. You know the following: There was a noise at the back door at about 8:00 a.m. Your husband went to the door to investigate. You heard a gun fire. You heard the back door slam and a noise that sounded like someone running away from your house. You got up and saw your husband lying by the back door. He was dead. You recall screaming "Oh, no! Oh, no!" You remember nothing more because you must have fainted. You may add any other information you care to fill in, but take care not to give contradictory information.

Neighbor woman: You live next door to the victim and his wife. About 8:00 a.m. this morning you heard a gunshot. You looked out your kitchen window in time to see a Caucasian youth, about nineteen or twenty, running from the house next door. He wore jeans and a brown jacket. He wore a baseball cap. He disappeared down the alley behind your house.

Neighbor man: You live across the street from the murder victim. You were watering your lawn this morning between 7:30 a.m. and 8:00 a.m. when you saw a yellow van drive very slowly down your street. It stopped at the corner and remained there for about twenty minutes. You were suspicious and thought maybe you should call the police. Just then the van turned the corner and disappeared. You thought nothing more about it. You shut the sprinkler off and went back into your house for a second cup of coffee. With coffee cup in hand, you went back to the front porch to collect the morning paper. That's when you saw a youth wandering down the street in the direction of your neighbor's house. He looked suspicious. He disappeared around their hedge, apparently headed for the alley behind their house. You heard a shot a few minutes later. Then you saw the same youth running between two other houses on your block; the youth turned around the corner and vanished from your view. Simultaneously, you heard a scream coming from your neighbor's house. You immediately called the police.

Another neighbor: You are the neighborhood snoop and gossip, but you missed seeing this one. You want to see your name in the paper and be quoted in the news story, so you offer lots of juicy and spicy information about the neighbors and the neighborhood. *Do not lie about not seeing the incident.* Do share local gossip with the reporter. For example, you might say that a lot of peculiar things go on in the neighborhood. The victim and his wife went to work at unusual hours, and would disappear for days throughout the summer months. When they were at home, they seemed to have an extraordinary amount of company (people went in and out of their house at all hours of the day and night). They never talked with the other neighbors, and so forth. They had the fanciest car in the neighborhood. This fact led you to believe there was something "fishy" about them. Feel free to add anything else you wish. Remember that your primary objective is to be quoted in the newspaper story.

An Advocacy Trial

Students love classroom trials, but when they merely take a criminal case from the news headlines and attempt to reenact or simulate the trial the results are often less than successful. An advocacy trial is an attractive alternative. The advocacy trial was suggested to your author by Drew Davey, a teacher of gifted students at Northridge Elementary School in Douglas County, Colorado. He based his model on a format used in the Public Television series "The Advocates." Mr. Davey employs the advocacy trial with fifth grade gifted students. He confronts them with this historical issue: Should the Confederate States be left alone to live in peace, or should the Union of the United States of America be preserved at all costs?

The advocacy trial contains many elements considered to be vital components of programming for gifted students: mentorships, independent research, critical thinking skills, creative problem solving, communication skills development, and interaction with gifted peers. In the advocacy trial, students choose roles as witness or lawyer and advocate for one of two points of view. All students then go to school to train for their roles; the lawyers go to "law school" and the witnesses go to "drama school." When possible, the "teachers" in the law and drama schools are volunteer mentors. The students independently research their roles thoroughly so their particular advocacy has credibility. Based on their research, attorneys and witnesses develop possible questions and responses they may ask or be asked during the trial. This question development employs the creative problem solving (CPS) model (see chapter 2). Once questions are determined, a script is written and memorized by each advocate team (attorneys and witnesses) and dress rehearsals are held. Finally, after considerable work and practice, the time arrives for the trial. The judge, typically the teacher (a retired judge might be willing to fill this role), gives a brief overview of the critical issues before the jury. The judge's opening statement is followed by the opening statements of the two chief counsels. The advocacy trial proceeds through the questioning and cross-examination of all witnesses and finishes with the closing arguments of the attorneys for the two sides. After deliberation, the jury presents its finding to the judge who then asks the jury foreman to read the final verdict.

Any topic or issue having at least two clear and defensible positions may be adopted for advocacy trials. Possible crime and punishment issues which could be used in advocacy trials might include: Should private ownership of hand guns be banned? Should crimes against the environment, such as the 1989 Alaskan oil spill, be made more punitive (e.g., mandatory prison terms for convicted offenders)?

The focus of the sample advocacy trial defined, described, and presented in the following twelve sections is a perennial topic related to crime and punishment—capital punishment. All components of the advocacy trial are described here. These components may be altered, compacted, or dropped to fit students' needs, abilities, and ages and teachers' time and resource constraints.

Roles in the Advocacy Trial

Drew Davey gives his fifth grade gifted students choices of real and fictional witnesses to portray. Possible Union Witnesses are John Brown, Harriet Tubman, Abraham Lincoln, Dred Scott, Clara Barton, a fictional slave, and a fictional Union soldier. Witnesses for the Confederacy could include Jefferson Davis, Robert E. Lee, Mrs. Rose Greenhow (a spy), a fictional plantation owner, and a fictional Southern belle. Before roles are determined and selected students should research the history and important social questions and issues related to capital punishment. Ideally, students will choose roles as lawyers or witnesses based upon their particular strengths and interests. There may be more than two students who want to be lawyers. Creative solutions can be found. There can be more than one counselor for each advocate team since the work load of lawyers is heavy. Legal teams may be created within each of the two advocate teams. In this case, there may be a senior member of each advocate legal team who is responsible for the opening and closing statements and the cross-examination of witnesses. Other members of the legal team may divide the work of creating questions and working with specific witnesses among themselves. There may also be paralegals, court reporters, and other roles created to fill student interests and points of view.

All students have individual and advocate team goals. The goals of the attorneys include the following:

interview witnesses

cross-examine opposing witnesses

persuasively present arguments

The goals of the witnesses include the following:

become an authentic character

present credible testimony

The goal of the pro-capital punishment team is to convince the jury of the rightness and efficacy of capital punishment. The goal of the anti-capital punishment team is to persuade the jury that capital punishment is inhumane and ineffective and that its usage should be halted in the United States.

Role Descriptions

Again all lawyers must attend "law school." In law school mentors will help the attorneys-to-be research issues related to the trial and assist them in building and presenting a case before the court. The lawyers must work hard because of the volume of research involved. They must know more about the issue at hand than any single witness. They must have a firm grasp of all the history and issues involved. They must be able to create salient questions for their own witnesses. Moreover, they must be able to think on their feet in order to effectively cross-examine the witnesses presented by the opposition. The lawyers must be familiar with courtroom procedures. They should know how and when to raise objections to the questioning and cross-examining strategies of adversaries. They should also know when, how, and why a courtroom recess may be petitioned. Finally, lawyers must be persuasive speakers who can present opening and closing arguments that will convince the jury of the rightness of the cause advocated.

In the witnesses's drama school, they will research their characters in order to create believable, credible portrayals and testimony. They must present a biographical sketch of their character to the legal counsel of their advocate team. Witnesses must assist in the writing of the script and memorize their testimony. Witnesses should also possess the desire to enhance their dramatic talents. Each witness must be convincing if he or she is to impress and convince the jury of the rightness of his or her position. Each advocate team may create its own witnesses based upon evidence collected during their research of capital punishment. Possible character lists might include the following:

Pro-Capital Punishment	**Anti-Capital Punishment**
relatives, friends and associates of murder victims	relatives, friends, and associates of executed persons
prosecutors in capital cases	defense attorneys in capital cases
prison wardens	prison wardens
criminologists	criminologists
theologians	theologians

Either of the advocate teams may seek additional witnesses. For example, parties associated with the 1972 U.S. Supreme Court case, *Furman v. Georgia*, might make excellent witnesses. In that decision the high court ruled that the death penalty, as then carried out, violated the Eighth Amendment.

Capital Punishment Issues

The issues related to capital punishment are complex, thought-provoking, and generate heated discussions among people, revealing fundamental differences of values and beliefs. If time and the maturity of students allow for it, confronting these issues may be an excellent opportunity to discuss Lawrence Kohlberg's moral development model.[2] At which level of Kohlberg's hierarchy, for example, is the state operating when it executes one of its citizens? The following list of possible issues represent concerns each advocate team may explore. Class discussions and team research may suggest other issues to confront.

Pro-Capital Punishment Arguments

1. Capital punishment is not an immoral practice of the state. It is the state acting to protect itself against the possibility that those who commit murder and treason will ever be able to commit such abominable acts again.

2. The murder rate within the nation is growing alarmingly. Society must have at its disposal every possible tool to halt the further growth of this trend.

3. Capital punishment serves as a deterrent to crime. Murder rates have declined as state executions of convicted murderers have increased.

4. If it is indeed true that the poor and minorities are executed more often than other citizens, the solution is not to eliminate capital punishment. Rather, the solution is in providing greater access to the legal system for the poor and minorities, and in the remediation of the social conditions and economic climates which may breed criminal behavior.

5. Capital punishment is not cruel and unusual punishment when the terrible finality of the executed person's crime is considered. The methods used by states to execute convicted murderers are quickly administered and are not instruments of torture.

Anti-Capital Punishment Arguments

1. Murder is murder regardless of whether the act is performed by individuals or the state. In a civilized society the state has no right to take the life of any of its citizens.

2. The "eye-for-an-eye" philosophical position which underscores the use of the death penalty is not in keeping with our nation's fundamental beliefs about compassion and justice.

3. Capital punishment does not serve as an effective deterrent to crime.

4. The possibility always exists that the state will execute an innocent man or woman. Because capital punishment is such an extreme and final act, there is no restitution the state can make to those who are wrongfully convicted and executed.

5. Capital punishment is carried out neither uniformly nor equitably. Not all states use capital punishment. Does this mean that the life of a citizen is more valued in some states than in others? The executed have more often than not been poor and/or minority citizens. They have been unable to pay for the legal counsel and the appeals processes which might have saved their lives. Such inequities are an affront to the principles of a democracy.

Mentors

Mentors for the law and drama schools need not be professionals in those fields. Some general understanding of courtroom procedures or character development and of the broad issues in the capital punishment debate is all they need. Potential mentors are all around. Parents of students associated with either profession may agree to be mentors for their own children or for their children's classmates. Local colleges and universities may have prelaw and drama students willing to mentor students for a brief period of time. High school debate students would make excellent mentors and instructors for the law school. Retired attorneys can also serve as mentors for the would-be lawyers. High school drama students and members of local drama groups are excellent mentors for the witnesses. Some of the best mentors for students are their own relatives, or a neighbor who will listen to, counsel, and advise them. Teachers should counsel mentors on the goals of the advocacy trial and the roles of the students. They can also share important information with the mentor about each student. Each student should be ready to tell the mentor his or her specific goals in playing the role as an attorney or witness. Each student should engage in considerable research prior to the initial meeting with the mentor. Drew Davey uses contract forms for his fifth grade students that outline their specific goals, the help and assistance requested of the mentor, and the times and dates when the mentor and student will meet. The form is signed by the teacher, the student, and the mentor.

Creating Questions

After each witness has determined his or her character, they research the background and/or issues so that his or her character can testify with credibility. Next, each witness should determine the primary goal of his or her character in the advocacy trial. For example, what would the primary goal of a theologian be if he or she is to be a persuasive witness for the advocate team? Each witness then brainstorms a list of perhaps twenty possible questions which might be asked during the advocacy trial by the advocate team lawyer. The next step is to narrow the list to five or six questions. Witnesses may work with their mentors at this point in the process to complete the evaluation stage of the CPS process. At the same time, the lawyers, knowing the general identities of their respective witnesses, may also work with their mentors to create questions utilizing the same format and guidelines. Figure 6.10 was designed by Drew Davey to help his students zero in on the best questions they might utilize in the advocacy trial.

Fig. 6.10. Form for evaluating questions.

Question Evaluation Form

Read the following criteria and discuss them with your mentor. Use the criteria to rank each of the possible questions. Use one criterion at a time to evaluate all the proposed questions. The top ranking should be a 10 (or the highest number which corresponds with the number of questions generated), and the lowest ranking should be 1. After ranking every question by the first criterion listed, move on to the second criterion and again rank all proposed questions from highest to lowest. Proceed to evaluate all questions in this manner. Next, total the points each question has received in the evaluation process. Record each sum in the TOTAL column. Use this information to help you decide upon the best 5 or 6 questions.

Criteria

1. Will the question elicit information in its answer that is beneficial to the advocate team's position?

2. Will the question elicit information in its answer that is detrimental to adversary advocate team's position?

3. Can the question be answered adequately in one or two minutes?

4. Is the answer to the question likely to provoke cross-examination?

5. Will the question be acceptable testimony to give in court without being challenged by an objection?

ALTERNATIVE QUESTIONS	CRITERIA					TOTAL
	1	2	3	4	5	
1.						
2.						
3.						
4.						
5.						
6.						
7.						
8.						
9.						
10.						

Now, what are your best questions? Write them below, along with suggestions for possible answers.

Question #1 _____

Suggestions for a possible answer: _____

Question #2 _____

Suggestions for a possible answer: _____

Question #3 _____

Suggestions for a possible answer: _____

Question #4 _____

Suggestions for a possible answer: _____

Question #5 _____

Suggestions for a possible answer: _____

The Opening Statement

While the witnesses are developing their respective characterizations, the lawyers (recall that there may be more than one attorney for each advocate team) are also occupied with research about the history and issues related to capital punishment and are writing their opening statements. The purpose of the opening statement of the advocacy trial is to inform the jury of the group and individual goals. The overall goal of the advocate team and the individual goals of each witness should be persuasively presented. The lawyer should try from the very beginning to create a positive image in the minds of the jurors about the integrity of their witnesses and the rightness of their team's cause.

Writing the Script

Except for the cross-examination of witnesses, most of the advocacy trial is rehearsed. The creation of a script is a collaborative process between the attorneys and their witnesses. Attorneys and witnesses meet and share the five or six questions each has created. Once again, the evaluation stage of CPS is utilized to narrow the ten to twelve questions down to the best five or six the attorney will ask the witness during the advocacy trial (see figure 6.11). After the questions have been determined, both parties begin writing the answers each witness will give. The time invested in selecting relevant, thoughtful questions via the CPS evaluation process should make the task of writing pertinent and persuasive answers relatively easy. Much of the criteria specified in figures 6.10 and 6.11 should assist students in the selection of questions which will yield answers supportive of the advocate team's position. Figure 6.12 is an example of a form supplied to students as they plan and write their advocacy trial script.

Advocacy Trial Script

Once the various questions and answers for *all* the witnesses on the advocacy team have been written, the order of appearance of each witness should be agreed upon. Further, a background question should be created for each witness identifying the witness for the jury and establishing his or her credibility as a witness. Once the order of witnesses has been set and the progression and content of the questions for each witness decided, the lawyers and witnesses create the best possible answers or responses and *write* them into the final advocacy trial script. Figure 6.12 provides a form which may be utilized by students in the creation of a script. When the script is completed, lawyers and witnesses memorize it and rehearse it at least once.

(Text continues on page 204.)

Fig. 6.11. Evaluation of final questions.

Final Questions Evaluation Form

Examine the five or six questions which both the witness and the lawyer have drafted. This will make a total of ten to twelve questions. Use the following criteria to pare the list down to the five or six best questions actually to be used in the advocacy trial.

Criteria

1. Will the question elicit information in its answer that is beneficial to the advocate team's position?

2. Will the question elicit information in its answer that is detrimental to the adversary advocate team's position?

3. Can the question be answered in one or two minutes?

4. Is the answer to the question likely to provoke cross-examination?

5. Will the question be acceptable testimony to give in court without being challenged by an objection?

ALTERNATIVE QUESTIONS	CRITERIA					TOTAL
	1	2	3	4	5	
1.						
2.						
3.						
4.						
5.						
6.						
7.						
8.						
9.						
10.						

(Figure 6.11 continues on page 202.)

Now, what are your best questions? Write them below, along with suggestions for possible answers.

Question #1 _____

_____

Suggestions for a possible answer: _____

_____

_____

_____

Question #2 _____

_____

Suggestions for a possible answer: _____

_____

_____

_____

Question #3 _____

_____

Suggestions for a possible answer: _____

_____

_____

_____

Question #4 _____

_____

Suggestions for a possible answer: _____

_____

_____

_____

Question #5 _____

_____

Suggestions for a possible answer: _____

_____

_____

_____

Question #6 _____

_____

Suggestions for a possible answer: _____

_____

_____

_____

Fig. 6.12. Script

Advocacy Trial Script

Name of Lawyer _____

Name of Witness _____

Background   Question: _____

_____

Witness Response: _____

_____

First   Question: _____

_____

First Answer: _____

_____

_____

Second   Question: _____

_____

Second Answer: _____

_____

_____

Third Question: _____

_____

Third   Answer: _____

_____

_____

Note to Students: Continue in this fashion until all questions and answers have been written into the script.

Closing Arguments

The most difficult assignment the lawyers must fulfill is the closing argument. The attorneys must first remind the jury of their respective team's primary goal. They must also stress points of impact their witnesses have made during the advocacy trial. They must refute the testimony given by the adversary lawyers and witnesses. For rebuttal, it is imperative that each lawyer have a thorough and accurate set of notes taken during the trial. (This is another reason for having more than one attorney for each advocate team.) The lawyer(s) for each team will also want to punctuate the closing statement with a dramatic sentence or story leaving a lasting and favorable impression on the jury.

Jury Duty

The jury makeup will vary. Students working on other projects and electing not to participate in the advocacy trial as witnesses or lawyers may serve as jurors. If all class members are witnesses or lawyers, the jury may consist of students from other classes or may be made up of parents and community members (e.g., retired teachers and attorneys). The jury members select a foreman from among themselves. Given the topic of capital punishment, the deliberative body in this example of an advocacy trial may be the United States Supreme Court rather than a jury.

Advocacy Trial Format

To begin the proceedings the advocacy trial judge makes an opening statement to the jury about the broad issues to be explored. A sample judicial opening might read as follows:

Ladies and gentlemen of the jury. In this advocacy trial you will hear testimony and arguments for and against the institution of capital punishment. This is a complex issue which requires that you give your full attention to these proceedings. Regardless of the beliefs and opinions you have about the use of the death penalty, I entreat you to erase such thoughts from your mind and to be at all times an impartial listener. To underscore the importance of your duty here as jurors, I would remind you that your decision in this advocacy trial may ultimately decide the future course of the justice system in our nation as well as the fate of many human lives.

The trial proceeds in this order.

1. Opening statement by pro-capital punishment lawyer

2. Opening statement by anti-capital punishment lawyer

3. Pro-capital punishment lawyer calls and interviews first witness for the side

4. Anti-capital punishment lawyer cross-examines that witness

At this point, two alternative procedures are possible. The pro-capital punishment lawyer can call and interview his or her remaining witnesses. Each witness will be cross-examined by the anti-capital punishment legal team. Then, the anti-capital punishment legal team proceeds to call all of its witnesses.

The second alternative involves alternate turns taken in the witness stand by the respective witnesses of the two advocate teams. That is, after the first pro-capital punishment witness is questioned and cross-examined, the first anti-capital punishment witness takes the stand to give testimony and be cross-examined. The lawyers for each side continue to take turns placing their respective witnesses in the witness box until all witnesses have been called, have given testimony, and have been cross-examined.

After all testimony is given, the chief counsel for each advocate team makes a closing statement. Next, the judge in the advocacy trial reminds the jury of its duties. The jury must consider all the testimony they have heard and must reach a reasoned and impartial decision. The teacher should decide in advance of the trial whether a unanimous decision is required or whether a majority decision is acceptable. In the case of unanimous decision, the possibility exists that the jury will realize after considerable deliberation that a consensus decision is impossible to effect. In this case, the jury foreman notifies the judge that the jury has reached a stage of impasse and cannot reach a decision. The jury must also provide positive feedback to each of the witnesses and lawyers. Figure 6.13 is an example of ballot and feedback forms the jury can use.

Once the jury has reached its decision, the jury foreman notifies the judge, who calls all parties back into court. The judge asks the foreman to read the jury's decision aloud. The jury also presents the feedback sheets to the judge who, in turn, distributes them to the witnesses and lawyers. While the jury deliberates, the judge may also complete feedback forms for the lawyers and witnesses. With this action, the advocacy trial is ended.

Fig. 6.13. Ballot and feedback forms.

Advocacy Trial Ballot

Carefully consider all the evidence you have received and place an "X" on the line beside the statement you believe to be the best course of action for the United States to adopt.

_____ Capital punishment should be retained as one of several forms of punishment for persons who have received a fair trial and have been convicted of crimes involving murder and/or treason.

_____ Capital punishment should be uniformly banned in the United States.

Witness Feedback Form

Name of Witness _____

Was the witness credible and convincing? Why or Why not? Did the witness meet his or her stated goal(s)?

Lawyer Feedback Form

Name of Lawyer(s) _____

Did the lawyer (or legal team) succeed in presenting a convincing case for his or her advocate team position? Why or Why not?

Did the lawyer (or legal team) fulfill the advocate team's individual and group goals?

Notes

[1]Doyle, Arthur Conan. *The Valley of Fear* in *The Annotated Sherlock Holmes*, Vol. 1, edited by William S. Baring-Gould. New York: Clarkson N. Potter, 1967, 472.

[2]United States Department of Commerce, Bureau of the Census. *Historical Statistics of the United States: Colonial Times to 1970*, Vol. 1, Washington, D.C.: U.S. Government Printing Office, 1975: 414. Also, *Statistical Abstracts of the United States*, 108th ed., Washington, D.C.: U.S. Government Printing Office, 1987: 160.

[3]The author acknowledges and thanks Renee Kayser for suggesting the use of this crime writing activity.

[4]Lawrence Kohlberg, "The Cognitive-Developmental Approach to Moral Education," in David Purpel and Kevin Ryan, eds., *Moral Education ... It Comes with the Territory*, Berkeley, Calif.: McCutchan, 1976: 215-16.

Teacher Resources

Block, Eugene B. *Famous Detectives: True Stories of Great Crime Detection*. Garden City, N.Y.: Doubleday, 1967.

    The lives and exploits of thirteen great detectives are detailed.

Butler, William Vivian. *The Young Detective's Handbook*. Boston: Little, Brown, 1981.

    This book for youthful, would-be detectives won a special Edgar Award.

Dale, Alzina Stone, and Barbara Sloan Hendershott, with maps by John Babcock. *Mystery Reader's Walking Guide to London*. Lincolnwood, Ill.: Passport Books, 1987.

    The authors provide a street guide for the delight of mystery lovers.

De Sola, Ralph. *Crime Dictionary*. New York: Facts on File, Inc., 1982.

    From "Alcoholics Anonymous" to "zwendel" which is Dutch for swindle, terms used in or related to criminology are defined.

Gustafson, Anita. *Guilty or Innocent?* New York: Holt, Rinehart, and Winston, 1985.

    Readers decide the guilt or innocence of defendants in famous trials. Includes Lizzie Borden, Sacco and Vanzetti, Dr. Samuel Sheppard, and John Hinkley, Jr.

Harrison, Michael. *In the Footsteps of Sherlock Holmes*. New York: Drake Publishers, Inc., 1972.

    A chronological *and* geographical tour of London as Holmes and Dr. Watson went about the great city.

Hindley, Judy, and Donald Rumbelow. *KnowHow Book of Detection*. London: Usborne, 1978.

    This excellent resource for younger detectives is available in the United States from Educational Developments Corporation, P.O. Box 470663, Tulsa, OK 74147.

Jett, Betty, and Peggy Grossman. *Mysteries for Group Detectives, Collection No. 1*. East Windsor Hill, Conn.: Synergetics, 1986.

    A collection of ten mysteries students solve through the use of critical thinking skills and cooperative learning. See also *Mysteries for Group Detectives, Collection No. 2* (Synergetics, 1988).

Jones, Richard Glyn. *Unsolved: Classic True Murder Cases*. New York: Peter Bedrick Books, 1987.
Famous mystery writers try their hand at solving real murder cases which remain unsolved.

_____. *Solved: Famous Mystery Writers on Classic True Cases*. New York: Peter Bedrick Books, 1987.
Sir Arthur Conan Doyle, Damon Runyan, Ellery Queen, and other eminent writers of the mystery genre analyze famous crimes.

Keane, John. *Sherlock Bones: Tracer of Missing Pets*. Philadelphia, Pa.: J. B. Lippincott, 1979.
The delightful story of the nation's first pet detective.

Kobayashi, Tsukasa, Akane Higashiyama, and Masaharu Uemura. *Sherlock Holmes's London: Following the Footsteps of London's Master Detective*. San Francisco, Calif.: Chronicle Books, 1986.
A superb photographic journey which follows the path of the great detective.

Laurie, Peter. *Scotland Yard: A Study of the Metropolitan Police*. New York: Holt, Rinehart and Winston, 1970.
Some of the history and much of the procedural work of Scotland Yard is detailed in this account of the famous British institution that figures prominently in British mystery literature.

McArdle, Phil, and Karen McArdle. *Fatal Fascination: Where Fact Meets Fiction in Police Work*. Boston: Houghton Mifflin, 1988.
Both authors have worked directly with large city police departments and provide highly creditable accounts of step-by-step procedures in police investigation work.

Nash, Jay Robert. *Bloodletters and Badmen: A Narrative Encyclopedia of American Criminals from the Pilgrims to the Present* (3 volumes). New York: Warner Books, 1975.
The stories of famous criminals are told.

_____. *Almanac of World Crime*. Garden City, N.Y.: Anchor Press/Doubleday, 1981.
The author begins with a discussion of the aliases and monikers criminals use and proceeds from there to describe and detail all kinds of criminal behavior, worldwide.

Peat, David. *The Armchair Guide to Murder and Detection*. Ottawa, Canada: Deneau Publishers, 1984.
The author provides a highly detailed account of police procedures in homicide cases.

Powers, Richard Gid. *G-Men: Hoover's FBI in American Popular Culture*. Carbondale, Ill.: Southern Illinois University Press, 1983.
The author examines the role of the FBI in popular culture.

Reader's Digest. *Great True Stories of Crime, Mystery & Detection from the Reader's Digest*. Pleasantville, N.Y.: The Reader's Digest Association, 1965.
Stories as seemingly improbable (but true) as that of felon Victor Lustig who "sold" the Eiffel Tower.

Reit, Seymour. *The Day They Stole the Mona Lisa*. New York: Summit Books, 1981.
Reit describes the theft of the world's most famous painting.

Rubin, Sol. *Juvenile Offenders and the Juvenile Justice System*. Dobbs Ferry, N.Y.: Oceana Publications, 1986.

This is an informative book about the rights juveniles have in the legal system.

Stanford, Gene, and Barbara Dodds Stanford. *Learning Discussion Skills through Games*. New York: Citation Press, 1969.

A fun book of classroom activities to stimulate problem solving and critical thinking. Out of print and hard to find but worth the effort.

Thompson, Ruth, and Judy Hindley. *The Good Spy Guide: Tracking & Trailing*. London: Usborne Publishing, 1978.

Younger readers will be delighted as they learn how to track and trail humans and animals. Available in the U.S. through EDC Publications, 8141 E. 44th Street, Tulsa, Okla. 74145.

Viney, Charles. *Sherlock Holmes in London: A Photographic Record of Conan Doyle's Stories*. Boston: Houghton Mifflin, 1989.

Dramatic photographs of Victorian London.

Williams, Roger M. *The Super Crooks: A Rogue's Gallery of Famous Hustlers, Swindlers, & Thieves*. Chicago, Ill.: Playboy Press, 1973.

The facts about thirteen famous crimes and criminals are summarized.

Computer Simulations

Portwood, G., L. Elliott, K. Bull, and L. Groody. "Where in the USA Is Carmen Sandiego?"® See also "Where in Europe Is Carmen Sandiego?," "Where in the World Is Carmen Sandiego?,"® and "Where in Time Is Carmen Sandiego?" Broderbund Software-Direct, P.O. Box 12947, San Rafael, CA 94913-2947. 1-800-522-6263.

"Sherlock: The Riddle of the Crown Jewels." Infocom, Inc., 125 Cambridge Park Drive, Cambridge, MA 02140. (no author cited)

Snyder, Tom. "Snooper Troops"®. Spinnaker Software Co. To date, two programs are available: "The Granite Point Ghost" and "The Disappearing Dolphin." Tom Snyder Productions, 90 Sherman Street, Cambridge, MA 02140. 1-800-342-0236.

Mystery Reading List for Crime and Punishment

Clemens, Samuel L. (Mark Twain). *Tom Sawyer, Detective*. New York: New American Library, 1985.

Twain based this mystery on a real-life trial of a criminal in Sweden.

Dixon, Franklin W. *The Short-Wave Mystery*. New York: Grosset & Dunlap, 1972.

The Hardy Boys emulate their father in solving crimes in this and many, many more mysteries which have delighted young readers for several generations.

Gardner, Erle Stanley. *The Case of the Troubled Trustee*. Roslyn, N.Y.: Walter J. Black, 1965.

Perry Mason, the shrewd defense attorney, solves the mystery in yet another courtroom drama.

Hillerman, Tony. *Talking God*. New York: Harper & Row, 1989.

Hillerman sets his mysteries in Navajo lands of Arizona and New Mexico. His sleuths are Navajo Police Officer Jim Chee and Lieutenant Joe Leaphorn.

Hitchcock, Alfred. *Solve-Them-Yourself Mysteries*. New York: Random House, 1986.

The master of cinematic mysteries provides young readers with five crime mysteries to solve.

James, P. D. *Cover Her Face*. New York: Warner Books, 1987.

This is another well-crafted mystery featuring Scotland Yard's Chief Inspector Adam Dalgliesh.

Keene, Carolyn. *The Mysterious Image*. New York: Simon & Schuster, 1984.

The most famous of girl sleuths, Nancy Drew, works with her father, Attorney Carson Drew, and the police to solve another mystery.

Marsh, Ngaio. *When in Rome*. New York: Jove Publications, 1983.

Marsh's sleuth is Scotland Yard's Roderick Alleyn. This time he solves a mystery set in Italy.

Mortimer, John. *Rumpole Omnibus*. New York: Viking Penguin, 1983.

Horace Rumpole is a British barrister with a droll sense of humor (and a bossy wife) who also manages to free most of his clients by solving the mysteries in which they have become embroiled. Rumpole is another sleuth greatly popularized via the Public Television *Mystery!* series.

O'Marie, Sister Carol Anne. *A Novena for Murder*. New York: Dell, 1984.

A terrible crime invades the tranquility of Mount St. Francis College for Women causing Sister Mary Helen to track down the murderer.

Tey, Josephine. *The Daughter of Time*. New York: Collier Books, 1988.

Tey's brilliant sleuth is Inspector Alan Grant of Scotland Yard. In this particular case, Grant is mending in the hospital when he decides to use his sleuthing skills to explore the historical mystery of Richard III and the little princes.

Van Gulik, Robert, trans. *Celebrated Cases of Judge Dee*. New York: Dover Publications, 1976.

Back in the seventh century, Chinese legal officials acted as both judges and detectives in discovering, capturing, and punishing criminals. These are real cases. In later volumes, Van Gulik creates fictional cases for Judge Dee.

Bibliography of Mysteries for Students and Teachers

Primary Grades

Adler, David. *My Dog and the Green Sock Mystery*. New York: Holiday House, 1986.

Adler proves that mysteries may be written for even the youngest readers with this entry in A First Mystery Book series.

————. *Cam Jansen and the Mystery of the Monster Movie*. New York: Dell, 1984.

A reel of the movie Cam and friends are watching suddenly disappears and Cam Jansen uses her detection skills to find it. This is but one of many entries in the Cam Jansen series by Adler.

Allard, Harry, and James Marshall. *Miss Nelson Is Missing!* Boston: Houghton Mifflin, 1977.

Allard and Marshall have created one of the most delightful, endearing, and popular children's books to be found. Miss Nelson reappears in *Miss Nelson Is Back* (Houghton Mifflin, 1982) and *Miss Nelson Has a Field Day* (Houghton Mifflin, 1985).

Bunting, Eve. *Jane Martin, Dog Detective*. New York: Harcourt Brace Jovanovich, 1984.

Jane Martin follows all clues, including paw prints, to locate missing canines in this delightful introduction to mysteries and sleuthing for younger readers.

Christian, Mary Blount. *Sebastian (Super Sleuth) and the Santa Claus Caper*. New York: Pocket Books, 1984.

Sebastian is a wonderful, lovable shaggy dog who is one great sleuth. Though he frequently must enlist the support of his owner, Detective John Quincy Jones of the City Police Department, most of the time Sebastian does just fine on his own, thank you! The fun of the Sebastian books is that there are many, many more titles in the Sebastian series for young mystery fans to enjoy.

Fleischman, Paul. *Phoebe Danger, Detective*. Boston: Houghton Mifflin, 1983.

Phoebe and her partner Dash investigate the disappearance of an old bottle of Dr. Mooseheart's Two Minute Cough Conqueror in this funny mystery.

Kellogg, Steven. *The Mystery of the Flying Orange Pumpkin*. New York: Dial, 1980.

A delightful tale of mystery at Halloween time.

Lawrence, James. *Binky Brothers, Detectives*. New York: Harper & Row, 1968.

Two brothers team to solve neighborhood mysteries.

Levy, Elizabeth. *Something Queer Is Going On*. New York: Dell, 1973.

This is a delightful story of sleuthing to recover a missing canine.

Quackenbush, Robert. *Sherlock Chick's First Case*. New York: Gruner & Jahr, 1986.

A case in need of a solution awaits Sherlock Chick as soon as Emma Hen and Harvey Rooster's new son pops out of his shell wearing a deerstalker cap. See also *Detective Mole and the Halloween Mystery*. New York: Simon & Schuster, 1989.

Razzi, Jim, and Mary Razzi. *The Sherluck Bones Mystery-Detective, Book 1*. New York: Bantam, 1981.

Sherluck Bones lives in Kennelwood, U.S.A. No mystery escapes the notice of this delightful and brilliant canine sleuth.

Sharmat, Marjorie Weinman. *Nate the Great*. Dell, 1972.

Nate is the shrewd detective who solves the mystery of his friend Annie's missing picture in this comical book. Happily, author Sharmat has continued the series with several more Nate tales.

Middle Grades

Anderson, Lena, and Ulf Svedberg. *Nicky, the Nature Detective*. New York: Farrar, Straus and Giroux, 1983.

Nicky is a naturalist and a detective. She uses detective skills to learn why birds sing and how spiders spin their webs.

Bellairs, John. *The Curse of the Blue Figurine*. New York: Bantam Books, 1983.

Bellairs books are extremely popular with middle school readers. This book skillfully combines mystery and fantasy.

Brooks, Walter R. *Freddy the Detective*. New York: Alfred A. Knopf, Inc., 1986.

The Freddy books were popular in the 1940s and 1950s. In 1986, Alfred A. Knopf reissued several titles including this one in which Freddy the pig tries his hand at being a detective on the Bean family farm. His excellent sleuthing uncovers a plot to frame Jinx, the farm cat, of killing a pigeon. For true followers of Freddy's adventures there is even a fan club: Friends of Freddy, Connie Arnold, 1-F Northway Road, Greenbelt, MD 20770.

Carey, M. V. *The Mystery of the Blazing Cliffs*. New York: Random House, Inc., 1981.

This is one entry in the Three Investigators series originally created by Robert Arthur. Jupiter Jones leads the investigators who live in the small coastal town of Rocky Beach, California.

Clemens, Samuel L. (Mark Twain). *Tom Sawyer, Detective*. New York: New American Library, 1985.

Twain's most famous characters, Tom Sawyer and Huck Finn unravel a case of murder and theft.

Dicks, Terrance. *The Case of the Missing Masterpiece.* New York: Elsevier/Nelson Books, 1978.

   The Baker Street Irregulars try to find a stolen Constable painting. This is just one entry in a series of mysteries solved by the Baker Street Irregulars.

Disney, Walt Productions. *The Detective Book.* New York: Random House, Inc., 1978.

   The centerpiece of this book is the retelling of *Emil and the Detectives.*

Dixon, Franklin W. *The Short-Wave Mystery.* New York: Grosset & Dunlap, Publishers, 1972.

   The Hardy Boys mysteries continue to be as popular today as ever.

Erwin, Vicki Berger. *Jamie and the Mystery Quilt.* New York: Scholastic Inc., 1987.

   Jamie finds a quilt that seems to tell a special secret. Then it is stolen and she must recover the quilt to learn the secret it holds.

Farley, Carol. *The Case of the Vanishing Villain.* New York: Avon Books, 1986.

   Two sisters determine the identity of an escaped convict who is one of many passengers on a car ferry crossing Lake Michigan.

George, Jean Craighead. *Who Really Killed Cock Robin?* New York: E. P. Dutton & Co., Inc., 1971.

   This work is subtitled *An Ecological Mystery*, and that is just what it is. A gifted young detective, Tony Isidoro, uses detection skills to find out why a robin has died. This work is both a good mystery and a good science lesson.

Giff, Patricia Reilly. *Have You Seen Hyacinth MaCaw?* New York: Dell Publishing Co., Inc., 1981.

   Junior detective Abby Jones and her friend Potsie go sleuthing for a missing bird.

Goodman, Burton. *The Reader as Detective: Book 1.* New York: Amsco School Publications, 1985.

   In this anthology of stories readers take an active role in the reading process. Authors represented include Arthur Conan Doyle and Isaac Asimov. The series is continued with book two (Amsco, 1986) and three (Amsco, 1988).

Hope, Laura Lee. *The Chocolate-Covered Clue.* New York: Pocket Books, 1989.

   Yes, the Bobbsey Twins are back and all dressed up for the 1990s. The two sets of twins, Nan and Bert and Freddie and Flossie, are on the trail of a thief who is smashing all the chocolate cakes in town.

Howe, James. *The Celery Stalks at Midnight.* New York: Avon Books, 1983.

   Howe's books share a popularity as great as the *Miss Nelson* books with young readers. In this adventure, Bunnicula, the vampire bunny, is missing and it is up to the other animals in the Monroe household to find him.

Kastner, Erich. *Emil and the Detectives.* May Massee, trans. Garden City, N.Y.: Doubleday, 1930.

   A band of child sleuths help Emil recover the money stolen from him in this German children's literature classic.

Keene, Carolyn. *Mystery of the Winged Lion.* New York: Simon & Schuster, Inc., 1982.

   Like the Hardy Boys, Nancy Drew has been a friend of young readers for generations. This episode takes Nancy to Venice.

Kenny, Kathryn. *Trixie Belden and the Mystery at Saratoga*. Racine, Wis.: Western Publishing Company, Inc., 1979.

The Trixie Belden mysteries, like the Nancy Drew and Hardy Boys mysteries, are strictly by formula, but nevertheless do provide enjoyable light reading for younger students.

Konigsburg, E. L. *From the Mixed-up Files of Mrs. Basil E. Frankweiler*. New York: Atheneum Publishers, 1967.

Konigsburg won the Newbery Medal in 1970 for this book which tells of an adventure a brother and sister have attempting to solve a mystery about a famous piece of sculpture.

McHargue, Georgess. *Funny Bananas*. New York: Dell Publishing Co., Inc., 1975.

This enjoyable mystery is set among the dinosaurs in New York City's Museum of Natural History. See also McHargue's *The Turquoise Toad Mystery* (Dell, 1982).

Montgomery, Ramsey. *The Mona Lisa Is Missing!* New York: Bantam Books, 1988.

This is one entry in the extremely popular Choose Your Own Adventure® series. In this adventure, the reader is transported to Paris where da Vinci's masterpiece, the *Mona Lisa*, has been stolen.

Naylor, Phyllis Reynolds. *The Bodies in the Bessledorf Hotel*. New York: Avon Books, 1986.

Comedy and mystery mix as Bernie Magruder and his friends try to find a villain who has raised havoc in the hotel his father manages.

Packard, Edward. *Where Is the Eye on the Pyramid on the One-Dollar Bill?* New York: McGraw-Hill Book Company, 1988.

The creator of the Choose Your Own Adventure® series is back with a new series, Earth InspectorsT, which combines the mystery and science fiction genres.

Raskin, Ellen. *The Westing Game*. New York: Avon Books, 1978.

This is a modern classic in children's literature which won the Newbery Medal. A host of gifted children are characters in this book which is not only a good mystery, but a puzzle to solve as well. Raskin also wrote two other puzzle/mystery novels for young readers, *Figgs & Phantoms* (Avon, 1974) and *The Tattooed Potato and Other Clues* (Avon, 1975).

Roos, Kelly, and Stephen Roos. *The Incredible Cat Caper*. New York: Dell Publishing Co., Inc., 1985.

Three children, a Siamese cat, Simba, and a cat burglar all become involved in this delightful mystery penned by Edgar Award-winning authors.

Simon, Seymour. *Einstein Anderson*. New York: The Viking Press, 1980.

Einstein Anderson is more apt to use test tubes than a magnifying class to solve mysteries that the science fans in the classroom will especially enjoy.

Snyder, Zilpha Keatley. *The Egypt Game*. New York: Dell Publishing Co., Inc., 1967.

This is an excellent book which defies categorization. There is mystery here, however, as modern-day children connect with ancient Egypt. Readers will be enthralled and entertained.

Titus, Eve. *Basil and the Pygmy Cats*. New York: Pocket Books, 1971.

Basil is the mouse equivalent of Sherlock Holmes, right down to dress and sleuthing style. The delightful story of Basil is revived in *Basil of Baker Street* (Pocket Books, 1988).

Treat, Lawrence. *You're the Detective!* Boston: David R. Godine, Publisher, 1983.

Following his success with *Crime and Puzzlement* (David R. Godine, Publisher, 1982) for adult reader-
ship, Lawrence Treat created a similar puzzle book of picture and word mysteries for children.

Wilson, Eric. *The Green Gables Detectives*. Toronto: Collins Publishers, 1988.

This excellent Canadian mystery is set in the very farmhouse on Prince Edward Island where Lucy Maud
Montgomery wrote *Anne of Green Gables*. Wilson has penned an entire series of mysteries which take
place in prominent Canadian locales.

Secondary Grades

Asimov, Isaac. *Casebook of the Black Widowers*. New York: Ballantine, 1980.

This is one of many anthologies by the man who is arguably the world's most prolific living author.
Readers may wish to also sample Asimov's *The Union Club Murders* (Ballantine Books, 1983).

Barnard, Robert. *Death of a Mystery Writer*. New York: Dell, 1978.

Barnard is for older readers, but he writes witty and literate mysteries.

Bentley, E. C. *Trent's Last Case*. New York: Harper & Row, 1978.

Dorothy L. Sayers ranked this work beside Collins's *The Moonstone* and Doyle's Holmes stories as a
genuine classic in the mystery genre.

Block, Lawrence. *The Burglar Who Liked to Quote Kipling*. New York: Pocket Books, 1979.
Block writes for an adult audience, but older students will enjoy his Bernie Rhodenbarr mysteries.

Braun, Lilian Jackson. *The Cat Who Ate Danish Modern*. New York: Berkley Publishing Group, 1986.
Cat fanciers will love the "Cat" mysteries Braun has crafted. Koko and Yum Yum are two Siamese cats who are the real sleuths in this mystery.

Chesterton, G. K. *The Father Brown Omnibus*. New York: Dodd, Mead, 1951.
The beloved Father Brown sleuths and solves mysteries.

Christie, Agatha. *The Mysterious Affair at Styles*. New York: Bantam, 1983.
Christie's first mystery. She is probably the best puzzle conjurer ever to write mysteries. Happily, most of her mysteries are entirely suitable for classroom use. She also wrote popular mystery plays that may be found in *The Mousetrap and Other Plays* (Bantam, 1981). *The Mousetrap* holds the record as the longest, continuously running play in the world.

Collins, Wilkie. *The Moonstone*. New York: Dodd, Mead, 1951.
Collins was the father of the English detective novel. This is his best work.

Doyle, Arthur Conan. *Adventures of Sherlock Holmes*. New York: Ballantine, 1975.
Doyle created the most famous fictional sleuth ever.

Dvorkin, David. *Time for Sherlock Holmes*. New York: Dodd, Mead, 1983.
This is an ingenious mystery in which the evil Moriarty has stolen H. G. Wells's time machine and Sherlock Holmes must go into the future to foil him.

Francis, Dick. *Twice Shy*. New York: Ballantine, 1982.
Students may already be familiar with the Dick Francis mysteries as several have been shown on Public Televison's *Mystery!* series. The books are for adult audiences, but may be read by high school students.

Gilman, Dorothy. *Mrs. Pollifax and the Golden Triangle*. New York: Doubleday, 1988.
Of Gilman's creation, the great actress Helen Hayes says, "Blessings on Mrs. Pollifax. She came along just when I was mourning the loss of Agatha Christie's Miss Marple."

Hammett, Dashiell. *The Maltese Falcon*. New York: Vintage, 1984.
The tough-guy private eye is created with the appearance of Sam Spade in this highly acclaimed mystery.

Hillerman, Tony. *Talking God*. New York: Harper & Row, 1989.
Hillerman's sleuths are Lieutenant Joe Leaphorn and Officer Jim Chee of the Navajo police force, and his mysteries are spell-binding thrillers laced with fascinating information about native American religion and customs. The crimes in the Hillerman novels, however, are frequently quite violent, and the books should be used with considerable care by teachers even at the secondary level.

Hitchcock, Alfred. *Alfred Hitchcock's Solve-Them-Yourself Mysteries*. New York: Random House, 1963.
In the introduction, Hitchcock recommends a game which the family may play while reading and solving the five mysteries presented.

James, P. D. *An Unsuitable Job for a Woman*. New York: Warner Books, 1982.

James has created a marvelous sleuth in Adam Dalgliesh, a Scotland Yard detective who also writes poetry. Her books are for mature readers, but are considered to be excellent works both within and beyond mystery circles. See also *Cover Her Face* (Warner Books, 1987).

Langton, Jane. *The Transcendental Murder*. New York: Viking Penguin, 1989.

Celebrated juvenile novelist Langton turns her attention to adult fare with this murder mystery featuring Homer Kelly, a celebrated Emersonian scholar, as her sleuth. See also Langton's *Emily Dickinson Is Dead* (Viking Penguin, 1985).

Lathen, Emma (Mary Jane Latsis and Martha Henissart). *By Hook or by Crook*. New York: Pocket Books, 1977.

"Emma Lathen" is not the real author of the John Putnam Thatcher mysteries, but there is nothing phony about the information packed into "her" mysteries. Thatcher, senior vice president of the world's third largest bank, this time finds himself involved in a murder in the Persian rug trade. There are nearly twenty mysteries in the series, each set in the atmosphere of a different industrial or commercial enterprise.

MacLeod, Charlotte. *Rest You Merry*. New York: Avon, 1978.

There is a whole body of Christmas-related mysteries, and this introduction to the Peter Shandy mysteries is probably the best of the lot. The author has many, many more grand mystery adventures, including many written under the pen name of Alisa Craig. (See her letter to students in the "Language Arts" chapter of *Mystery and Detection*.)

Marsh, Ngaio. *When in Rome*. New York: Jove Publications, 1983.

Inspector Roderick Alleyn is Marsh's sleuth and this time the Scotland Yard sleuth explores both an ancient civilization and a modern crime.

Milne, A. A. *The Red House Mystery*. New York: Dell, 1984.

Secondary readers who loved Winnie-the-Pooh will be delighted that his creator also wrote a very fine mystery.

O'Marie, Sister Carol Anne. *A Novena for Murder*. New York: Dell, 1984.

The writer here is a nun and so is her sleuth, Sister Mary Helen. Readers have great fun matching wits with Sister Mary Helen who must solve the crimes which plague the campus of Mount St. Francis College for Women.

Poe, Edgar Allan. *The Short Fiction of Edgar Allan Poe: An Annotated Edition*. Indianapolis, Ind.: Bobbs-Merrill, 1976.

Here are the classic short stories by the man who created the mystery story genre.

Rich, Virginia. *The Cooking School Murders*. New York: Ballantine, 1982.

Now here is a real treat. Not only do readers get a good mystery yarn, they also get first-rate recipes to try. See also *The Baked Bean Supper Murders* (Ballantine, 1983).

Sayers, Dorothy L. *The Five Red Herrings*. New York: Harper & Row, 1986.

Lord Peter Wimsey, Sayers's aristocratic sleuth solves the mystery.

Taylor, Phoebe Atwood. *The Crimson Patch*. Woodstock, Vt.: Foul Play Press, 1986.

The Vermont publisher, Foul Play Press, has lovingly reproduced and brought back into print Taylor's wonderfully evocative 1930s Cape Cod mysteries featuring a most delightful sleuth, Asey Mayo.

Tey, Josephine. *The Daughter of Time*. New York: Collier Books, 1988.

Many mystery fans would argue that this is the best mystery novel ever written. It is a spellbinding tale of a modern-day inspector, Alan Grant, who probes the mystery behind the tale of Richard III, accused of the heinous crime of murdering his brother's children who stood between him and the throne of England.

Van Gulik, Robert, trans. *Celebrated Cases of Judge Dee*. New York: Dover, 1976.

Celebrated cases of Judge Dee, a seventh-century Chinese judge who performed duties as both detective and judge. Van Gulik has gone beyond the translations to create several original Judge Dee mysteries.

Watson, Clarissa. *Somebody Killed the Messenger*. New York: Atheneum, 1988.

Murder and intrigue in the art world. The sleuth is Persis Willum of the Gregor Olitsky's posh North Shore Galleries.

Teachers and Library Media Specialists

Dexter, Colin. *Service of All the Dead*. New York: Bantam, 1988.

The sleuth is Inspector Morse who loves Mozart and T. S. Eliot and who must solve the grizzly murders taking place in Oxford's Church of St. Frideswide.

Hansen, Joseph. *Fadeout*. New York: Holt, Rinehart and Winston, 1970.

Hansen's mysteries are very well written, but they are really for the teacher or librarian. His detective is insurance investigator David Brandstetter who is gay. While the works are certainly not pornographic, they do revolve around adult issues.

Huxley, Elspeth. *Murder on Safari*. New York: Harper & Row, 1982.

A 1930s mystery set in Kenya involving a safari party.

Grafton, Sue. *"A" Is for Alibi*. New York: Bantam, 1987.

Like Hansen's well-crafted mysteries, Grafton's work is also excellent but primarily for adult reading audiences. Kinsey Millhone is a smart, independent, and modern woman. She is also a California private investigator who gets into more than her share of intrigue. Grafton's alphabet mysteries make great vacation reading for teachers and librarians. See also *"F" Is for Fugitive* (Henry Holt, 1989).

Moyes, Patricia. *Dead Men Don't Ski*. New York: Holt, Rinehart and Winston, 1984.

Moyes introduced Inspector Tibbett of Scotland Yard in this murder mystery set in a ski resort in the Italian Alps.

Teachers and library media specialists searching for additional mysteries for the secondary grades may wish to consult Bill Pronzini and Marcia Muller's *1001 Midnights: The Aficionado's Guide to Mystery and Detective Fiction* (New York: Arbor House, 1986).

Answer Key

Chapter 2: The Language Arts

Mystery Desk—The desk shown in figure 2.4, p. 25, might have been one used by the Brontë children: Charlotte, Emily, Anne, and Branwell. For further details, please see the accompanying drawing and also read the letter to students in "The Arts" chapter, p. 70.

SCENE: Haworth Parsonage when Brontë children were young (Charlotte, Emily, Branwell, Anne).

1 Their father was a minister.
2 Church at Haworth 1831.
3 Graveyard
4 Books written by Charlotte, 1830's.

5 Quill and ink symbolize writer.
6 Small desk circa 1750's.
7 Map drawn by Branwell, an artist.
8 12 wooden soldiers (circa 1800's), a gift from their father around which the Brontë children created Great Glass Town and other adventures.

Traces—Figure 2.5, p. 27, is a scene from the wicked witch's death in *The Wizard of Oz*. The animal tracks were made by "Toto." Dorothy is wearing the ruby slippers so she does not leave human footprints. The witch's crystal ball is on the table. The torch the witch used to frighten the scarecrow lies on the floor along with her hat and the empty bucket and water which was her undoing. The flying monkeys may be seen in the distant sky. The wizard's face may be detected in the clouds directly above the drawbridge.

Sleuth Search—figure 2.7, pp. 35-36.

Puzzle A	Puzzle B
1. B	1. K
2. F	2. I
3. G	3. G
4. C	4. H
5. H	5. A
6. A	6. L
7. J	7. B
8. L	8. D
9. E	9. C
10. P	10. E
11. M	11. J
12. K	12. F
13. I	
14. O	
15. N	
16. D	

Chapter 3: The Arts

Mystery Desk—Figure 3.4, p. 76, is a desk/table which might have been in the studio where famed American artist Georgia O'Keeffe worked. For the identification of specific drawings, please see the accompanying drawing.

SCENE: Adobe style house "Ghost Ranch" in New Mexico.

1 Desert
2 Mexican and Indian art.
3 Pelvic bone
4 Skull
5 River rocks

6 Lots of Indian rugs
7 Painter's art materials.
8 Long time association with Chicago Institute of Art.
9 Tickets to New York to visit husband, Alfred Stieglitz.

Traces — Figure 3.6, p. 79, is a scene from *Pinocchio*. The accompanying drawing identifies the footprints.

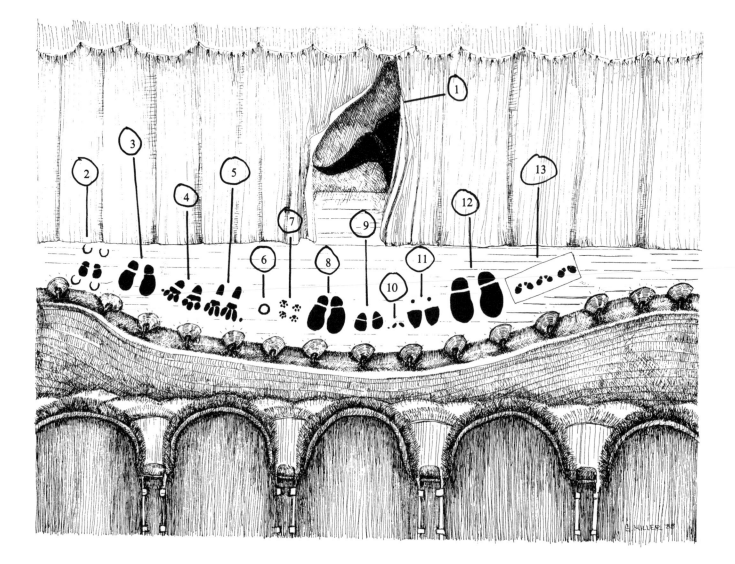

1 Monstro	8 Geppetto
2 Lampwick (all boys that were turned into donkeys)	9 Pinocchio
3 Shady Coachman	10 Jiminy Cricket
4 Gideon	11 Blue Fairy
5 Honest John	12 Stromboli
6 Cleo (fish)	13 Other puppets
7 Figaro (cat)	

"Picture Gallery," figure 3.9, pp. 95-96.

Solution to *Picture Gallery*

1. Yes. There are hundreds of examples of fooling the public.

2. Not with absolute certainty. Controversy still rages over some paintings which experts have studied to the best of their ability without being able to ascertain their authenticity.

3. Probably, as pointed out in answer 2. Experts can usually spot copies, but not always.

4. No. The canvas has rotted on many works of art, either because of age or the poor quality of the medium painted on, and a technique has been developed for placing the painting face down, removing the old canvas without hurting the painting, and then pasting a new canvas onto the back. Then presto! You have an old painting on new canvas.

5. Yes. These methods are commonly used to give sure proof of the age of a painting.

6. The still life of the flowers, which casts the same shadow as all the paintings in A. On the second visit Whiz noted that all the paintings with one exception cast shadows different from what he'd seen the first time. He concluded that he was seeing a painting of a painting, and that it had been copied with the shadow as it existed in A. The thief removed the real painting, pasted the painting of the painting in its place, and nobody noticed the difference until Whiz pointed it out.

   The kind of painting that looks so real that it fools you is called *trompe l'oeil*, which is French and means "fools the eye." It goes back thousands of years ago to the legend of the Greek painter who painted grapes so realistically that birds came and pecked at them.

   In the nineteenth century it was fashionable for wealthy people to have someone paint these *trompe l'oeil* paintings on their walls, so that it looked as if there were a lake or a beautiful garden outside. Sometimes they just had a door painted, but the fashion has disappeared, maybe because *trompe l'oeil* is so hard to pronounce—except, of course, for a Frenchman.

Picture Mystery, figure 3.10, p. 98. Please see accompanying drawing provided by Walden Books.

HOW MANY HIDDEN WEAPONS CAN YOU FIND?

Chapter 4: The Social Studies

Tools of the Trade—Figure 4.3, p. 109. An archaeologist suggests that the following tools would be found at a site such as the one pictured. Tools found inside the tent would include:

microscope	scales
drafting board	light box
various chemicals (to clean found artifacts)	sponges
glue	

Tools found inside or outside the tent would include:

brushes	dental tools
notebooks	tags
plastic bags	boxes
brown paper sacks	pens
graph paper	

Tools found outside the tent would include:

trowel	camera	line level
plumb bob	string	stakes
hammer	screens	backhoe
tape measure	compass	foil
cotton	transit	marker pens
pin flags	signboard/letterboard	tarp
shovels (flat-nosed and pointed)	gloves	buckets
flagging tape	canteen	first aid kit

Mystery Desk—Figure 4.4, p. 110 is a desk and office space which might have belonged to famed anthropologist Margaret Mead. See the accompanying drawing for more detailed information about the desk.

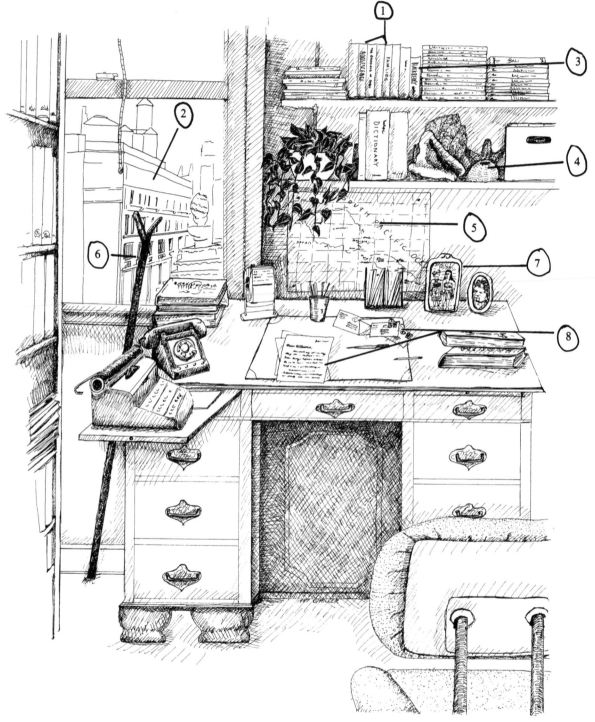

SCENE: Meads office as curator of American Museum of Natural History.

1 Focus of research.
2 View out of tower office of American Museum of Natural History in New York.
3 Autobiography
4 Shells from South Seas.

5 Map of South Pacific.
6 Staff she carried in later life.
7 Picture of Mead with native.
8 Prolific correspondence with people around the world.

Traces—Figure 4.5, p. 111 is a drawing of an archaeological site. Fort Boonesborough was created by Daniel Boone in 1774 on a bank beside the Kentucky River. Students should note the clearing around the fort that was created so that enemies could not hide. Timber cut for the clearing was used to build the fort. There were thirty cabins built around a rectangular piece of ground. all the windows and doors faced into the middle courtyard. The cabins were joined by timber fence to form a stockade. The cabins in the four corners were two-story to allow riflemen better aim. The post holes were dug for the placement of the cabin and stockade timbers. The square holes were dug for the posts securing the gates. The stones were collected and used to build chimneys and fireplaces for the cabins.

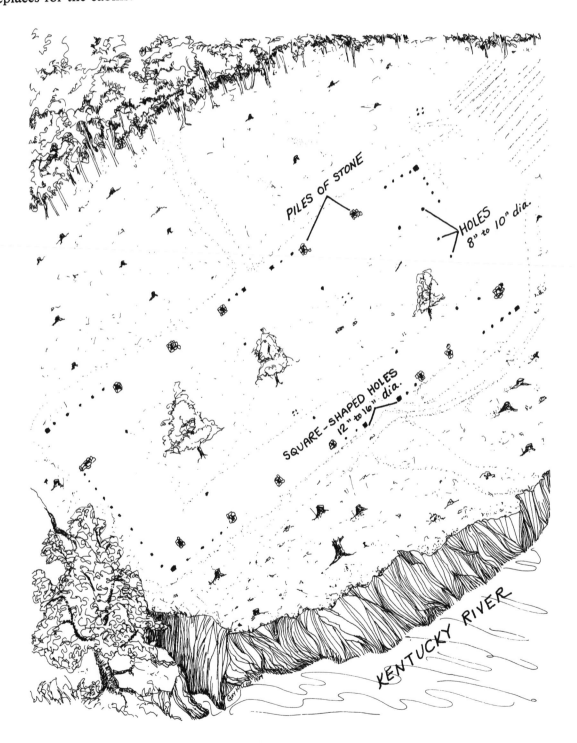

Chapter 5: Future Studies

Mystery Desk—The desk in figure 5.4, p. 146, might belong to Isaac Asimov. See the accompanying drawing for the identifications of details found in the drawing.

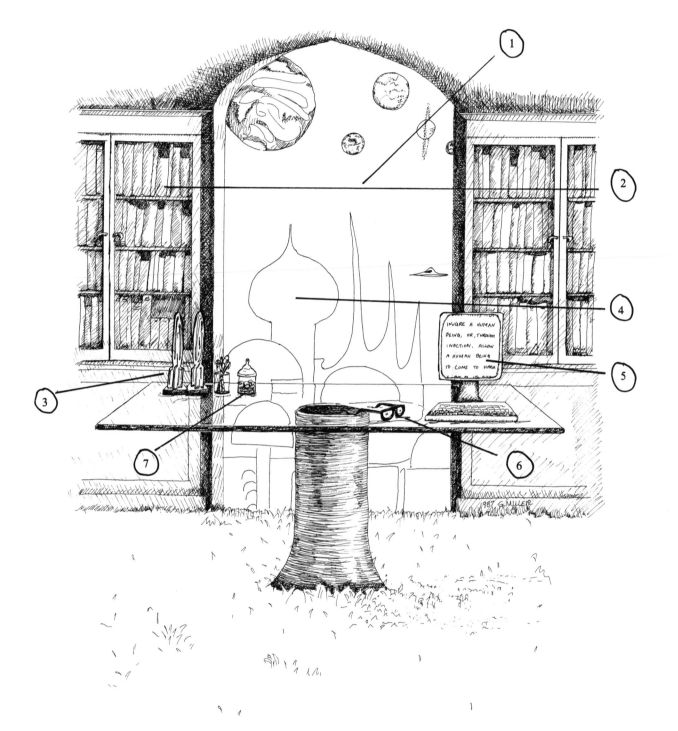

1 Futuristic scene
2 Many books symbolize prolific writer.
3 Two Hugo awards
4 Russian architecture (he was Russian born)

5 Three laws of robotics
6 His glasses
7 Jars of candy. Father owned a candy store. Isaac worked there as a young boy.

Traces — Figure 5.5, p. 147, represents the first landing on the Moon during the *Apollo 11* mission in 1969. The human footprints belong to Neil Armstrong and Edwin Aldrin. The tripod prints were made by the lunar landing module.

Chapter 6: Crime and Punishment

Mystery Desk — Figure 6.4, p. 173, is the desk of the world's most famous detective, Sherlock Holmes. See the accompanying drawing for references to many of his famous cases which are featured in the drawing.

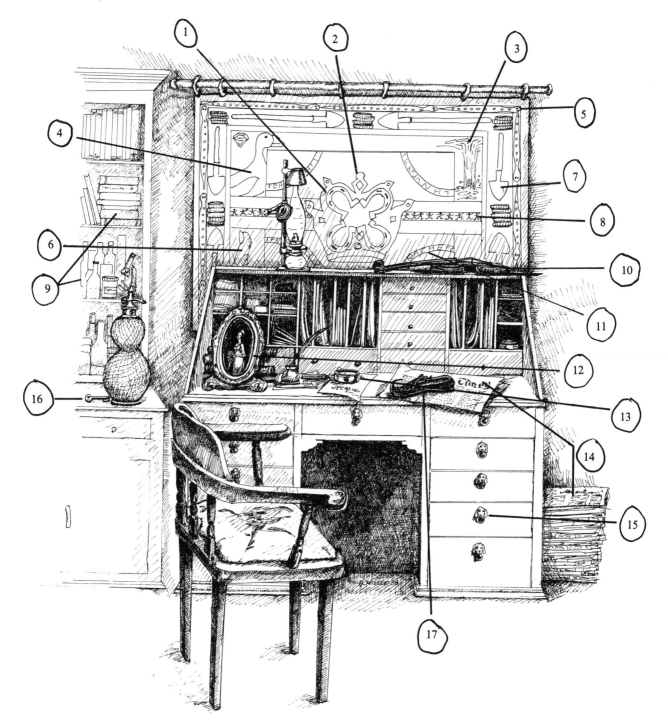

Eleven adventures are represented in this drawing.

1 Horseshoes from "Silver Blaze."
2 Crown from "The Musgrave Ritual."
3 Waterfall from "The Final Problem."
4 Goose and stone from "The Blue Carbuncle."
5 Swamp adder from "The Speckled Band."
6 "The Engineer's Thumb"
7 Spades and coins from "The Red-Headed League."
8 Stick figures from "The Dancing Men."
9 Chemicals, books, etc.

10 Sherlock's violin
11 "Rache" from "A Study in Scarlet."
12 Irene Adler from "A Scandal in Bohemia."
13 Magnifying glass
14 London Times
15 "The Hound of Baskervilles"
16 Key to unlock mysteries.
17 Persian slipper for pipe tobacco.

Traces—Figure 6.5, p. 175, represents a possible stage setting for a dramatization of one of Sherlock Holmes's most celebrated cases, "The Speckled Band." The stage is sectioned to show two adjoining bedrooms. The room on the left belongs to the evil Dr. Roylott. The room on the right is Miss Stoner's. A small passageway in the wall between the rooms may be noted. This is the route through which Dr. Roylott passes the deadly swamp adder.

Index

AT&T, 11
Abrell, Ron, 4, 5-8(fig.), 17
Acceptance-finding stage of creative problem solving, 58-59
Acrostic puzzle, 12, 15(fig.)
Adam Dalgliesh, 10, 32, 35, 126, 182
Adams, Tom, 93
Adler, David, 36
Adventures of Conan Doyle: The Life of the Creator of Sherlock Holmes, 40
"Adventure of the Dancing Men," 43, 93
"Adventure of the Speckled Band" (story), 21-22, 31
"Adventure of the Speckled Band" (video), 29
"Adventures of the Empty House," 21
"Adventures of Sherlock Holmes" (television series), 29
Adventures of Sherlock Holmes (book), 16, 28
Adverb walk, 81
Advocacy trial, 180, 194-206
  creating questions, 197-202
  jury duty, 204
  mentors, 197
  opening statements, 200
  roles, 194-95
  trial format, 204-5
  trial script, 203
"Advocates" (television series), 194
Aeschylus, 28
Afghanistan, 128
Agatha Christie: An Autobiography, 41
Agatha Christie Collection (film series), 28
"Agatha Christie: How Did She Do It?" (video), 39
Aldersgate, 129
Aldershot, 129
Allan, John, 42
Allan Pinkerton: First Private Eye, 39, 40
Allen, Woody, 87
Allied troops, 72
Almanac of World Crime, 180

Alphabet books, 97
American Bar Association, 176-77
American Revolution, 143
Amsterdam museums, 72
Analogous reasoning, 22, 30
Analysis. *See* Problem solving model
Anasazi, 132
Anderson, LeVere, 39
Angel (fictional sculpture), 93
Animalia, 97
Anno, Mitsumasa, 97, 99
Anno's Journey, 97, 99
Anno's U.S.A., 97
Anthropologist, 106
Appointment with Death (movie), 28
Archaeological investigations, 131-34
Archaeology site, 109, 111
Aristotle Detective, 125
Arizona State Law Journal, 167
Arizona State University, 167
Armchair Detective, The (periodical), 10
Art projects, 93-100
  alphabet books, 97
  calendar art, 99
  desk intrigue, 100
  draw a crime, 94
  draw a residence, 93
  draw a sleuth, 93
  fingerprint art, 100
  gameboards, 94
  greeting cards, 100
  Harris Burdick puzzles, 99
  illustrated art mysteries, 99
  mystery by the dozen, 99
  mystery chess set, 100
  picture mysteries, 97
  rebus codes, 93
  sculpting heroes, 100

Art forgery. *See* Case studies/Arts
Asch, Rosalind, 93
Asey Mayo, 16, 35
Ashleigh Brilliant, 161
Asimov, Isaac, 51, 56, 160-61
Asimov's Sherlockian Limericks, 51
Asking questions (research skills), 114-15
Assassinations (Kennedy and Lincoln), 124
Attorney, 167
Aunt Sadie's will, 127-28
Australia, founding of, 143-44, 180
Author's League, 62
Awareness activities, 80-81

Backplanning, 121-23(fig.)
"Baker Street" (musical), 88
Baker Street (221 B), 5, 93, 123, 128-29, 183
Barry, John, 88
Base, Graeme, 97
Baseball scandal, 180
Baskerville Hall, 93
Bassett, Carol Ann, 133
Bellaris, John, 36
Bergman, Ingrid, 28
Bible, 21, 132
Bigley, Betsey (a.k.a., Cassie Chadwick), 180
Billy the Kid, 180
Biography studies and activities, 39-43
Black Bart, 51
Black Socks scandal, 180
Block, Eugene B., 182
Bloodletters and Badmen: A Narrative Encyclopedia of American Criminals from the Pilgrims to the Present, 180
Bloomsbury (England), 129
"Blue Carbuncle" (video), 29
Board games, 94, 123
"Body in the Library" (video), 28
Boesky, Ivan F., 128
Bogart, Humphrey, 29, 32
Boles, Charles E. (Black Bart), 51
Bonnie and Clyde, 128, 179-80
Booth, John Wilkes, 180
Borden, Lizzie, 44, 51, 124, 180
Boston police, 170
Botany Bay, 143-44
Bradbury, Ray, 161
Brandeis, Louis, 182
Bredius, Abraham, 72
Breton, Andre, 16
Brett Connor, 89-90(fig.)
Brett, Jeremy, 29
Brinks robbery, 99, 167-70(fig.)

British literature, 119
British Museum, 129
British Travel Authority, 128
Broadway Journal (periodical), 42
Brontë children, 70-71
Brother Cadfael, 35
Bruce, Nigel, 29
Buck, Pearl, 55
Bull, Ken, 131
Bulletin board displays, 93, 117, 123, 129, 179, 191
Bulwer-Lytton Contest, 57
Burger, Warren, 182
Burns, William J., 182
Burr, Aaron, 180
Burr, Raymond, 62
Bush, George, 100
Butler, William, 178

C. Auguste Dupin, 35, 43
Calendar art, 99
Cam Jansen, 36
Cambridge, 129
Cape Cod Mystery, 16
Capital punishment, 136, 194-96
Capone, Al, 180
Card catalog, 119
Carmen (role of), 88
Carter, Howard, 132-33
Cartooning, 89, 191
Case of the Vanishing Victim, 36
Case studies, 9
    arts, 72-74(fig.)
    crime and punishment, 169-70(fig.)
    futures, 143-44(fig.)
    language arts, 21-22(fig.)
    social studies, 107-8(fig.)
Casebook of the Black Widowers, 56
Cassidy, Shaun, 29
Cassidy, "Butch," 131
Cassiday, Bruce, 28
Castle, 134
Catching crooks, 178
Cats (musical), 52
Celery Stalks at Midnight, 85
Central Park (New York), 97
Chandler, Raymond, 35
Charing Cross Station, 129
Chess set (mystery), 100
Chesterfield (England), 129
Chesterton, G. K., 28, 29, 35, 56
Choctaw, 108
Choose Your Own Adventure Series, 60
Christ and the Disciples at Emmaus (painting), 72-73

Christie, Agatha, 28, 35, 36, 39, 40, 51, 56, 83, 97, 99, 100, 112, 118, 136. *See also* Hercule Poirot and Jane Marple
  autobiography, 41
  characters, 10
  disappearance, 39
  limerick tribute, 51
  works, 28
Cinquains, 50
Class detectives club, 56-57
Classroom environment, 10
Claudia Kincaid, 93
Clearing House (periodical), 4, 5-8(fig.)
Clemens, Samuel L. (Mark Twain), 44, 56, 62, 87
Clemm, Virginia, 43
Close Encounters of the Third Kind (movie), 159
Clue (board game), 10, 40
Codebreakers, 108
Codes, 107-8(fig.)
Collins, Wilkie, 16, 41, 58
Colorado College, 106
Colorado history and geography, 131
Columbo, 90
Companion to the Mystery of Edwin Drood, 59
Complete Guide to Sherlock Holmes, 45
Complete Sherlock Holmes, 183
Computer Crime, 156
Computer crimes, 155-56
Constructive speeches, 135
Convivial Codfish, 19
Cook, Captain James, 143
Coopersmith, Jerome, 88
Coremans, P. B., 73
Corpse in Oozak's Pond, 19
Corpus delicti, 176
Courbet, 99
Covent Garden, 129
Craig, Alisa, 19
Create-a-mystery game, 84
Create-a-Sleuth: Writing a Detective Story, 60
Creative dramatics activities, 80-84, 192
  adverb walk, 81
  awareness activities, 80-81
  create-a-mystery game, 82-83
  environmental walks, 82
  improvisations, 82-83
  pantomime crimes, 81-82
Creative problem solving (CPS) model, 58-59, 194, 197-99
CPS activity: *Mystery of Edwin Drood*, 58-59
Creating radio dramas, 85-87
Cricket (periodical), 19
Crime and Puzzlement, 94
Crime Dictionary, 177
Crime reporter, 192-93(fig.)

Crime terms, 176-78
Criminals, 149, 160, 179-80
Criminologist (periodical), 19
Critical reading, 30
Critical reading questions, 30
Critical thinking, 1-2, 3(fig.), 152, 186. *See also* Reasoning
Cross-examinations, 135-36
Cross-impact matrix, 150, 151(fig.)
Cryogenics, 149, 161
Cryptography, 43, 93
Cuckoo's Egg: Tracing a Spy through the Maze of Computer Espionage, 155
"Culture Thieves," 133
Current Science (periodical), 92
Curriculum webs, 12, 13-14(figs.), 152
  webbing technique, 112
Currier & Ives, 97
Curse of the Blue Figurine, 36

Dale, Alzina Stone, 129, 183
Dance activities, 101
Dangerous Edge, 41
Darrow, Clarence, 182
Darwin, Charles, 42
Dashiell Hammett: A Life, 40
Data-finding stage of creative problem solving, 58-59
Daughter of Time, 125
Davey, Drew, 194, 197
Davis, Scott, 162
Da Vinci, Leonardo, 72
Day, Doris, 88
Day They Stole the Mona Lisa, 180
De La Torre, Lillian, 47
De Sola, Ralph, 177
Death Comes at the End, 125
Death at the 50 Yard Line, 48, 49(fig.)
Death on the Nile (movie), 28
Death Tolls, 141
Debate activities, 135-36, 156
Debater's Guide, 135
Deductive reasoning, 22, 30
Deep Quarry, 141
Dendrochronology, 132
Desk intrigue, 100
Desks. *See* Mystery desks
Detection Club. *See* Class detectives club
Detectionary, 45
Detective, The (movie), 29
Detective agency, 184-85
Detective Cuff, 16
Detectives, 119, 148. *See* Sleuths
DeVere, Edward, 44
Dick Tracy, 16, 89

Dickens, Charles, 36, 58-59
Dillinger, John, 180
Disney, Walt, 62
Disney World, 127
Dixon, Franklin W., 10, 36, 122
Doddy, Margaret, 125
Don Quixote (character of), 99
Donald Duck, 62
Doolittle, Eileen, 97
Dossiers, 83
Douglas, William O., 182
Doyle, Arthur Conan, 21, 28, 35, 36, 41, 43, 51, 53, 60,
    82, 88, 93, 100, 112, 118
  Piltdown hoax, 39, 134
  works, 28
  writer, 31, 43
Dr. Livingston, 131
Dr. John H. Watson, 5-8(fig.), 16, 21, 36, 100, 128, 132,
    149, 161, 171
Dr. Roylott, 21-22(fig.)
Dr. Sam: Johnson, Detector, 47
"Dragnet" (radio program), 30
Drama school, 194-97
Drawing
  a crime, 94
  a residence, 93
  a sleuth, 93
Driving under the influence (DUI), 168(fig.)
Dutch art world, 72-73(fig.)

E.T.: The Extraterrestrial (movie), 159
Eames, Hugh, 41
Earhart, Amelia, 124
Edalji, George, 39
Edgar Allan Poe, 40
Edison, Thomas Alva, 61
Egypt Game, 36, 125
Eleventh Hour: A Curious Mystery, 97
Eliot, T. S., 52, 55
Elizabeth I, 143
Ellery Queen, 45, 93
Elliot, Lauren, 131
Encyclopedia Brown: Boy Detective, 36
Encyclopedias, 119
"Engineer's Thumb," 183
English Journal, 57
English countryside, 52, 128-29
Environmental walk, 82
Erickson, Douglas, 135, 167-68(fig.)
Erickson, Jon, 135
Erle Stanley Gardner: The Case of the Real Perry
    Mason, 40

Ethics. See Moral development model
Evaluating the inquiry process (research skills), 124,
    194-202(fig.)
Everyman sleuths, 32
Evil under the Sun (movie), 28
Extrapolations, 150

Fairy tales, 55
Fairy tale trials, 55
Fala Factor, 125
Family Vault, 19
Famous Detectives: True Stories of Great Crime
    Detection, 182
"Far Side" (cartoon), 191(fig.)
Farley, Carol, 36
Farnham, 129
Fatal Fascination: Where Fact Meets Fiction in Police
    Work, 10, 60, 100
Fatal Shore: The Epic of Australia's Founding, 144
Father Brown, 29, 35, 52
Father Brown Omnibus, 28
Faulkner, William, 55
Federal Bureau of Investigation (FBI), 113, 170, 176, 183
Ferber, Edna, 88
Fictional biographies, 45
Fighting Computer Crime, 156
"Final Problem," 21, 53, 171
Find Waldo Now, 97
Finding and evaluating resources (research skills), 118
Fingerprint art, 100
Fingerprinting, 100, 112
Finney, Albert, 28
Five (5) W's, 125
Five Red Herrings, 28
Flack, Jerry, 69, 143
Floating Admiral, 56
Floyd, "Pretty Boy," 180
Forensic science, 106, 176, 178, 190
Forensics simulation, 190
Frances, Dick, 32
Frank Hardy, 117. See also Hardy Boys
Freud, Sigmund, 56
From the Mixed-Up Files of Mrs. Basil E. Frankweiler, 93
Frommer, Arthur, 128
Funny pages sleuthing, 89
Furman v. Georgia, 196
Futures activities, 148-54
  cross-impact matrix, 150, 151(fig.)
  future's wheels, 152, 153-54(fig.)
  Mayflower III simulation, 157-59(fig.)
  3 P's, 148, 149(fig.)
  trending, 150
Futures wheels, 152, 153-54(fig.)

Galsworthy, John, 55
Gameboards, 94, 123
Games (periodical), 92, 183
Gardner, Erle Stanley, 35
Garrett, Pat, 182
Geography activities, 128-31
George, David, 190
German occupation of Holland, 72
Gertz, George, 134
Gifted students, 4, 9, 47, 51, 58, 60, 62, 69, 84, 87, 88,
     93, 100, 115, 121, 123, 131, 135-36, 174, 178,
     182, 186, 190, 194
Gilman, Dorothy, 32
Gorey, Edward, 53
Goering, Hermann, 72
"Gold Bug," 35, 42-43, 93
Gould, Chester, 16
Graham's Magazine (periodical), 43
Grammar, 48-49
Grand Old Opry, 88
Great Brain (character), 32
Great British Train Robbery, 180
Great Depression, 127
Great Detectives: Seven Original Investigations, 45, 93
*Great True Stories of Crime, Mystery & Detection from
     the Reader's Digest*, 180
Great Waldo Search, 97
Green, Richard Lancelyn, 47
"Green Hornet" (radio program), 85
Greenberg, Harry, 161
Greeting cards, 100
Grossman, Peggy, 190
Grub-and-Stakers Quilt a Bee, 19
Grudeff, Marian, 88
Gruesome grammar, 48-49
Guinness, Alec, 29

Halloween, 82, 100
Hallucinogenic drugs, 29
Hals, Frans, 72
Hamilton, Alexander, 180
Hamlet, 44
Hammerstein, Oscar, 88
Hammett, Dashiell, 28, 32, 35, 39, 41, 48
Handford, Martin, 97
Hardwick, Michael, 10, 45
Hardy Boys, 1, 29, 32, 36, 45, 54, 117, 122-23,
     161
Hardy Boys' Detective Handbook, 10, 117, 177
Harris, Sydney, 44
Harris Burdick mysteries, 99
Harrison, Michael, 129, 183
Hart, Ann, 45

Hauptmann, Bruno, 124, 180
Heinrich, Edward Oscar, 182
Helen Stoner, 21
Hemingway, Ernest, 55
Hemitage Museum, 93
Hendershott, Barbara Sloan, 129, 183
Henissart, Martha, 32
Henry VIII, 124
Hercule Poirot, 1, 16, 22, 28, 32, 35, 45, 46, 100, 132,
     180
   profile, 46(fig.)
Herfordshire, 129
Heyerdahl, Thor, 133
Hickok, "Wild Bill," 180
Highashiyama, Akane, 129, 183
Higham, Charles H., 40
Hillerman, Tony, 32, 35
Hindley, Judy, 178
*Historical Statistics of the United States: Colonial Times
     to 1970*, 179
Hitchcock, Alfred, 29, 41, 62, 88
Hitchman, Janet, 40
Hoffman, James Michael, 106-7(fig.)
Holland (Netherlands), 72-74(fig.)
Holmes, Rupert, 58, 88
Homicides, 176
Hoomes, Eleanor, 60
Hoover, J. Edgar, 116
Horace Rumpole, 135. *See also* "Rumpole of the Old
     Bailey"
Horner, Captain E. W., 108
Horning, Jane, 10, 16
Hound of the Baskervilles, 94, 97
Hoving, Thomas, 133
Howe, James, 85, 87
Hubert, Karen, 60
Huckleberry Finn, 56, 62
Hughes, Dorothy B., 40
Hughes, Robert, 144
Human Factor in Computer Crime, 156
Huston, John, 29
Hypothesis. *See* Problem solving model

I, Robot, 160
Ian Fleming Thriller Map, 129
Idea-finding stage of creative problem solving, 58-59
Illustrated art mysteries, 99
Impression poems, 51
Improvisations, 82-83
Improvisations, character, 82-83
In the Footsteps of Sherlock Holmes, 129, 183
Independent study. *See* Research skills
"Indestructible Man" (scenario), 162-63(fig.)

Individual Education Plan (IEP), 123
Inductive reasoning, 22, 30
Industrial Revolution, 143
Inspector Clouseau, 30
Inspector Lestrade, 32
Inspector Smug, 57
"Ironsides" (television series), 62
Irwin, James, 132
Isaksen, Scott G., 58
It Was a Dark and Stormy Night, 57

Jack the Ripper, 180
Jacobson, Wendy, 59
James Bond, 88
James, Henry, 44
James, P. D., 31, 35, 126-27
Jane Marple, 22, 32, 45, 50, 93, 97, 118
Jefferson, Thomas, 42
Jepson, Edgar, 56
Jessel, Raymond, 88
Jessica Fletcher, 19,90
Jett, Betty, 190
Jim Chee, 32, 35
Joe Hardy, 117. *See also* Hardy Boys
John Putnam Thatcher, 32, 35, 128
Johnson, Diane, 40
Junior Achievement, 185

Kahn, David, 108
Kaminsky, Stuart, 125
Kauffman, Draper L., 151
Kawamura, Jan, 131
Keane, John, 185
Keene, Carolyn, 36
Keller, Helen, 100
Kemelman, Harry, 35
Kennedy, Robert, 182
Kennedy assassination, 124
Kern, Jerome, 88
Key word search (research skills), 118, 119(fig.)
Keystone Cops, 101
KGB, 93
Kid detectives, 32
King, Martin Luther, Jr., 24
King Lear, 44
King Tut's (Tutankhamun) Tomb, 132
King George III, 143
Kinsey Millhone, 90
Kipling, Rudyard, 55
Knapp, Bettina, 40
KnowHow Book of Detection, 178

Kobayashi, Tsukasa, 129, 183
Kohlberg, Lawrence, 196
Konigsburg, E. L., 93
Kraus, W. Keith, 113

L'Engle, Madeleine, 57
Lambert, Gavin, 41
Lansbury, Angela, 28
Larson, Gary, 191
The Last Supper (painting), 73
Lathen, Emma, 32, 35, 128
Latin derivations, 47
Latsis, Mary Jane, 32
Laurie, Peter, 183
Law enforcement, 176
Law school, 194-97
Learning center, 10, 117, 123
Learning Discussion Skills through Games, 185
Leonard, Elmore, 28
Leopold and Loeb, 124
Letter writing, 47
Letters from professionals, 9
    art, 70-71(fig.)
    crime and punishment, 167-68(fig.)
    future studies, 141-42(fig.)
    language arts, 20-21(fig.)
    social studies, 106-7(fig.)
Letters to Sherlock Holmes, 47
Lewis, Sinclair, 55
Lewis and Clark, 131, 147
Library Media Center, 40, 84, 86, 118, 134
Library Media Specialist, 9, 10, 30, 60, 80-81, 94, 108,
    112-14, 120, 142, 147, 151, 176, 179, 186, 190
Library Reference Sheet (research skills), 118, 120(fig.)
Life and Crimes of Agatha Christie, 40
Life and Times of Jane Marple, 45
Limericks, 51
Lincoln, Abraham, 24, 39, 42, 56
    assassination, 124
Lindberg kidnapping case, 60, 124
Listening skills, 30, 85
Literary Homes, 93
Literature of Crime and Detection: An Illustrated History,
    28
Little Red Riding Hood, 99
Local history society, 113
London, 128-30
London Underground, 128
Lord Peter Wimsey, 1, 32, 35
Lord Sydney, 143-44
Louisiana Purchase, 131
Louvre Museum, 180
Lovesey, Peter, 125

Loy, Myrna, 29
Luck Runs Out, 19
Lytton, Edward Bulwer, 57

McArdle, Karen, 10, 60, 100
McArdle, Phil, 10, 60, 100
McGinnis, Joe, 169-70
McGlinn, John, 89
Macaulay, David, 134
"Macavity: The Mystery Cat," 52-53
Macbeth, 44
MacLeod, Charlotte, 19, 20-21(fig.), 35
Mad*Libs, 48
Magnum P.I., 90
Maid of Honor, 19
Maigret, 45, 93
Maldive Mystery, 133
Maltese Falcon (movie), 29
Man Who Knew Too Much (movie), 88
Mancini, Henry, 88
Manderley, 93
Manson, Charles, 180
Mark Treasure, 93
Marshall, Thurgood, 182
Mayflower III (simulation), 157-59(fig.)
Mayflower Compact, 158
Max Bittersohn, 19
Melin, Linda, 84
Mellon Institute, 73
Memoirs of Sherlock Holmes, 28
Memory Blank, 141
Mentors, 197
"Mercury Theatre" (radio program), 159
Mess-finding stage of creative problem solving, 58-59
Meyer, Alfred, 134
MGM Records, 88
Michelangelo, 93
Michigan State University, 69
Mickey Mouse, 62
Military intelligence, 107-8(fig.)
Miller, Jamie, 33(fig.), 89, 90(fig.)
Miller, Gay, 69, 70-71(fig.), 100
Miranda v. Arizona (Supreme Court case), 136, 176
Mirror Crack'd (movie), 28
Mirror exercise, 82
Miss Marple. *See* Jane Marple
Mona Lisa (painting), 93
Montague Street, 129
Montgomery, R. A., 60
Moonstone, 16, 28, 58
Moral development model, 196
More Literary Homes, 93
Morgan, Janet, 39

Morgan, J. P., 128
Mortimer, John, 28
Motel of the Mysteries, 134
"Mr. Sherlock Holmes: Teaching Exemplar
　　　Extraordinary," 5-8(fig.)
Mrs. Emily Pollifax, 32
Mrs. Pym, 183
Murder and the First Lady, 125
Murder in the Dark (English parlor game), 83-84
"Murders in the Rue Morgue," 56
Murder in the Smithsonian, 41
Murder Ink: The Mystery Reader's Companion, 10, 30,
　　　55, 160
"Murder Is Announced" (video), 28
Murder, Mischief, and Mayhem, 113
Murder on the Orient Express (movie), 28
Murder on the Orient Express (novel), 60
"Murder, She Wrote" (television series), 127
Murderess Ink: The Better Half of the Mystery, 10, 160
Murphy, James F., 135
Music criticism, 88
Mussorgsky, 88
My Fair Lady (movie), 29
Mysteries for Group Detectives, 190
Mysteries of Harris Burdick, 99
Mysterious Affair at Styles, 28
Mysterious William Shakespeare, 44
"Mystery!" (television series), 28-29, 53
Mystery by the dozen, 99
Mystery desks, 9, 70, 100
　　arts, 76(fig.)
　　crime and punishment, 173(fig.)
　　future studies, 146(fig.)
　　language arts, 24, 25(fig.)
　　social studies, 110(fig.)
Mystery cartoons, 89-91
Mystery catalogs, 160
Mystery chess set, 100
Mystery dramatizations, 82-84
Mystery games and simulations. *See* Simulations
Mystery Lover's Book of Quotations, 10, 16
Mystery newspapers, 54, 191
Mystery of Edwin Drood (book), 36, 58-59
"Mystery of Edwin Drood" (musical), 58, 88
Mystery of Edwin Drood (CPS activity), 58-59
"Mystery of King Tut's Tomb" (video), 29
"Mystery of Marie Roget," 60
Mystery Reader's Walking Guide to London, 129, 183
Mystery Scene Magazine, 141
Mystery story elements, 31
Mystery story starters, 60, 61-62(fig.), 161
Mystery themes (music composition), 87-88
Mystery trivia, 55-56
Mystery webs, 12, 13-14(figs.)

Mystery windows, 77, 78(fig.)
Mystery writer's notebook, 16, 37, 58, 117, 121, 124, 191
"Mysteryland," 127

Nancy Drew, 1, 32, 36, 45, 54, 123, 132, 161, 178
Nash, Jay Robert, 180
National Association for Gifted Children, 69
National Council of Teachers of English, 113
National Public Radio, 87
Native Americans, 107-8(fig.). *See also* Anasazi
Navajo, 107-8
Nazis, 72-74
Nelson, "Baby Face", 180
Nene College, 190
Nero Wolfe, 35, 45, 93
Ness, Eliot, 182
New York Times, 45, 113-14
Newsweek (periodical), 126
Nick and Nora Charles, 29
Nielsen, Elizabeth, 3, 70
"Night on Bald Mountain" (musical composition), 88
Nile River, 131
Noah's Ark, 132
North by Northwest (movie), 29
Northern Arizona University, 106
Norville, Barbara, 10, 31, 60
Note-taking (research skills), 121

O'Connor, Sandra Day, 182
O'Keefe, "Specs", 169-70
O'Keeffe, Georgia, 100
O'Neill, Gerard, 162
Observations (research skills), 117
Ockenga, Starr, 97
Ode, 52
Ogburn, Charles, 44
Old Possum's Book of Practical Cats, 52
Organizing and outlining data (research skills), 121
Osborne, Charles, 40

Packard, Edward, 60
Paget, Sidney, 77, 93
Palace Guard, 19
Pall Mall (England), 129
Pantomime, 81-82
Parker, Donn B., 156
"Partners in Crime" (video), 28
Paul Clifford, 57
Paulis, Chris, 57
Peel, Robert Sir, 182
Penal space colonies, 144, 152, 153(fig.)

Penzler, Otto, 45
"Perpetrator at Piltdown," 134
Perry Mason, 35
Persis Willum, 93
Personalized poems, 50
Peter Shandy, 19, 35
"Peter Gunn" theme (musical composition), 82, 88
Peters, Ellis, 35, 125
Philip Marlowe, 35, 45, 93
Phillips, Arthur, 143
Photo crimes, 92
Photo mysteries, 92
Photography, 92
Piccadilly Circus, 129
"Picture Gallery," 95-96(fig.)
Picture mysteries, 97
Pike, Zebulon, 131
Pikes Peak, 131
Piltdown forgery, 39, 134
Pink Panther (movie), 30
Pink Panther theme (musical composition), 82, 88
Pinkerton, Allan, 10, 39, 116, 182
Pino, Tony, 169-70
Planning a study (research skills), 121-22
"Pocketful of Rye" (video), 28
Poe, Edgar Allan, 28, 31, 35, 36, 39, 48, 50, 56, 60, 82, 87, 93, 100
   profile, 42-43(fig.)
Poe, Elizabeth Arnold, 42
Poe, David Jr., 42
Poe, Virginia Clemm, 42
Poetry activities, 50-53
Police detective methods, 176
Political science, 135
PolyGram Records, 88
Portwood, Gene, 131
Powell, William, 29
Price, Vincent, 28
Private eyes, 32
Problem solving, 2-3, 58-59. *See also* Creative problem solving
Problem solving model, 2, 3(fig.), 72
Problem-finding stage of creative problem solving, 58-59
Professor Moriarty, 53, 152, 160, 171, 191
Professor Moriarty's den, 171-72(fig.)
Psychological sleuthing, 125-26
Psychology of mysteries, 126-27
"Purloined Letter," 43
Puzzle pictures, 97
Pylypczuk, Nancy, 91(fig.)
Pyramid, 134

Que Sera Sera (musical composition), 88
Question asking (research skills), 114-15
Quick, Dorothy, 62
Quotations (mystery), 16-17

Rabbi David Small, 35
Radio broadcasts, 30, 85
Radio Days (movie), 87
Radio dramas, 85-87
Radio scripts, 85-87
Radio sound effects, 86
Raskin, Ellen, 36, 85
Rathbone, Basil, 29, 127
"Raven, The" (poem), 50
Raymond Chandler Mystery Map, 129
Readers' Guide to Periodical Literature, 119
Readers theatre, 87
Reagan, Ronald, 85
Rear Window (movie), 62
"Reason," 160
Reasoning. *See also* analogous, deductive and inductive
         reasoning
Reasoning by analogy, 136
Reasoning by example, 136
Reasoning, causal, 135-36
Reasoning, sign, 135
Rebecca, 93
Rebus codes, 93
Rebuttals, 135-36
Recycled Citizen, 19
Redshift Rendezvous, 141
Regent Street, 129
Rehnquist, William H., 182
Reit, Seymour V., 180
Renoir, 99
Reporting crime, 192-93
Reporting mysteries, 36
Research skills, 112-25
     asking questions, 114-15, 116(fig.)
     evaluating the inquiry process, 124
     finding and evaluating resources, 118, 119-20(figs.)
     observations skills, 117
     organizing and outlining data, 121
     planning the inquiry, 121, 122(fig.), 123
     selection of a topic, 113-14
     sharing information, 123
     taking notes, 121
Resolution. *See* Problem solving model
Rest You Merry, 19
Return of Sherlock Holmes, 28
Rice, Scott, 57
Richard III, 124
Robin Hood, 179

Robocop (movie), 160
Robots, 149, 160
Rogers, Mary Cecilia, 60
Roman à clef, 60
Roosevelt, Eleanor, 24
Roosevelt, Elliott, 56, 125
Roosevelt, Franklin D., 56
Rotterdam Museum Boymans, 72
Royal Canadian Mounted Police, 183
Rumbelow, Donald, 178
"Rumpole of the Bailey" (television series),
         28
Russell, Bertrand, 55

Sacco, Nicola, 180
St. Mary Mead, 22, 52, 118
Salem witch trials, 180
Sam Spade, 29, 32, 35, 39, 41, 162
Sanctuary Sparrow, 125
Sarah Kelling, 19
Save Tomorrow for the Children, 162
Sayers, Dorothy L., 28, 31, 35, 39, 56
"Scandal in Bohemia" (story), 16, 88
"Scandal in Bohemia" (video), 29
Scapescope, 141, 161
Scenario writing, 162
Schindler, Raymond, 182
"Science Fiction/Science Fact" (television special),
         141
Science 83 (periodical), 134
Science 86 (periodical), 133
"Scotland Yard" (game), 184
Scotland Yard: A Study of Metropolitan Police,
         183
*Scotland Yard Photo Crimes from the Files of
         Inspector Black*, 92
Scotland Yard studies, 183-84
Scotland Yard Times (hypothetical newspaper),
         54
Selection of a topic (research skills), 113-14
Sellers, Peter, 30
Selznick, David O., 29
Sergeant Cribb, 32
Seurat, 99
"Shadow, The" (radio program), 30, 85
Shakespeare, William, 16, 21, 44
Sharing information (research skills), 123
Shaw, George Bernard, 55, 97
Sheppard, Samuel, 180
"Sherlock: The Riddle of the Crown Jewels" (game),
         191
Sherlock Bones: Tracer of Missing Pets, 185

Sherlock Holmes, 1, 10, 29, 31, 35, 41, 48, 53, 54, 56, 60, 62, 77, 80, 81, 82, 85, 87, 88, 93, 94, 100, 118, 119, 123, 127, 128-30, 131, 132, 134, 136, 148, 152, 156, 160, 161, 171, 178, 180, 183, 190-91
  characteristics, 32, 45
  demise, 21
  letters to, 46
  model problem solver, 1, 4, 5-8(fig.)
  quoted, 5-8(fig.), 16
Sherlock Holmes in London, 129, 183
Sherlock Holmes: My Life and Crimes, 10, 45
Sherlock Holmes Mystery Map, 129
Sherlock Holmes's London: Following the Footsteps of London's Master Detective, 129, 183
Sherlock Holmes through Time and Space, 161
Shippensburg State College, 113
Short Fiction of Edgar Allan Poe, 43
Shot in the Dark (movie), 30
"Show Boat" (musical), 88
Signal (catalog), 29
Simulations
  bank robbery, 188-89(fig.)
  computer, 131, 190-91
  forensics, 190
  Mayflower III, 157-59(fig.)
  murder mystery, 185-86, 187(fig.)
  newspaper, 192, 193(fig.)
Sirius (ship), 143-44
"Six Million Dollar Man" (television series), 160
Slaughter on Tenth Avenue (musical composition), 101
Sleuthing model, 2, 3(fig.), 72
Sleuthing, psychological, 125-26
Sleuths, 32, 45, 89, 99, 115, 135, 145, 160
  all-purpose sleuth, 33(fig.)
Sleuth search, 34-35(figs.)
Snooper Troops, 191
Snyder, Zilpha Keatley, 36, 125
Sobol, Donald J., 36
Solution-finding stage of creative problem solving, 58-59. *See also* Evaluation stage of CPS, 197-201.
Somebody Killed the Messenger, 93
Something the Cat Dragged In, 19
Sophocles, 28
"Sound of Thunder," 161
Soviet Union, 93
Speke, Captain, 131
Sperry, Robert L., 156
Spielberg, Steven, 29, 159
Spolin, Viola, 81
Stanford, Barbara Dodds, 185, 189
Stanford, Gene, 185, 189
Starr, Belle, 180
Statistical Abstracts of the United States, 178-79

Steinbeck, John, 55
Stevenson, Parker, 29
Stewart, James, 62, 88
Stith, John, 141-42(fig.), 161
Stoke Moran, 21, 129
"Stolen White Elephant," 62, 87
Stoll, Clifford, 155
Storm Cloud Cantata (musical composition), 88
Stout, Rex, 35
Strand Magazine, 77
Student activities
  acrostic puzzle, 12, 15(fig.)
  advocacy trial, 194-206
  archaelogical investigations, 131-34
  art projects, 93-100
  biography studies, 39-43
  case studies. *See* Case studies
  class detectives club, 56-57
  create a mystery game, 84
  creating radio mysteries, 85-88
  creative dramatics projects, 80-84
  crime reporting, 192, 193(fig.)
  crimebusters research, 182
  cross-impact matrix, 151, 151(fig.)
  dance activities, 101
  debate studies, 135-36
  fairy tale trials, 55
  famous criminals research, 179-80
  fictional biographies, 45
    with (Venn diagram), 45, 46(fig.)
  futures activities, 148-62
  geography studies, 128-31
  gruesome grammar, 48, 49(fig.)
  letters to Sherlock Holmes, 47
  mystery catalogs, 160
  mystery desks. *See* Mystery desks
  mystery newspapers, 54
  mystery trivia, 55-56
  mystery windows, 77-78
  mystery writer's notebook, 16
  "Mysteryland," 127
  photography projects, 92
  poetry, 50-53
  psychological sleuthing, 125-26
  readers theatre, 87
  reporting mysteries, 37, 38(fig.)
  research skills and projects, 112-25
  scenario writing, 162
  simulations. *See* Simulations
  sleuth searches, 34, 35-36(figs.)
  solving mysteries creatively, 58-59
  starting a detective agency, 184-85
  traces. *See* Traces
  trending, 150, 179

tools of the trade. *See* Tools of the trade
Venn diagrams, 45, 46(fig.), 180, 181(fig.)
vocabulary studies, 176-78
writing projects, 59-62, 161-62. *See also* Writing activities
Study in Scarlet, 128
Such a Strange Lady: A Biography of Dorothy L. Sayers, 40
Super Crooks: A Rogue's Gallery, 180
"Suspense" (radio program), 30, 85
Symons, Julian, 45, 93

Tabor, "Baby Doe," 131
Tamerlane and Other Poems, 42
Tarkenton, Fran, 56
Taylor, Phoebe Atwood, 16, 35
Teaching and Writing Popular Fiction, 60
Teaching the Future, 151
Ten Little Indians, 83
Tey, Josephine, 125
Thin Man (movie), 29
Third Man (movie), 29
39 Steps (movie), 29
Thoreau, Henry David, 16
3 P's: possibles, probables, preferables, 148, 149(fig.)
Timelines, 123, 180
Titian, 72
Tom Sawyer, 56
Tom Sawyer, Detective, 56, 62
Tommy and Tuppence Beresford, 36
Tools of the trade, 9
    arts, 74, 75(fig.)
    crime and punishment, 171, 172(fig.)
    future studies, 145(fig.)
    language arts, 22, 23(fig.)
    social studies, 108, 109(fig.)
Torrance, E. Paul, 162
Traces, 9
    arts, 79(fig.)
    crime and punishment, 174, 175(fig.)
    future studies, 147(fig.)
    language arts, 26, 27(fig.)
    social studies, 111(fig.)
Treasure in Roubles, 93
Treat, Lawrence, 94, 95-96(fig.)
Treffinger, Donald J., 58
Trending, 150
Trends in crime, 179
Trivial Pursuit, 40
Trixie Belden, 32
Trojan Horse attack, 155-56
Trouble in the Brasses, 19
Truman, Harry, 40

Truman, Margaret, 40, 41(fig.), 56
Turtle Wexler, 36
Tutankhamun: The Untold Story, 133
Twain, Mark. *See* Samuel Clemens
20 questions, 115, 116(fig.)
2081: A Hopeful View of the Human Future, 162
Tyrannosaurus rex, 161

UFO's, 159-60
U.S. Supreme Court, 136, 196
Uemura, Masaharu, 129, 183
Ultimate Alphabet Book, 97
Unabridged Edgar Allan Poe, 28
Union Club Mysteries, 56
Ustinov, Peter, 28

Valentine's Day, 100
Valley of Fear, 171
van Meegeren, Han, 72-73(fig.), 93
Van Allsburg, Chris, 99
Van Duyn, J., 156
van Gogh, Vincent, 72, 99, 100
Vane Pursuit, 19
Vanzetti, Bartolomeo, 180
Venn diagrams, 45, 46(fig.), 180, 181(fig.)
Verification. *See* Problem solving model
Vermeer (Jan van der Meer), 72-73(fig.)
Vertical files, 119
Victorian England, 118-19
Viney, Charles, 129, 183
Vocabulary of crime, 176-78
Vollmer, August, 182

Wade, Henry, 56
Walden Mystery Club, 97, 98(fig.)
Wall Street, 128
War communications, 108-9
Warren, Earl, 182
Waterloo Bridge, 129
Watson, Clarissa, 93
Waugh, Charles G., 161
We Dare Not Go A-Hunting, 19
Web. *See* Curriculum webs
Weber, Andrew Lloyd, 52
Welles, Orson, 159
Wells, H. G., 159
West Point (U.S. Military Academy), 42
Westing Game, 85, 94
Westlake, Donald, 28
Westminster, 129
"Where in the World Is Carmen Sandiego?" (computer simulation), 131, 209

"Where in the USA Is Carmen Sandiego?" (computer simulation), 131, 209
"Where in Europe Is Carmen Sandiego?" (computer simulation), 131, 209
Where's Waldo?, 97
"Whistler, The" (radio program), 30
Whistling Gallery, 96(fig.)
Whiz McGonnigle, 96(fig.)
Whitehall, 183
Who Censored Roger Rabbit? (book), 62
Who Framed Roger Rabbit? (movie), 62
Wilks, Mike, 97
Williams, Roger, 180
Wimpole Street, 129
Winn, Dilys, 10, 160
Winslow, John, 134
Withdrawing Room, 19
Wizard of Oz (movie), 9
Wobble to Death, 125
Woeller, Waltraud, 28
Woking and Ripley, 129
Wolf, Gary K., 62
Woman Taken in Adultery (painting), 72
World War II, 107-8, 127
World of Wonders: A Trip through Numbers, 97

Wrack and Rune, 19
Wrinkle in Time, 57
Writer's Digest (periodical), 84
Writing activities
  biography, 39-40
  collaborative writing, 56-57
  letters to Sherlock Holmes, 47
  Mayflower III simulation, 158-59(fig.)
  Mystery of Edwin Drood completion, 58-59
  mystery parody, 57
  mystery stories, 60-62
  mystery writer's notebook, 37
  newspapers, 54
  poetry, 50-53
  scenarios, 162
Writing a Modern Mystery Story, 10, 30-31, 60

Yankee (periodical), 19
Yorkshire, 71
You're the Detective, 94, 95-96(fig.)
Young Christ Teaching in the Temple (painting), 73
Young Detective's Handbook, 178
Young Sherlock Holmes (movie), 29
"Yours Truly, Johnny Dollar" (radio program), 30